Praise for *Leverage Leadership 3.0*

"Leverage Leadership has already transformed how tens of thousands of school leaders worldwide invest their time to drive student learning. With *Leverage Leadership 3.0*, Paul Bambrick-Santoyo takes it further than ever: he seamlessly integrates AI not as a replacement for human leadership, but as a tool that gives leaders more time for what matters most—developing their teachers face-to-face. Essential reading for anyone who believes every student deserves an exceptional school."

—**Ezequiel Molina**, Senior Education Economist, World Bank

"*Leverage Leadership 3.0* redefines what effective school leadership looks like for today's complex reality, combining instructional excellence with adaptive, people-centered leadership. Paul Bambrick-Santoyo brings unmatched experience translating real school challenges into practical, actionable guidance."

—**Ana Fernandez**, Principal, Nathaniel Hawthorne Elementary School, Dallas, Texas ISD

"*Leverage Leadership 3.0* makes one thing clear: AI doesn't replace great leaders, it amplifies them. Paul shows how instructional excellence, powered by intelligent tools, becomes scalable, human, and relentless, especially for the children who need us most."

—**Dr. Herminder K. Channa**, OBE
Regional Director, Department for Education, United Kingdom

"This is Paul Bambrick-Santoyo at his best—helping leaders raise the ceiling and save time doing it. *Leverage Leadership 3.0* takes it even further with updated content, learnings from a new group of successful leaders, fresh videos, and more. By leveraging AI to access all of it instantly and reduce prep work, leaders will spend more time where real growth happens: coaching teachers, developing teams, and building community."

—**Tera Carr**, Regional Superintendent, Boston, Massachusetts

"*Leverage Leadership 3.0* pairs Paul Bambrick-Santoyo's practice-ready guidance with the LL AI app that turns theory into daily action. It makes key leadership protocols visible, measurable, and coachable—supporting Instructional Leadership development, disciplined implementation, and real growth in schools."

—**Windy Dorsey-Carr**, Assistant Superintendent of Curriculum, Instruction, and Accountability, Robeson County, North Carolina

"*Leverage Leadership 3.0* has been a core text I return to year after year, and 3.0 is its most powerful update yet. By using AI to streamline planning, leaders will spend less time on logistics and more time in classrooms where we need to be—observing, coaching, and building great instruction."

—**Colleen Colarusso**, Superintendent, RISE Prep Mayoral Academy, Woonsocket, Rhode Island

"The Leverage Leadership app provides just-in-time guidance and exemplars that strengthen leader and teacher capacity—while still preserving professional judgment and voice. It's a powerful tool for improving practice without losing what makes great teaching human."

—**Ginger Conroy**, Principal, Barney Ford Elementary School, Denver, Colorado

"*Leverage Leadership 3.0* reflects what's next in education—equipping leaders with practical, actionable strategies that evolve with today's demands. Paul Bambrick-Santoyo continues to raise the ceiling, empowering educators to drive sustainable growth and results for both teachers and students. He makes AI practical, accessible, and customized to the demands of instructional leadership."

—**Latoya Jeems**, Principal, Journey Coleman Academy, Memphis, Tennessee

"One of the biggest barriers to consistently coaching teachers—looking at student work, lesson planning, and feedback—is the time it takes to prepare. The Leverage Leadership app is a game-changing tool that drastically reduces prep time so leaders can spend more energy where it matters most: face-to-face coaching."

—**Rachel Willcutts**, Managing Director of Leader Development, IDEA Public Schools, Buda, Texas

"The Leverage Leadership app that accompanies *Leverage Leadership 3.0* is the first AI technology I've used that puts the power of instructional leadership directly into the hands of school and system leaders. With just a click, it saves time and strengthens the quality of the work."

—**Denise de la Rosa**, Managing Partner, National Leadership Academies, Relay Graduate School of Education, New York City

"With *Leverage Leadership 3.0*, Paul Bambrick-Santoyo stays true to his mission of giving instructional leaders the 'what' and the 'how' to increase student achievement, while solving the timeless challenge of time. With AI as a planning partner, leaders can prepare meetings and feedback in minutes, freeing more time for face-to-face coaching, classroom observation, and staff development."

—**Ross Lunceford**, Director of Equity and Access, Ogden (Utah) School District

"*Leverage Leadership 3.0* is more than a tool; it's a game changer. By automating the 'how-to' with the companion app, it removes the administrative burden of instructional leadership by streamlining the most time-consuming prep work. This frees leaders to focus on what actually moves the needle: high-impact coaching and teacher development."

—**Amanda McDonald**, Managing Director, DSST Public Schools, Denver, Colorado

"As every successful instructional leader knows, great coaching requires great preparation—but preparation takes time. The Leverage Leadership app helps teams prep smarter and faster so they can spend more energy perfecting the work that matters most: internalization of lessons, data-driven action, and instructional excellence. What a gift!"

—**Susan Hernandez**, Senior Executive Director, Richardson, Texas ISD

"*Leverage Leadership 3.0* and the LL app are revolutionary tools for instructional leaders. With AI support reducing preparation time, leaders can spend more face-to-face time developing educators and closing student learning gaps."

—**Tammy Finch**, Director of Education and Curriculum, The Expedition School, Hillsborough, North Carolina

"Time and quality—that's what the Leverage Leadership app gives school leaders. By leveraging this powerful tool, leaders can reduce preparation demands while increasing the strength and consistency of instructional leadership."

—**Nicole Veltzé**, High School Principal,
Colegio F. D. Roosevelt—American School, Lima, Peru

"*Leverage Leadership 3.0* shows what's possible when proven leadership practice is used collectively and at scale. I've seen these ideas help system and school leaders build shared clarity and ownership for delivering dramatically improved student outcomes. By integrating AI into this edition, Paul equips leaders with powerful new tools to see more clearly and act together more effectively for students."

—**William Robinson**, Executive Director,
UVA Partnership for Leaders in Education

LEVERAGE LEADERSHIP 3.0

LEVERAGE LEADERSHIP 3.0

A Practical Guide to Building Exceptional Schools

Paul Bambrick-Santoyo

JOSSEY-BASS™

A Wiley Brand

Library of Congress Cataloging-in-Publication Data

Names: Bambrick-Santoyo, Paul, 1972-author
Title: Leverage leadership 3.0 : a practical guide to building exceptional
 schools / Paul Bambrick-Santoyo.
Description: Third edition. | Hoboken, New Jersey : Jossey-Bass, [2026] |
 Includes bibliographical references and index.
Identifiers: LCCN 2026010563 (print) | LCCN 2026010564 (ebook) | ISBN
 9781394324439 paperback | ISBN 9781394324453 adobe pdf | ISBN
 9781394324446 epub
Subjects: LCSH: School management and organization | School improvement
 programs | School principals—Professional relationships
Classification: LCC LB2805 .B245 2026 (print) | LCC LB2805 (ebook)
LC record available at https://lccn.loc.gov/2026010563
LC ebook record available at https://lccn.loc.gov/2026010564

Cover Design: Wiley
Cover Image: © Stillfx/stock.adobe.com

For children like Peter—that we can build you schools
of excellence that allow you to fly

Contents

Online Content

Here is a quick overview of all the materials available on the Leverage Leadership App and Online:

VIDEO CONTENT

Here is an overview of the video clips for your quick reference. Click or scan the QR code within the text and follow the instructions to access the videos.

Data-Driven Instruction (Chapter 1)

Clip	Technique	Description	Where referenced in the book
1	See It. Weekly Data Meeting	**"I want to dive into standard 3.R.2. . ."** Rick Romain guides his teachers to unpacking students' ability to identify the central idea of a text.	p. xxviii, xxxv
2	Do It. (Plan) Weekly Data Meeting	**"I'm going to give you five minutes to plan your reteach. . ."** Candace Young and her teachers plan their upcoming reteach lesson on arithmetic patterns.	p. 4
3	Reteach Modeling (Teaching Clip)	**"I'm going to model for you how I ask myself questions..."** Ashley Oliver prepares her students to pay attention to the thinking she does in her model.	p. 32

Clip	Technique	Description	Where referenced in the book
4	Reteach Modeling (Teaching Clip)	**"What questions did you hear me ask myself?"** Ashley Oliver models the thinking for her students.	p. 32
5	Reteach Guided Discourse (Teaching Clip)	**"Give me your thoughts: when a zero is included in the decimal. . .."** Dienabou Magassa guides her students to evaluate incorrect mathematical reasoning.	p. 33
6	Academic Monitoring (Teaching Clip)	**"Go back and re-read: what part of this passage is the central idea?"** Melissa Erberti gives every student in her class multiple pieces of feedback in just 15 minutes.	p. 36
7	See It. (Exemplar) Weekly Data Meeting	**"Let's dive into the exemplar for 3.OA.9. . ."** Candace Young and her teachers dive in looking at student work by reviewing the standard and the exemplar response.	p. 41
8	See It. (Exemplar and Gap) Weekly Data Meeting	**"So the gap is how the details of the setting help illuminate the central idea. . . "** Michelle Coleman works with her teacher to identify the gap in student work.	p. 44
9	See It. Name it. (Gap) Weekly Data Meeting	**"So what is the highest leverage gap?"** Candace Young leverages her Know-Show Chart to identify what went wrong and lead teachers to find the way to fix it.	p. 44
2	Do It. (Plan) Weekly Data Meeting	**"I'm going to give you five minutes to plan your reteach. . ."** Candace Young and her teachers plan their upcoming reteach lesson on arithmetic patterns.	p. 45
10	Do It. (Plan) Weekly Data Meeting	**"Should we use or model or discourse?"** Michelle Coleman guides her teacher to plan the upcoming reteach.	p. 45
11	Do It. (Practice) Weekly Data Meeting	**"So, class. . ..what is the prompt asking me to do?"** Michelle Coleman coaches her teacher as she rehearses her reteach plan.	p. 46

Clip	Technique	Description	Where referenced in the book
12	Do It. (Follow-Up) Weekly Data Meeting	**"When will you be reteaching this lesson?"** Alicia Iwasko locks in the date of the teachers' reteach plan to be able to observe and follow up.	p. 47
13	See It. Monitor the Learning	**"Where do you anticipate students will struggle?"** Taro Shigenobu anticipates student and teacher struggles in preparation to observe the class.	p. 53
14	Do It. Monitor the Learning	**"What are you seeing?"** Taro Shigenobu coaches his leader to identify the gap in student work and the teacher action step.	p. 53

Planning (Chapter 2)

Clip	Technique	Description	Where referenced in the book
15	Do It. (Practice) Weekly Planning Meeting	**"Let's add complexity with an imperfect answer. . ."** Taro Shigenobu and his teacher rehearse key moments of discourse in class.	p. 75, 89
16	See It. (Exemplar) Weekly Planning Meeting	**"What makes this text complex?"** Jessica Mullins breaks down the challenge of the text the teacher is planning to teach.	p. 87
17	See It. (Model) Weekly Planning Meeting	**"I'm going to model for you. . ."** Jessica Mullins models not only what to teach but how to teach it.	p. 88
18	Do It. (Practice) Weekly Planning Meeting	**"Let's practice your monitoring. . ."** Jessica Mullins coaches her teacher to monitor student work effectively while the students are reading.	p. 89

Observation & Feedback (Chapter 3)

Clip	Technique	Description	Where referenced in the book
19	See It. (Model) Feedback Meeting	"I'm going to model for you. . ." Katie Harshman uses a model to help her teacher understand her action step.	p. 106
20	See It. (Model) Feedback Meeting	"Looking back at our PD, what is the purpose of naming a lap. . ." Rick Romain leverages a video and PD to guide his teacher to see a model.	p. 135
21	See It. Name It. Feedback Meeting	"Today we are going to focus on discourse to respond to student misconceptions. . ." Marie Culihan works with her teacher on elevating the quality of her discourse.	p. 137
22	Do It. (Plan and Practice) Feedback Meeting	"Let's go to your classroom and practice in real-time. . ." Marie Culihan guides her teacher to rehearse the lesson while in her classroom.	p. 138
23	Do It. (Practice) Feedback Meeting	"You ready to take it live?" Katie Harshman engages her teacher in planning and practice.	p. 139

Leading PD (Chapter 4)

Clip	Technique	Description	Where referenced in the book
24	Do It (Practice). Leading PD	"Remember to emphasize your thinking questions. . ." Jasmine Woodward gives teachers the opportunity to practice their think aloud for their lesson.	p. 158
25	See It. Name It. (Model) Leading PD	"How I think aloud to unpack this text. . ." Jasmine Woodward models for her staff the questioning in a think aloud.	p. 166
26	Do It. (Plan) Leading PD	"Take 7 minutes to plan and then we'll compare with a partner. . ." Jesse Corburn guides his teachers in the design of the lesson plan before they practice.	p. 170

27	Do It. (Practice) Leading PD	**"Partner 1: you will go first. . ."** Yanela Cruz and Monique Cincore offer step-by-step instruction to ensure quality practice.	p. 171
28	Reflect Leading PD	**"Take a moment to write down: what are your takeaways?"** Jasmine Woodward locks in learning with facilitated reflections.	p. 173
29	Do It. (Plan) Practice Clinic.	**"Take a moment to plan your batch feedback. . ."** Matthew Rooney and Eddie Rangel give teachers time to plan during a practice clinic.	p. 180
30	Do It. (Practice) Practice Clinic	**"Ok. Final round. Re-do implementing the feedback. . ."** Matthew Rooney and Eddie Rangel lead a Practice Clinic.	p. 180

Student Culture (Chapter 5)

Clip	Technique	Description	Where referenced in the book
31	See It. (Model) Student Culture	**"Good morning!"** Anabel Ruiz and Cecilia Jackson set the culture of their schools starting from arrival.	p. 195
32	Do It. (Roll Out) Student Culture	**"Be sure to monitor both the hallway and the classroom. . ."** Katie Harshman trains staff down to the smallest details to get routines running smoothly.	p. 208, 210
33	See It. Name It. (Roll Out) Student Culture	**"Thank you for starting your Do Now. . ."** Katie Harshman models the entry routine for the classroom.	p. 209
34	See It. (Roll Out to Students) Student Culture	**"I'm going to model for you the transition. . ."** Trennis Harvey leads a reset of classroom dismissal by modeling the actions students should take.	p. 213, 219
35	Do It. (Roll Out to Students) Student Culture	**"Nice work moving with purpose. . ."** Trennis Harvey encourages his students as they implement the routine.	p. 213, 219

TOOLS AND RESOURCES

Enter the Leverage Leadership App to access any of these materials:

One-pagers

Every one-pager, rubric and exemplar mentioned in the text can be found on the LL App in printer-friendly format. The power of the one-pagers that you've seen presented in each chapter is that they can be easily printed for daily use. A number of schools and school districts have created what we call "Rainbow Guides": a small spiralbound resource that includes all of the following documents in the following order double-sided:

Overall:

- Get Better Faster Sequence of Action Steps
- Leverage Leadership Implementation Rubric

AI:

- AI Primer one-pager

DDI:

- Weekly Data Meetings one-pager
- Reteaching structures one-pager
- Monitoring the Learning one-pager

Planning:

- Weekly Planning Meetings one-pager

Observation and Feedback:

- Giving Effective Feedback one-pager
- Realtime feedback one-pager

Leading PD:

- Leading PD one-pager
- Practice Clinic one-pager

Student Culture:

- Student Culture one-pager

Staff Culture:

- Staff Culture Toolkit (launch culture, cultivate culture carriers, emotional resilience, accountability conversations)

Leadership Teams:

- Leadership Team Meetings one-pager

The "Rainbow Guide" gets its name by printing every one-pager on differently colored paper within the guide, making it easy for leaders to quickly reach the guide they need without any additional tabs. Leaders can carry this around with them and put it into daily use as so many of the leaders highlighted in this book already have been doing so for years!

Exemplars, Rubrics & Templates

In addition to the one-pagers, you will find exemplars, rubrics, and templates for your use. The below list is not exhaustive, but it will continue to be updated so check out the latest on the app:

Resource	Description
Data-Driven Instruction	• Implementation Rubric for DDI • Assessment Results Spreadsheet • Exemplar Teacher Analysis and Action Plans (ES, MS and HS) • Interim Assessment School Calendar (ES, MS and HS)

Resource	Description
	• Monthly Map for DDI • Exemplar Weekly Data Meeting Plans • Weekly Data Meeting templates
Planning	• Evaluating lesson plans one-pager • Exemplar Weekly Planning Meeting Plans • Weekly Planning Meeting Templates
Observation and Feedback	• Exemplar Feedback Meeting Plans • Feedback Meeting Templates • Observation Tracker • Observation Schedule
Leading PD	• Leading Professional Development Rubric • Exemplar PD Plans • PD Plan Template
Culture	• Exemplar Minute-by-Minute Plans (All School and In-Class Routines) • Exemplar Accountability Meeting Plans • Student Culture Rubrics (ES and HS) • Staff Culture Tracker Template
Finding the Time	• Weekly Schedule Template • Sample Leader Weekly Schedule (ES, MS, and HS) • Monthly Map Template • Sample Monthly Maps • Daily Action Plan Template • Principal Playbook Template

How to Learn and Train More

Want to learn and train more? The Leverage Leadership Institute offers one-day to two-day workshops, both in person and virtually. Check out the website for more details: www.leverageleaders.org

Acknowledgments

When I was growing up, school was my refuge: the place where I felt loved and pushed to be the best that I could be. Fast forward many decades later, and I feel incredibly blessed to have had the chance to work with and learn from some of the most amazing school leaders in the world. This book is my gratitude for them and for how they have changed the belief of what is possible in schools. You will meet these leaders throughout this text—leaders like Rick, Candace, Taro, Jasmine, Katie, Stephanie, LeVar, Tiffany, and Marie. To every leader I have had the chance to work with through the Leverage Leadership Institute (LLI) and beyond, I say simply . . . thank you. You are the everyday heroes that guide and inspire me. I'm so grateful to walk alongside you.

In the spring of 2025, I embarked on a new adventure, shifting to working full-time at the LLI that I founded many years ago. It was exhilarating and daunting to dream big, but a village of supporters—colleagues and thought partners, friends, and family—have helped make this new LLI take shape.

I cannot imagine where I would be without the transformational support of Debra Cottone. She is the companion writer of this text—putting in countless hours to synthesize the research in the field, interview school leaders, edit sections, and provide fresh insights into the lever of staff culture. And as if that were not enough already, she was also a personal coach and advisor who taught me how to build strategic plans to turn a dream into a reality. This book is a completely refreshed text because of her. Thank you, Debra!

It takes a village to write and lead, and this book is no exception. Kathleen Sullivan, my long-term co-leader of LLI, continues to prove that sustained excellence and compassion go hand in hand. Justin Pigeon at Ideal Instruction (ideal-instruction.com) stepped up in a time of need to help me film and collect all the videos for this book.

Justin, your extraordinary generosity will not be forgotten! For every leader at LLI who submitted videos, testimonials, and experiences, thank you!

One of the most exciting new additions to this book is the Leverage Leadership App. I never would have explored AI if I hadn't been invited by my friend Ezequiel Molina at the World Bank to co-author *El Director Libre*. Then I still needed a push from my college roommate Steve Winch to embrace this new world as our future. The app also wouldn't have been possible without the support of Charleston County School District and its leaders Anita Huggins (Superintendent) and Daniel Prentice (COO). And a huge thanks goes to the developers: Carl Fyffe and Ed Kelley. You made this dream come true!

In the end, this is a book of hope, a renewed hope that I have felt since the passing of my brother Peter more than a year ago. And no one helped me see the hope in moments of despair more than my family. Ana, Zach, Maria, and Nico: thank you for letting me find joy in every interaction with each of you. Thank you for allowing me to participate in your own dreams and always believing in me. And Gaby—you are the love of my life. By the time this book is published, we will be celebrating 30 years of marriage. You have been there for me through the highs and lows, and you teach me, every day, what it looks like to live a life full of love.

Thank you to each and every one of you. This book is a tribute to all of you.

About the Author

Paul Bambrick-Santoyo is the Founder and Dean of the Leverage Leadership Institute, creating proof points of excellence in urban schools worldwide. Author of multiple books, including *Get Better Faster 2.0, Driven by Data 2.0, A Principal's Guide to Leverage Leadership, Make History,* and *Love & Literacy,* Bambrick-Santoyo has trained more than 50,000 school leaders worldwide in instructional leadership, including hundreds of schools that have gone on to become the highest gaining or highest achieving schools in their districts, states, and/or countries.

When you first meet Rick Romain, he seems more like a shy college professor or a quiet librarian than a principal: He constantly avoids center stage and deflects to others. Yet the fruits of his leadership deserve the spotlight. When Rick Romain started as a principal at PS 268 Emma Lazarus School in New York City in 2019, his school was the lowest performing in the district. At his first staff meeting, Rick declared that the school would one day be #1 in the district and his teachers laughed. "I understand why," he shared. "All they had experienced was failure."

Fast forward to 2025, and PS 268 was indeed the #1 school in the district, an extraordinary and unimagined turnaround. His superintendent came to observe and said, "I cannot believe these are the same teachers and this is the same school!" Lazarus School was aptly named indeed!

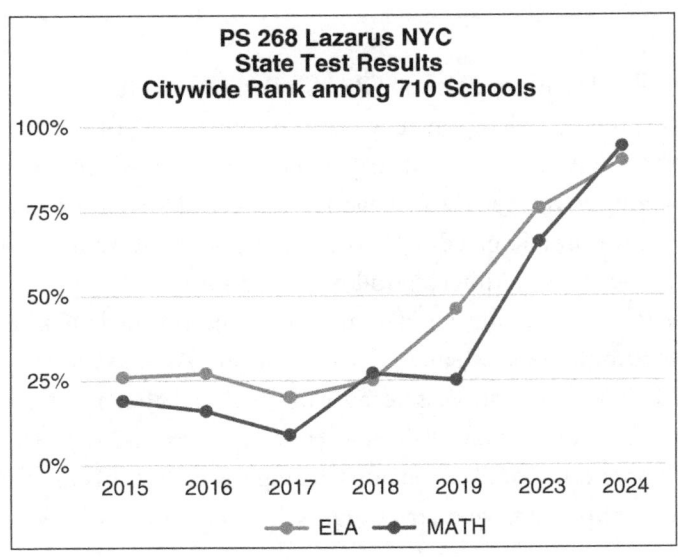

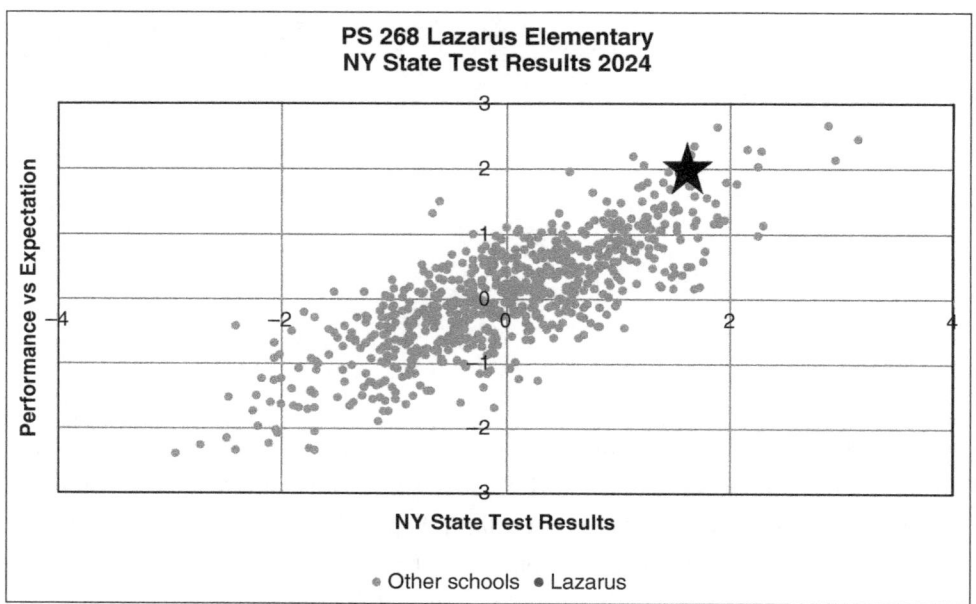

PS 268 Lazarus Elementary
NY State Test Results 2024

Performance vs Expectation

NY State Test Results

• Other schools • Lazarus

Here is a glimpse of Rick in action leading a weekly data meeting for his fourth-grade Math teachers:

WATCH Clip 1: Romain—See It—Weekly Data Meeting
See It. Name It. Do It.

Numbers like this leave no question: Rick's mission of getting students who enter school at a disadvantage to college may be ambitious, but it's far from impossible. Rick was facing the same challenges nearly all educators have faced—the return from COVID-19's learning loss, the rise in negative impact of social media, and so much uncertainty. Yet he was not deterred. "We just put our heads down and worked: one day at a time, one high leverage action step followed by another."

Rick's success is not a one-off wonder, and he is not a miracle worker (his school's name notwithstanding). He is talented, driven, and incredibly hard working, but ultimately, he has led his school to success because of the choices he makes in using his time: what he does, and how and when he does it. How do we know? Because Rick's success is not an isolated phenomenon. We see outstanding results like his in schools and cities of all types: from comprehensive district high schools to small schools serving largely

Native American students. We see them from the east coast to the west and across the ocean. From DC to Chile to South Africa to the United Kingdom, these leaders are making conscious deliberate choices to focus their time on what matters most to create exceptional schools.

At the time of this writing, more than 50,000 leaders worldwide experienced the practices that made Rick and so many others successful. They are not perfect schools, but thriving ones, where student learning is dramatically better than it was before. And the best thing about it? You can do it, too.

What did all these leaders have in common? They knew how to invest their time, and how to lead others to do the same.

Core Idea

Exceptional school leaders succeed because of how they use their time: what they do, and when they do it.

A PARADIGM SHIFT: LEADERSHIP IN THE AI AGE

The world is transforming and schools are adjusting. While great teaching still drives great learning,[1] the rate and scope of change is escalating. Among many changes, the Science of Reading and the rise of High Quality Instructional Materials have put instructional quality and curriculum front and center.[2] And now artificial intelligence has taken us to a whole new frontier that is exciting and threatening. Will these and other transformational changes undermine great teaching or help us take it to new heights?

The answer lies in how we respond to this wave of change. Run from it, or embrace it (with guardrails)? We choose the latter.

So, what does it look like to lead a highly effective school today? And how do you get there?

By standing on the shoulders of giants.

Core Idea

If I have seen further or more clearly,
it is because I stand on the shoulders of giants.
—Isaac Newton

Just like Newton's research advanced because of the scientific giants who went before him, you can stand on the shoulders of outstanding leaders who have blazed a trail for you to go further.

This book offers guidance and tools derived from the collective work of thousands of successful leaders who fearlessly share both their wins and their struggles for the benefit of leaders everywhere. We highlight a few of them in the book, and they all meet two basic criteria:

> **Exceptional Results that Exceed Expectations:** By any metrics, these leaders achieved staggering academic successes. Their state test or AP results marked each leader's school as a top performing or top gaining school in its city or state. What makes this even more impressive is the population that these schools served. In all cases, the schools served large free and reduced lunch populations and were mostly students of color. But the point bears noting: The schools we found are not "good urban schools;" they are superlative schools outright.

> **Replicable Results:** These leaders didn't succeed in some idiosyncratic way: they used replicable systems and structures that others can follow. The successes these leaders built were not the products of unique charisma; they came from strategies and systems that any leader can apply.

Are you wondering if this can work for you? The question takes many forms:

- Can these solutions really work for my school?
- We serve a particularly challenging population and are a traditionally labeled "failing" school; will this turn my school around?
- I lead a big district; is this feasible for us?
- I work in a small rural school isolated from others—what about my school?
- I lead a school that is doing fine academically, but not great. What about me?
- I have enough on my plate; will adapting to new technology really help?

The answer to each of these questions is a resounding *yes*.

But don't take my word for it right away; in fact, given the number of impractical solutions and changes you've seen in the past, don't take my word for it at all. Instead, read and listen to the leaders presented in this book. They are here not simply to *tell* their stories about leadership but to *show* how success is possible anywhere. What separates their practices from those of other school leaders I observed who were doing "well" but not achieving the same dramatic results is simple: each of them leveraged more out of each minute of the day. They carefully and intentionally chose the actions that would have the biggest impact on student learning—and they avoided those actions that don't.[3] None of their practices were revolutionary in their own right: it was the combination of practices and the precision to which they were implemented that made the difference. The precision with which a leader uses their time for what matters most is what marks a paradigm shift.

So, what really makes schools effective? The answer is high leverage leadership that ensures great teaching to guarantee great learning for every student.

Core Idea

So, what really makes school leaders effective?
High leverage leadership to guarantee high-quality learning
for every student.

What Leverage Leadership is Not: Myths

The Leverage Leadership paradigm has the potential to re-shape any school in any context. Here is what it is *not*:

> **Principals as administrators and fire fighters, not instructional leaders.** Administrative burden is real. But the driver of change is instructional leadership. And with AI, leaders can even more easily reduce this burden to keep their actions and their eyes squarely on instruction.

> **High Quality Instructional Materials (HQIMs) solve everything.** They don't. HQIMs are important, yes, but what a teacher does with them determines whether students learn. And that depends on good coaching.

> **Sweat the pedagogy, and results will follow.** Pedagogy, whether it be the science of reading or something else, only works when it doesn't forget its core purpose: if students don't learn, it doesn't matter how we taught it. And well-delivered leadership is what keeps that focus.

> **Change (or turnaround) is slow.** There is a common sentiment in the educational field that only slow, gradual change is effective.[4] The leaders in this book dispel that

myth quite dramatically. Principal Kim Tymkowych turned around Winona Elementary School in Loveland, Colorado, and she says, "In school, even in turnaround, it's not 'go slow to go fast' but 'go fast right away.' Focus on what matters most and go."

➤ **The "Principal Personality."** You don't need to be extroverted, forceful, and charismatic to be successful. All you need is a willingness to work hard and work "smart"— differently than you might have before. Exceptional leaders have a "Good-to-Great" mentality—they are far more motivated by self-improvement than simply by the results themselves.

The Seven Levers

The leaders who have implemented the practices in this book follow a core set of seven levers to achieve consistent, transformational, and replicable growth.

The Seven Levers
Executing Quality Instruction and Culture

Instructional Levers:

1. **Data-Driven Instruction**—Continuously prioritize the learning: start from a high-quality end goal and adjust your teaching to meet students' needs
2. **Instructional Planning**—Plan backward to guarantee strong lessons
3. **Observation and Feedback**—Coach teachers to improve the learning
4. **Professional Development**—Strengthen teams with hands-on training that sticks

Cultural Levers:

5. **Student Culture**—Set the expectations, routines, and values that create an environment where learning can thrive
6. **Staff Culture**—Build shared values and behaviors that unite and guide adults to a common purpose
7. **Managing School Leadership Teams**—Increase instructional leadership capacity to achieve consistent coaching for every teacher every week

By shifting to an intentional focus on the seven levers, leaders dramatically improve learning within the same amount of time. Fundamentally, each of these levers answers the core question of school leadership: what should an effective leader do? Nearly 15 years have passed since the original publication of *Leverage Leadership*, and these levers have stood the test of time—they continue to be the biggest drivers of school improvement.

The levers tell you what to do. See It, Name It, Do It tells you how.

How: See It, Name It, and Do It

Over 20 years, we've honed a unifying framework to illuminate what it really takes to implement each of these levers. It can best be encapsulated in my experience learning to cook cod—and then passing on that learning to my son-in-law.

Growing up, I never liked fish. Fast forward years later to my first year living in Mexico City: my father-in-law Miguel prepared a delicious cod dish called Bacalao a la Mexicana. I was hooked! But I had no idea how to prepare it myself. I watched Miguel cook it once and wrote down the ingredients and instructions, but when I got around to cooking it myself, I couldn't remember the details. So, I watched him again, this time noting the subtleties and writing them down: strain the diced tomatoes before adding to the mix, skim the water off the top, and stop when only oil is bubbling along the edges of the pot. I asked Miguel to watch me, and he let me cook, just adding subtle tips. Sure enough, I was successful (although not quite as good as Miguel himself).

Fast forward 25 years later, and I found myself taking the same approach with my son-in-law Zach. He wanted to learn our family recipe for grilled hangar steak (a definite family favorite!). So, he watched me once, and the next time I let him do all the preparation. He pounded out the steak to break up the fibers and seasoned it with a marinade that we didn't keep on for too long to avoid the meat from getting mushy. Then he learned the trick for removing the marinade before grilling, getting the right temperature on the grill, turning it at just the right moment, and finish with cutting the steak against the grain. He could try to follow that from a recipe book, but real-time feedback from me moved him so much faster. Now it's his go-to recipe for guests.

My experience in the kitchen mirrors what we saw when observing and cataloging instructional leadership. Each lever boils down to a core process in three actions: see a model of success, name it in concrete steps, and do what it takes to make it real. See it. Name it. Do it.

> ## Core Idea
>
> The fastest way to develop a skill?
> See It. Name It. Do It.
> And repeat until you've mastered it.

Think about how that played out for me and my son-in-law in the kitchen. If we had not seen someone else prepare the meal (see the model), we wouldn't have captured the subtleties that made the preparation magical and far better than our own (see my gap). Then we needed to write down those steps to remember them (name it), and finally we needed to do it ourselves with guidance (do it).

This clearly doesn't just apply to cooking. We recognize it in other professions as well; we'd never ask an aspiring doctor to perform an operation before seeing one, studying the particulars, and training the execution. *Leverage Leadership 3.0* simply brings a clarifying language, tools, and performance-proven methods to education. See It, Name It, and Do It are the three essential steps to implementing any one of the seven levers of school leadership: *seeing* a model of excellence in clear detail (and the gap between that model and our own practice); *naming* the qualifying characteristics that make that model effective (so that others can name it as well); and *doing* those actions repeatedly, first behind the scenes in extensive practice sessions and then daily in the classroom.

A "PRACTICAL GUIDE": WHAT YOU'LL FIND IN THE BOOK

Leverage Leadership 3.0 is a practical guide that you can apply right away. After a primer on AI (which will be a core mechanism for implementation throughout your leadership), there's one chapter on each lever. Embedded in each chapter are the exercises and the tools to apply it immediately (don't skip those and grow faster by doing as you read). We end with a chapter on how to put it all together and manage your time—this is the cornerstone of tailoring all of this to your context and your school.

Here are the tools at your disposal that are embedded throughout:

Leverage Leadership AI App

To accompany this book, we have developed the AI-driven Leverage Leadership App. This not only allows you to get the best resources possible at the touch of a button, it goes further. You can prepare all your meetings, your PD, your schedule, and your tools in a fraction of the time. Rather than spending 50 minutes researching a standard for a weekly data meeting or writing a script for a PD, the Leverage Leadership App can draft it for you in minutes, allowing you to invest more time anticipating teacher responses and adjusting your coaching to meet them where they are. What makes the Leverage Leadership AI App unique is our proprietary library of application-rich video clips, exemplar preparation, PD materials, and more from the top school leaders from around the world. What's more, we teach you how to tailor the materials to your specific needs—no cookie-cutter approach! (You'll learn more in the AI Primer chapter, and when you start to use it.)

Videos

Throughout this text and in the app, we've included a brand new selection of video clips of top-tier leaders in action (no repeats from previous books!) working directly with their teachers. These videos are not staged, nor are they videos of principals' interactions with their strongest teachers. These videos show teacher-leader interactions with all types of teachers: struggling teachers, new teachers, and everyone in between. You can scan the QR code to watch them, and you can also find links to them in our accompanying app.

This is what we mean by "See It": when you see leadership in action, it is much easier to replicate than by just reading about it. Although it is possible to use this book without watching the accompanying videos, we doubt it will be as effective (or engaging!). Look for this logo:

  WATCH: Video Clip 1 (Rick Romain)

Tools: One-Pagers, Core Ideas and Materials

The power of a common language to describe best practices is impossible to overstate. Leaders repeatedly tell us that concise, brief guides to specific skills are among the most useful tools in the practice. We call these "one-pagers." Catchy and precise, they name key words and actions we observed in thousands of hours of video clips of the most effective leaders. They consolidate the most important information to remember about any topic onto a single sheet (or two). Here's an example of part of the one-pager that sums up the process for weekly data meetings:

Data Meetings

Leading Teacher Teams to Analyze Student Daily Work

See It 13–18 mins	See Past Success, See the Exemplar, and See and Analyze the Gap
	See Past Success (1 min):
	• "Last week we planned to re-teach _____ and we went from ___ % proficient to ___%. Nice job!"
	• "What actions did you take to reach this goal?"
	See the Exemplar (8 min):
	• Narrow the focus: "Today, I want to dive into [specific standard] and the following assessment item."
	• Interpret the standard(s):
	○ "Take 1 min: in your own words, what should a student know or be able to do to show mastery?"
	• Unpack the teacher's written exemplar:
	○ "Take 1–2 min to review the exemplar: What were the keys to an ideal answer?"
	○ "How does this [part of the exemplar] align with the standard?"
	• Analyze the student exemplar:
	○ "Take 1 min: How does your student exemplar compare to the teacher exemplar? Is there a gap?"
	○ "Do students have different paths/evidence to demonstrate mastery of the standard?"
	○ "Does the student exemplar offer something that your exemplar does not?"
	See the Gap (5 min):
	• Move to the sample of un-mastered student work (look only at representative sample):
	○ "Take 2 minutes: What are the gaps between the rest of our student work and the exemplar?"
	○ "Look back at our chart of the standard and exemplar: What are key misconceptions?"

This book includes at least one one-pager like this one in every chapter. Print them out and use them as a daily guide in your work, and distribute them among your staff after PD on each of these subjects so that they can do the same!

In addition to one-pagers, we have countless other tools throughout the book. We have a "Turnaround" box at the end of each chapter, if your school is in serious turnaround, with tips from a leader who was in your shoes on where to focus. There are other guides and worksheets you can work with right in the book, or you can complete them in the Leverage Leadership App.

Here is an example.

Pulling the Lever
Action Planning Worksheet for OBSERVATION AND FEEDBACK

Self-Assessment

- How frequently are your teachers being observed? ___/year or ___/month
- What are your strengths in implementing See It. Name It. Do It. feedback?

_____

_____

_____

- What are your biggest areas to improve in See It. Name It. Do It?

_____

_____

_____

Chapter 8 will give you the opportunity to put it all together to create your own schedule to show exactly how you can make change feasible even as it is transformational.

Finally, throughout the text, you will also find yellow Core Idea boxes that highlight the most important key ideas from each section:

Core Idea

Effective instruction is not about whether we taught it.
It's about whether the students learned it.

The goal of each Core Idea is to make the complex ideas in this book simple and memorable. If you take nothing else away from this reading, take these and share them with your colleagues at your school!

A Word On . . . What's New Here?
Key Differences Between *Leverage Leadership 2.0* and *Leverage Leadership 3.0*

Readers who are familiar with the Leverage Leadership model may be curious to know exactly how this text differs from the earlier versions of *Leverage Leadership*. Although the seven levers themselves remain the same, we've re-written nearly all of the text in *Leverage Leadership 3.0*. Here are the key changes:

- **AI-centric.** The biggest hurdle for many leaders to start being an instructional leader is to reduce the administrative burden and the amount of time taken to prepare to lead. Throughout each chapter, you will learn how to use the Leverage Leadership App to save hours of time daily in planning your meetings, preparing your PD, completing administrative tasks, and organizing your schedule. This leaves you with more time for what matters most: face-to-face coaching.

- **Globally field-tested.** Since the publication of *Leverage Leadership*, more than 50,000 school leaders have tested and used the seven levers. Following up with these leaders has given us far greater insight into which Leverage Leadership methods and tools worked well, which were feasible for leaders to implement as they were written, and which ones needed fine-tuning. Those insights are reflected in *Leverage Leadership 3.0*.

- **New, refreshed materials.** All materials in the book and the Leverage Leadership App have been substantively revised to capture the latest lessons learned from leaders worldwide. You'll find all new videos, models, and exemplars that can guide your implementation of the See It. Name It. Do It. Framework.

- **A more diverse, international array of leaders.** With the sheer number of leaders who have made the seven levers their own in the past 15 years, we are able to highlight an even broader set of the most successful. These leaders have lifted the levers in every context: bilingual schools, turnaround schools, small schools and large ones, domestic and worldwide. What all these leaders have in common is they were able to optimize their time to transform their students' lives. The diversity of their experiences with the Leverage Leadership model enrich this book, showing how any school can use these steps to become not just a good "urban" school or a good turnaround school but a superlative school by *any* measure.

WHO SHOULD USE THIS BOOK—AND HOW

This book is for school leaders. While each leader highlighted is a principal, most schools have many more than a single instructional leader. As such, this book is for anyone who plays a leadership role in school culture or instruction: instructional coaches, department chairs, lead teachers, and teachers. It also extends up to the level of superintendents and district directors of curriculum, instruction and assessment.

As we have noted, the methods we offer here have worked in some of the most challenging conditions in American education and worldwide. The fact that our case studies are drawn from underserved mostly urban areas is no accident; the schools and students who most need dramatic change are those that are currently least well-served. Although our main setting is urban schools, when used well, the systems we propose here can—and do—deliver significant impact in all schools.

How to Read This Book

For Principals

The order in which you implement the Leverage Leadership model will depend on you—your needs, and your school's level of progress. However, after studying the impact of each of these levers in schools across the country, there has emerged a common order of implementation that is often most effective. You'll need to adapt this to your school, but here are some global recommendations.

> ➤ **Step 1: Read the AI Primer; Next Move to The Super Levers—Data-Driven Instruction and Student Culture:**
> The Leverage Leadership App will be your personal assistant, saving you dozens of hours. So, read the primer to understand it. Then, of the seven levers, two are the fundamental foundation of any school's success. We have dubbed these the "super levers:" Beyond being vital, robust data-driven instruction (Chapter 1) and student culture (Chapter 5) systems determine your school's *instructional capacity*, which is the upper bounds for how successfully your school can teach its students. Without such capacity, transformational growth is not possible: in nearly every case (pre- and post-COVID-19) where once-struggling schools experienced significant turnarounds or good schools became great, these levers were the game-changers. By contrast, schools that had not mastered data-driven instruction or student culture found it impossible to significantly boost student achievement, notwithstanding persistent investment on the other levers. **If in doubt, data and culture take priority.**

Before you determine if your school has mastered these levers, read those chapters. They will help you identify your next steps even if you have already implemented these to a certain extent.

➤ **Step 2: Build a Coaching Cycle:** If student culture and data change the game plan, the coaching cycle (plan and practice, observe, and plan and practice again) is the driver to develop teachers to execute it. As the backbone of this text, the coaching cycle exists in all levers, particularly observation and feedback, planning, data-driven instruction, and leading PD. Coaching creates consistency that is so important for effective implementation. It needs to be habitual and routine. For leaders who have not "found the time" to do instructional leadership frequently or consistently, the transition can be daunting. Using the tools and the Leverage Leadership App makes it doable and the strategies in Chapter 8 (Finding the Time) are your blueprint for consolidated scheduling.

➤ **Step 3: Implement Remaining Levers as Much as Is Feasible In Year One**
Once leaders have solid data-driven instruction, strong student culture, and a consistent coaching cycle, the remaining levers can turn good schools into great ones. Whatever you cannot focus on in Year 1 can then become a project for your second year of leadership. It is worth repeating: all levers are doable simultaneously. We have given you a leader's schedule throughout the book to prove this. But you do not need to launch all of them simultaneously to enact effective change (in fact, if you don't yet have a solid foundation, trying to tackle all seven at once can easily hinder your success). But you know the needs and capacity of your school best to determine the speed of implementation beyond these first levers.

For Coaches and Other Instructional Leaders
➤ **Step 1: Start With Data-Driven Instruction**
Many coaches do not have a prominent role in leading schoolwide student culture. If that is the case, focus on Chapter 1: Data-Driven Instruction. The systems for data-driven instruction are the backbone for instructional leadership: start from student work, and the rest will follow.

➤ **Step 2: Build In Planning and/or Observation and Feedback**
With data-driven instruction in place, coaches can shift their focus to developing a coaching cycle via Planning or Observation and Feedback. Planning can simply be seen as a deeper dive on observation and feedback that prioritizes the most important learning objectives of the day and the unit.

➤ **If Applicable: Add Professional Development**

Additionally, if coaches have been assigned to lead group training for peers or teachers, you will benefit from focusing on delivering effective professional development sessions (Chapter 4).

For Principal Managers and Superintendents

➤ **Step 1: Start with the Top 2 Levers—Data-Driven Instruction, Student Culture—and Build the Coaching Cycle:**

If you have limited time and are not sure where to begin, start from the super levers of data (Chapter 1) and student culture (Chapter 5). Then create a coaching cycle in the school, whether it be through weekly data meetings (Chapter 1), weekly planning meetings (Chapter 2) or observation and feedback meetings (Chapter 3). For consolidated scheduling of these levers, see Chapter 8.

➤ **Step 2: (If Time) Read the Rest of the Book**

If you cannot read all of it, read Finding the Time (Chapter 8) before transitioning to the companion guide.

➤ **Step 3: Move to the Companion Guide Specifically Designed for You**

In talking with principal managers and superintendents across the country, there has been so little practical guidance written as to how to be effective in leading multiple schools. *The Principal Manager's Guide to Leverage Leadership* is published intentionally as a companion to this book to fill that void. The guide offers a deeper dive into the critical role you play in driving school quality. There you will find resources specifically designed for principal managers, including examples and testimonials from superintendents and principal managers from across the country.

THE PATH AHEAD

Over the course of the past 20 years, I have observed first-hand the challenges facing school leaders, some specific to their unique regions and others startlingly similar. And if all these leaders have taught me one thing, it's that no challenge is too great to be overcome. I have seen schools rise above endemic illiteracy, hunger, centuries-long legacies of systemic racism, and more; and I have seen them soar. I have seen leaders achieve success at one school then move on to another with different challenges and achieve similar success. That's because the solutions are largely universal even though the challenges vary.

This book is about the action steps behind those success stories. It's about the leaders who have built oases for learning even in the harshest of landscapes. School leadership is hard, no doubt—I think it is the toughest job in the world. But one thing we've noticed across the country is that most school leaders already work very hard. The power of these steps is that they help you work "smart"—they lock in the results you strive for and your students deserve. If we've learned anything from these transformational school leaders, it is this: work both hard and smart, and results will follow.

Are you ready? All you need is a pen (to take notes), a phone or a laptop (to immediately use the AI app), curiosity, and a desire to implement. Turn the page.

AI Primer—Leverage Leadership App as Your Personal Assistant

One of the most precious resources you have as an instructional leader is your time. It is also what seems scarcest.

From your first day on the job, you will immediately confront the biggest obstacle—how do I find enough time?

Do you feel like you are racing all day but rarely spend time on the work that most changes student learning? If so, you are not alone. In our survey of 5,000 principals in Latin America, on average 70% of a principal's time is consumed by logistics, compliance, and firefighting.[1]

Those same leaders, using AI productively, shaved admin and prep time by 10 hours per week—that's two more hours a day for instructional leadership. That is a game-changer.

Whether you are a first-year principal or a veteran, this chapter—and this book—is an invitation to experience a new way of working. Welcome to your new personal assistant: the Leverage Leadership AI-driven App. This app has been tested and honed by high-achieving school leaders who have used it in their schools, and it is now ready for you.

But let's be transparent; it's your choice.

You can read this book and never open the app. You'll adopt new methods including how you schedule your time (see Chapter 8). But the "alone time" you need to prepare a coaching meeting, plan a PD, or draft a weekly memo won't change. Planning and preparation tasks may bleed into your personal time, tempting you to cut back on face-to-face instructional leadership.

You can also read the book through a filter of skepticism or resistance. "AI is just a troubling trend that will take away the humanity of coaching." "It is just more bells and whistles." You are right to be cautious. Too often technology has done little or nothing to advance learning. And some of the first uses of AI into education have been disturbing—principals typing up AI-generated email feedback rather than meeting face-to-face, teachers getting direct AI feedback with no interaction with an adult, AI tutors, etc. What AI will never change is the importance of human connection. A motivated few can do machine learning (as the COVID-19 online experiment taught us); the rest of us need a human teacher.

But what if . . . this tool is different? What if you can use it to get more time to connect with your teachers? The mantra of this tool—and this book—is the following: spend less time on your laptop and more time face-to-face coaching.

Core Idea

Spend less time on your laptop and more time face-to-face coaching.

At the heart of every chapter, you will see repeatedly that face-to-face coaching is the irreplaceable driver of schoolwide achievement—not computer tutors, ChatGPT coaches, or written feedback. We are guided and inspired by social connection and mentors we know and trust. AI is not a leader. It cannot build community or inspire with purpose. Let AI handle your preparation so you can do what no machine can: develop people.

I invite you to try a new pathway: give it a chance. As you are reading, stop every time you see the LL App logo and open it.

Try it once a chapter. Measure the impact in the time you can spend face-to-face coaching. Then you can decide, based on your own experience, whether it's worth continuing. I'm not asking for blind faith—just 30 minutes. Thirty minutes that could immediately give you time for one more coaching meeting, and then more.

If it works—and Leverage Leadership leaders worldwide believe it will—you'll begin your journey toward more frequent high-leverage leadership. And if it doesn't, you'll have lost less time than you do in one unproductive meeting. Are you willing to try it? Let's start with how it works.

WHAT IS AI . . . AND WHY IS IT LIMITED?

To understand how AI tools work (and specifically tools that are called Large Language Models— or LLMs for short), it helps to start with a simple comparison. The abacus was the original computer: a tool that represented numbers by moving beads into one position or another—much like a yes-or-no choice. Like the Abacus, computers make simple yes-or-no decisions at every step. That's the foundation of the digital world and all coding: a series of 0s and 1s (yes or no) for every decision. These instructions are literally coded into the machine, so the outcome is predictable. That's why when you take any action on a laptop (like pressing "send" to send an email), you are certain it will happen.

AI works differently. Rather than live in the world of certainty, it lives on a foundation of probability. A Large Language Model (LLM) is a type of artificial intelligence designed look for patterns in trillions of pieces of information (more than we can possibly imagine!) and scans them all for the most probable answer. For example, you could ask, "Who is the leader of the Catholic Church?" AI will then look for all the possible responses. It might find that 90% of all websites/sources list "The Pope", but 5% say "President Obama" and 5% say a myriad of other responses. AI then simply picks the more probable response: The Pope.

Understanding this premise can explain one of the first limitations you have likely experienced using AI: it can produce the wrong answer. Why? Because it's calculating probabilities. If there are enough incorrect answers on the web (and we certainly know there are with "fake news" and every other inaccurate source!), AI will sometimes give you errors.

There is a second major limitation in the framework of AI. By being built around probability, it falls prey to the flaw of the average. When it recommends the most probable answer, it relies on the midpoint average. As AI eliminates infrequent incorrect responses, it also eliminates the most desirable and essential: outstanding ideas that are the outliers:

Thus, if you search AI for guidance on best practices in education, it will give you average practices, not exceptional ones.

So how can we leverage the power of AI and remedy these errors? By prompting and specializing.

FIXING PROBLEM #1—REDUCING ERRORS: THE POWER OF PROMPTING (ME. YOU. WHAT. HOW.)

Imagine you have to write a communication to your school community about an upcoming Family Fun Day. You could spend a few hours writing it yourself, or you could prompt AI for help.

Here is a prompt a school leader gave to AI. What are the characteristics of this prompt and what makes it effective?

AI PROMPT

- I am a principal of Smith Elementary School and we are about to have a Family Fun Day at the local park
- Here are the details you need
  - Saturday, April 1, 10:00 am -1 pm
  - Cost: free
  - To bring: one snack or dessert to share with others
  - Registration link here. RSVP by March 20th
- Here is a sample message I've written from a previous event so you can emulate my writing voice. [attached]
- Be my multi-audience school communications specialist
- Generate email messages for different audiences:
  - Create versions for my district, staff, and families
  - Create one version for email and one for a social media blast
  - Highlight dates in bold
  - Keep facts consistent across all versions
  - Preserve my writing voice

Stop & Jot

What are the characteristics of this prompt?
What helps make it effective?

_____

_____

_____

AI doesn't know who you are, what you need, or how to do it unless you tell it, explicitly. Think of AI as a newly hired special assistant who is ready for an assignment anytime. The clearer your instructions, the better the output:

➤ **ME:**   Who you are (context for your school and the problem you are trying to solve)
➤ **YOU:**   What role you want AI to play (in this case, your communications specialist)
➤ **WHAT:** What you want AI to do (write multiple communications)
➤ **HOW:**   How you want AI to do it (the details)

Good prompts take you 90% of the way there. There are two final moves that get it to 100%:

➤ **Revise:** Evaluate the final product to make sure it meets your needs. This is critical. Getting it 90% of the way there is not the same as getting it right. So prompt it to revise and correct. It will respond in seconds. There is no limit on the revisions you can make and the more you do it, the quicker you will get.
➤ **Personal Touch:** Make it your own with your own voice and style. Insert your school's language, examples, or routines so teachers hear your voice in the plan. The best outputs feel authentically you!

CORE IDEA

The more precise your prompts, the better the response:
Me. You. What. How. (Revise. Personal Touch.)

FIXING PROBLEM #2—INCREASING EXCELLENCE: THE POWER OF SPECIALIZATION

Part of the reason that AI LLMs gives average responses is that they don't have the ability to determine which outlier responses are actually desirable. For one, they cannot download proprietary content, so they are lacking key books and tools that are not in the public domain. This limitation can introduce errors and unreliable—even dangerous—outcomes. You may have heard about errors in medical diagnosis from doctors using generic AI. Here's an example that came to me from a lawyer: he was trying to find court cases that set precedent for his current case, and AI gave him inaccurate citations; some were completely fabricated (because they existed on the web somewhere!). So how do fields like law and medicine avoid this trap and still take advantage of AI's power? They specialize.

MedPalm (a leading medical LLM at the time of this writing) restricts AI's source material to proprietary content—approved medical textbooks and guidelines. The result? A targeted, specialized LLM with all the power of AI but a limited resource library. Remember the bell curve graph? MedPalm, and other specialized LLMs searching for answers exclusively in the far right hand section where excellence resides. And while it's the go-to LLM for doctors, it doesn't replace their humanity—listening to patients, conducting physical exams, refining treatment plans, and training Residents. Using MedPalm, Doctors have more time for patients because they spend less time researching and scanning for knowledge. Other professions have adopted the same, like Chat Law and BloombergGPT.

THE LEVERAGE LEADERSHIP APP—A SPECIALIZED LLM FOR YOU

The Leverage Leadership App applies the same principles of specialized LLMs for instructional leadership. What makes it unique and irreplicable is that we have uploaded the proprietary content of all my books and tools in one place—including one-pagers, exemplar scripts, systems, and a guide to access our brand new library of videos. Every exemplar in the app has been proven in one of the highest-achieving or highest-gaining schools worldwide. No other sources are included, thereby eliminating the "average." It has been beta-tested with Leverage Leadership leader-champions who iterated on those resources to create unlimited tools for you.

What's more, it includes immediate updating. As we make improvements to Leverage Leadership implementation resources, we immediately upload the new tools and guidance in the LL App. So rather than wait for the next book release or revised workshop, you can access best practices instantaneously. With the touch of a button, preparation has never been easier.

Table of Contents
Leverage Leadership App

NOTE: Contents will expand over time, so open the app to see the latest.

1. **Where to Start if I Don't Know**
   - "My Current Reality Diagnostic"—Leverage Leadership Implementation Rubric
   - "Choose Your Lever" Wizard (interactive prompt flow)
   - "I Have 1 Hour" Fast-Start Options

2. **Coaching and Leading**
   - Observation and Feedback
     - Plan an Observation-Feedback Meeting
     - Select the highest-leverage action step
     - Real-Time Feedback (feedback while observing)
   - Data-driven Instruction
     - Plan Weekly Data Meetings (unpack standards/exemplars/assessments, ID the student gap, reteach lessons)
     - Monitor the Learning
   - Weekly Planning Meetings
     - Plan Weekly Planning Meetings (unpack standards/texts/exemplars, create/revise tasks/exit tickets, ID moment of productive struggle)
     - Evaluate lesson plans for their rigor and alignment to standards/end-goal assessments
   - Leading PD
     - Faculty Meetings
     - Practice Clinics
     - Full-day PD
   - Leading Leadership Team Meetings
     - Planning Leadership Team Meetings
     - Follow up

- Coaching Principals or Instructional Leaders
  - Coaching principals/instructional leaders 1-on-1
  - Coaching principals in teams (e.g., Playbook Meetings)
  - Follow up
3. **Culture**
   - Culture Systems (Routines, Minute-by-minute plans, rollouts)
   - Rubrics and Walkthrough Protocols
   - Staff Culture Tracker
   - Accountability Conversations
4. **Systems**
   - Yearlong Systems (schoolwide calendar, DDI calendar, PD calendar)
   - Quarterly Systems (playbooks, monthly maps, 6-week reteach plans)
   - Weekly Systems (leader schedules, time/task management tools, delegation of tasks)
5. **Schoolwide Communication** (weekly memo and communications, emergencies, updates)

You haven't even read the book yet, and you are already ahead of the game! And the more you read each chapter, the more you'll be able to glean from the app.

Here we learn a powerful lesson about what AI can be when used well. It doesn't replace your judgment; it amplifies it.

Core Idea

AI doesn't replace your judgment; it amplifies it.

THE GOAL OF THE LL APP

The metric that matters is simple: Does the Leverage Leadership App save you time to allow you to do more face-to-face instructional leadership? And does it make you more effective—positively impacting the learning? If it does, it works. If not, it's just tech.

> ## Core Idea
>
> If AI isn't giving you more face-to-face time with teachers—
> and more effective coaching—It's just tech.

So keep this measure in mind. If face-to-face time doesn't increase, and neither does the learning, this is a waste of time. Period.

DO THIS NOW—A SMALL WIN

You might feel the urge to keep reading or put the device down. Stop. Give it a chance. Any new practice requires a first rep. Take 60 seconds and try one of these right now—we dare you.

Click on the App anytime you see it in the text.

Stop & Do

Open the Leverage Leadership App. Do one of the following tasks. It will take you no more than a few minutes:

1. Evaluate a lesson plan to see if it is aligned to the rigor of your state test and state standards. (Have any lesson plan ready to upload—in any format!)

2. Analyze student work: "Here are anonymized exit ticket samples. Identify the gap and propose reteach moves for Friday."

3. Plan one feedback meeting that you have next week.

LL App

What are your takeaways?

_____

_____

_____

BUILD THE HABIT (SO IT STICKS)

The hardest part isn't using the tool once—it's building the routine to make it a habit that sticks (more about habits in Chapter 8). Try this progression:

➤ **Chapter checkpoints:** During each of the Leverage Leadership chapters you read, stop and do each AI task even if you don't use it—just to build the habit.

➤ **30 minutes a day:** Choose a consistent time slot to work 30 minutes in the app (most leaders choose right before or after school). Set an initial daily goal of generating one plan and evaluating one of your own resources.

➤ **Two focused days—One "Meeting Build" and one "Task":** Choose one day a week as your "meeting build" day—plan all your meetings for that day in one chunk (e.g., feedback meetings, leadership team meeting, faculty PD, PLCs). Choose a second day for your tasks/tools (e.g., schedule, weekly memo, communications).

➤ **Expand to your Full Task List:** Start using the app to manage your time and tasks— let it build your schedule each day and lay out your tasks.

READY. SET. GO.

If you took the leap, tried out the app, and began accelerating your preparation --bravo! It will only get faster. In the rest of the book, we'll teach you how to use your AI-enhanced preparation to coach teachers face-to-face.

AI doesn't have a heart and it can't lead, but it is a game-changing tool when leveraged effectively.

> ### Core Idea
>
> AI doesn't have a heart and it cannot lead.
> But it can give you more time to do so.

It can allow you to do more of what we'll talk about next: the seven levers of leadership. Remember: you don't have to fear the tool. You just have to leverage it well.

Here is the precise one-pager for using AI:

AI Primer
Me. You. What. How.

Prepare	**Prepare**

	• Determine your deliverable (plan a meeting, evaluate work, build a schedule, etc.)
	• Have your tools and data in hand:
	  ○ Tools: relevant Leverage Leadership one-pagers, any exemplars you plan to use
	  ○ Data: relevant student work, lesson plans, calendar, etc.

Me. **You.** **What.** **How.**	**Me. You. What. How.**
	Me—Who you are and context • State your role, school, grade/subject, and relevant context **You—What you want AI to be** • "Today, be my Leverage Leadership coach and help me prepare for this meeting." **What—What you want produced:** • Ask for the exact artifact (script, bullets, agenda, schedule): "Write the full script for my Weekly Data Meeting." **How—How you want it built** • Name the precise details of what you want, e.g., name standards, artifacts to analyze, and formatting.
	• Example: "Review TEKS 6.4 (ratios), analyze attached student work, find the highest leverage gap, and include a Know–Show Chart plus a reteach lesson script. Embed all of it into one script I can run in the meeting."

Refine it	Give it feedback. Add your personal touch.
	Quality check—Give it feedback: • Do *not* assume it will be perfect: review for errors or gaps • Tell it what to adjust (tone, length, examples, steps) • "Shorten it to 30 minutes, keep only three questions per section, and add a model reteach aligned to the gap." **Add your personal touch:** • Insert the personal details of your school, team, students • Adjust it to meet your voice

Part I

Instruction

Chapter 1

Data-Driven Instruction

Peer-to-Peer: 30 Minutes that Tell it All

If you want to see the magic happen at Northeast Elementary school, don't just visit classrooms—also enter the conference room. At 11:10 AM on a Thursday morning, Principal Candace Young is seated at a table with her third-grade team for prep. Her leadership team's newer members are also in the room to observe and learn—real-time PD. What is most striking is the prevalence of charts—multiple charts on every surface filled to the brim with information. One such chart has been pulled to the front for this meeting. You see the following:

Standard: 3.OA.9: Identify arithmetic patterns (including patterns in the addition table or multiplication table) and explain them using properties of operations. (patterns in columns and rows)	
Know	**Show**
• Multiples are the numbers reached when skip counting by a given factor	• Show a strategy to use place value to multiply by multiples of 10

(Continued)

• Even and odd numbers are repeated arithmetic patterns.	• Multiply by multiples of 10 by first decomposing the multiple of 10 into (a) × 10 and using the associative property to group the two smaller factors before multiplying by the 10
• All numbers with a 0 in the ones place are multiples of 10	
• Naming the tens (9 tens) is equivalent to the number times ten (e.g., 9 tens is the same as 9 × 10)	
• Understand the multiplying by ten pattern: "When I multiply by ten, I write the factor in the tens place and add a 0 in the ones place"	
• Skip counting by a multiple of 10 can be done by skip counting by the tens digit and adding the 0 (80s, count by 8s, then add 0)	
• A multiplication equation with one multiple of 10 factor can be decomposed into three factors and solved using the associative property: for example, 20 × 3 can be decomposed into (2 × 3) × 10 to help solve.	

There is something else noteworthy: the room is quiet as teachers are bent over samples of their students' most recent exit tickets looking for patterns.

The timer goes off, and Candace asks, "Ok! Now that we looked at non-mastered student work, using the language of the chart, what is the highest leverage gap you see?"

The teachers immediately jump in, as one teacher says, "The gap was in the explaining of the arithmetic patterns using the properties of operations." "Do you agreed that this should be our gap?" Candace asks the rest of the team. "Yes," they say convincingly.

 WATCH Clip 2: Young—Do It (Plan)—Weekly Data Meeting

When Candace Young first arrived at Northeast Elementary School in Farmington, New Mexico, it was the only F school in the district and one of the lowest performing schools in the state. "People had given up on the school," shared Candace. But Candace was undeterred. "You don't just talk about belief. You act on it."

Candace leaned on her friend, fellow Principal Justin Pigeon in New York City, borrowing resources to start leading Weekly Data Meetings for the third-grade team. They set a goal of 85% mastery on every standard, and if students didn't reach that percentage on the exit ticket, they immediately addressed it next period. Candace commented, "We moved away from the idea that you just teach it hoping they learn; so, if they don't learn it, you have to try again until they do."

Step by step, one data meeting at a time, Northeast started to climb. They didn't just move up from F rating; they became an A school and consistently outperformed the state, becoming a National Blue Ribbon school:

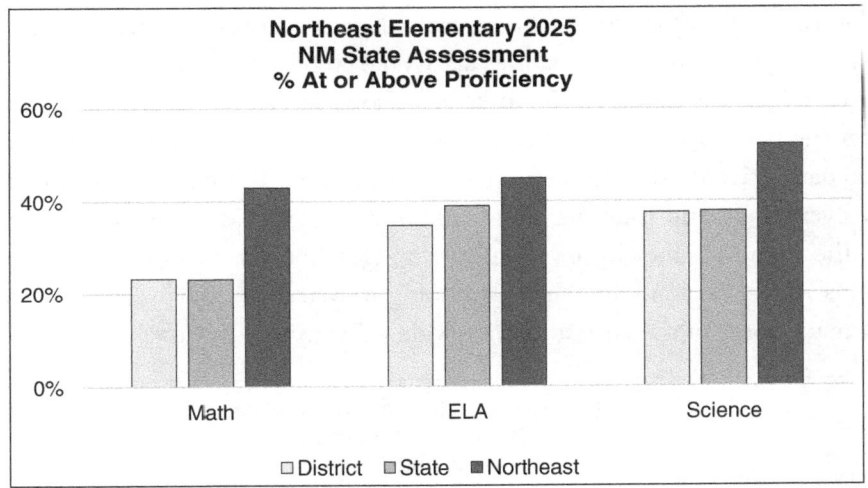

Candace is not alone. Countless leaders have followed these same principles to stay laser-focused on student learning by asking themselves a set of basic questions:

- How do we know if students are learning?
- And when they're not, what do we do?

Candace didn't get results like these by changing her students' economic situations (most of them are economically disadvantaged) or their racial backgrounds. She did it by embracing data-driven instruction.

"Data" has long been a contentious word in some educational circles. But effective data-driven instruction isn't about limiting the content we teach nor about reducing our students to numbers. On the contrary, data-driven instruction is about knowing precisely what our students need and meeting them there every step of the way. It's about shifting our daily focus from "Did we teach it?" to the much more pertinent: "Did they learn it?"

Core Idea

Effective instruction isn't about whether we taught it.
It's about whether students learned it.

Putting this simple principle to work fundamentally transforms schools. More importantly, it transforms *all* types of schools, from district schools to turnaround schools to charter schools, forging success stories across the globe. "'Did they learn it' isn't just for turnaround," affirms Candace. "It works for schools at every lever wherever you are!"

Over the past 20 years, I have observed and worked with leaders who have implemented data-driven instruction effectively to get results. Those leaders have come from nearly every state and multiple countries,[1] and they include leaders who have been either the highest-achieving or highest-gaining school in 100 different cities. They aren't just doing it alone; they are also doing it system-wide like in Charleston, SC, which made some of the largest district-wide gains in the country:

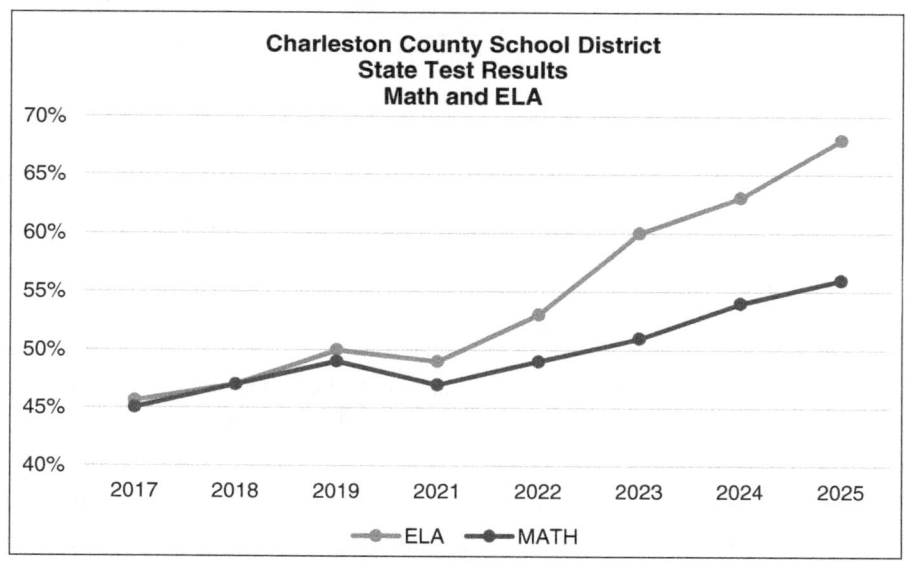

In working with them, I can affirm without question that data-driven instruction is the single most effective use of a school leader's time. Candace's 40-minute weekly data meetings are the highest-leverage, most game-changing 40-minute conversations possible—week after week, and she knows if students are learning. And when they aren't, she fixes it. Leaders like Candace do the same.

Core Idea

The most effective teachers and leaders know when teaching is working. And when it isn't, they fix it.

In this chapter, we'll examine and show the powerful actions that leaders like Candace use to guarantee student learning. They fall into three phases in the ongoing cycle of teaching and learning:

1. **Assess:** Set the road map for rigor.

2. **Analyze:** Identify the gaps in student understanding.

3. **Act:** Reteach key content to get students on track.

The pages that follow will cover all of these in depth plus the systems you'll need in place to roll them all out. Without further ado, let's dive in.

ASSESSMENT: WHAT WILL STUDENTS LEARN?

Imagine a group of sixth-grade Math teachers who are all charged with teaching their students the following standard:

Seventh-Grade Math Standard
Expressions and Equations

- Use variables to represent numbers and write expressions when solving real-world or mathematical problems; understand that a variable can represent an unknown number.

- Use variables to represent quantities in a real-world or mathematical problem and construct simple equations to solve problems by reasoning about the quantities.

- Write and solve word problems leading to equations of the form $px + q = r$, where p, q, and r are specific rational numbers. Solve equations of these forms fluently.

—CCSS.Math.Content.7.EE.B.4.

Each of these seventh-grade teachers is given a curriculum and a Math textbook that is aligned to this standard, and they start teaching. At the end of the week, all the teachers create their own one-question assessment/exit ticket to see if students have mastered the standard. As you look at their questions below, consider this question: What is the difference between what students have to know and be able to do to solve each assessment item?

The Power of Assessment

Seventh-Grade Math Assessment Questions

1. Write an equation that matches this sentence: *A number decreased by 7 equals 15.*
2. Solve for x: $3x + 1 = 28$.
3. A student earned $24 for mowing three lawns. If she earns the same amount for each lawn, write and solve an equation to find how much she earns per lawn.
4. A plumber charges a flat service fee of $45 plus $25 per hour of work. Write an equation for the total cost C in terms of hours h, and find how many hours she worked if the total bill was $145.
5. A moving company charges a one-time equipment fee of $40, plus $25 for each hour of labor. Last weekend, Maya and her friend hired the company for a short job. The total bill came to $190. Two workers completed the job, and each worked the same number of hours. How many hours did each worker work?

Stop & Jot

What is the difference in what students have to know and be able to do to solve each assessment item?

_____

_____

_____

_____

_____

_____

_____

If you take a moment to solve each of these problems, you will quickly notice how different they are. Generally, each question ratchets up the rigor from the question before it. Question 1 is simple and procedural, and you can solve it almost instantly (and it also misses the more challenging part of the standard). Question 2 is more complex algebraically, but it is still a basic equation with relatively easy numbers to solve. Question 3 asks students to translate a simple word problem into an equation and solve it, but it doesn't fully address the standard because it doesn't address both constants and variables. Question 4 moves into true multi-step reasoning: students must recognize that the total cost includes both a fixed amount and a variable rate, then represent that relationship algebraically before solving. Question 5, the most challenging, demands layered reasoning within a single equation, and students must understand that two workers contribute equally to the total, so the variable must represent their combined work. This final problem asks not only for procedural fluency but also for conceptual understanding of how multiple quantities relate in an equation.

Now imagine five teachers planning instruction around this same standard. Teacher #1 might report that 90% of her students "mastered" it, while Teacher #5, using the most complex problem, might say that only 40% did. Both are technically correct—but they aren't speaking the same language. They're measuring mastery at completely different levels of rigor. Even when teaching the same standard, from the same curriculum, they're assessing entirely different expectations.

And that's the heart of the matter: Standards are meaningless until you determine how to assess them.

Core Idea

Standards are meaningless until you determine how to assess them.

The best-worded standard and most sophisticated curriculum don't tell you what students need to do; the question you ask them does. The assessment, then, sets the bar for rigor.[2]

This core principle has upended how we design instruction. Traditionally, we tell teachers to backward plan from standards. Plan your lessons to help students master the standard and, after teaching, plan an assessment that you will use to measure it. This thinking process, however, is backward. What this leads teachers to do is to design an assessment that matches how they taught, which may or may not guarantee the rigor like question #5 above. Essentially, we are allowing the teachers to define their own bar for rigor, which means every classroom will learn content at highly varying degrees of difficulty.

Now contemplate the reverse. Imagine if *before* you start planning the teaching, you design the end assessment. Then you ask yourself, "How do I have to teach the content so my students master this level of assessment?" You have changed the order of instruction: you make assessment the starting point, not the end.

Core Idea

Assessments are the starting point for instruction, not the end.

Candace's teachers understand this idea, and it changes the way they plan and execute their teaching. They work backward from assessments that demand the level of rigor they need their students to be capable of doing, and they plan what to teach from there. With assessment as their starting point, they travel a much more direct journey to get to the proper destination.[3]

A Word On . . .
Rigor, Multiple Choice, and Open-Ended Responses

One of the most common criticisms of data-driven analysis is that it reduces learning to "rote-level" or "basic" skills, preventing students from engaging in "real" thinking. Beneath that critique lies a mistaken belief—that the format of a question determines its rigor. By this reasoning, assessment types like multiple-choice questions are inherently "un-rigorous" and lack analytical value. Let's test that claim by looking at a question from F. Scott Fitzgerald's *The Great Gatsby*.

Directions: In this passage, the narrator, Nick Carraway, observes Gatsby standing alone at the end of his dock. Read the excerpt and answer the question that follows.

"And as I sat there, brooding on the old, unknown world,
I thought of Gatsby's wonder when he first picked out the green
light at the end of Daisy's dock.
He had come a long way to this blue lawn,
and his dream must have seemed so close that he could hardly fail
to grasp it.
He did not know that it was already behind him,
somewhere back in that vast obscurity beyond the city,
where the dark fields of the republic rolled on under the night."

1. **Question:** The description of Gatsby's dream as "already behind him" contributes to the meaning of the passage primarily by—

   a. contrasting Gatsby's optimism with the narrator's growing cynicism.

   b. symbolizing the fading of Gatsby's hopes and the illusory nature of the American Dream.

   c. suggesting Gatsby's dream will soon be realized through his persistence.

   d. illustrating the distance between wealth and love in Gatsby's pursuit of Daisy.

To answer this question correctly, students must interpret symbolism ("the green light"), perspective (Nick's reflection), and theme (the unattainable nature of the American Dream).

Even if they understand the literal meaning, they might still choose A or D unless they can discern that the line "already behind him" carries irony and finality, not anticipation—leading to the correct answer, B.

That's sophisticated textual analysis. And, yes, this is precisely the sort of question that appears on AP Literature and SAT Evidence-Based Reading exams.

Now, consider an open-ended alternative:

- **Prompt:** Analyze how Fitzgerald uses imagery and symbolism in this passage to convey the novel's central theme about the nature of the American Dream.

There's no doubt that this prompt is rigorous and valuable. It asks students to generate their own argument, select evidence, and synthesize meaning across text and theme.

In the end, both the multiple-choice and open-ended questions add value, and they complement each other in essential ways. One (open-ended) demands that students generate their own thesis; the other (multiple-choice) challenges them to discern between several viable interpretations and identify the strongest one. In our world today, both skills matter. We need readers who can distinguish between subtle shades of meaning as much as writers who can construct meaning from the ground up. And we need both pragmatically: throughout life, we are called upon to perform in both formats—the SAT, LSAT, and professional certification exams on one side, and the essays, reports, and presentations of college and career on the other.

To teach only one skill is to shortchange the intellect. To teach both is to develop thinkers who can reason, write, and discern—the true hallmarks of rigorous education.

Where is the Starting Line? Keys to Effective Assessments

Almost all schools strive to offer instructional "rigor." Authors from Dagget to DuFuor have offered definitions of rigor.[4] Barbara Blackburn and others have defined it: ". . .creating an environment in which each student is expected to learn at high levels, and each is supported so he or she can learn at high level, and each student demonstrates learning at high level."[5] And as Del Stover underscored for the *American School Board Journal*, setting the right assessments to give students the opportunity to demonstrate high-level learning is an indispensable step to creating a rigorous environment.[6] But all of this just goes to raise the question: what does a rigorous assessment actually look like?

At Northeast, and at schools that achieve similar results, leaders and teachers use the following criteria to design their assessments:

Common: If assessments define rigor, then they must be common across all classes and grade levels if we want to guarantee equal rigor in each classroom. "You're not talking the same language without a common assessment," Candace comments. If not, we will have some teachers that push their students to the highest levels of learning and others who don't. This is not just true for elementary schools; instead, it applies at every level. Taro Shigenobu is the principal of the Henderson Collegiate High School, one of the highest-achieving high schools in North Carolina (more on him in Chapter 2 on Planning). Taro explains, "In high school, it's easy to unwittingly lower expectations by starting where students are. Establishing a common end goal first gets all the teachers shooting higher toward a clearer target."

Transparent: If standards are meaningless until we define how to assess them, then teachers and leaders need the assessment *before* teaching. Without it, teaching to the defined degree of rigor is left up to chance. To conceal assessments from educators is something akin to asking a group of hikers to climb a mountain without telling them which peak they need to scale. Teachers need to see the destination to be able to navigate the route.

> ## Core Idea
>
> To conceal assessments is akin to asking a group of hikers to climb a mountain without telling them which peak they need to scale. Teachers need to see the destination to be able to navigate the route.

Interim: Great schools like Candace's schedule interim assessments to identify problems while change is still possible. Rick DuFour was one of the first educators to make the analogy to health care decisions. If you have a sick child, what do you do? You seek medical help. You don't wait until she is close to death because that would be insanity! Yet schools do just that with student achievement. Rather than identifying what's making a child's learning "sick" during the school year and finding the right medicine to attack the disease (that is, make it possible to learn more effectively), schools wait to analyze year-end assessment results after some students have failed to learn.

Rick DuFour said it best in 2004: "The difference between a formative and summative assessment has also been described as the difference between a physical and an autopsy. I prefer physicals to autopsies." The top-tier school leaders highlighted throughout this book give school-wide assessments four to six times a year, and never more than eight weeks apart. This distribution rate permits teachers to make changes, while not overwhelming students (and faculty) with "test fatigue."[7] In addition to those interim assessments, Candace and other successful school leaders also develop systems to work with fellow leaders and teachers to review student work on a weekly basis—more on that later in this chapter.

Aligned: To make sure that they have sufficient rigor, interim assessments must be carefully aligned to the end-goal assessment of that class (state test, AP exam, etc.). Remember from our earlier Math question example: if you only aspire to vague goals like "critical thinking" or "problem solving," you will have totally different levels of rigor in each classroom. There are a few levels of alignment:

- **State test-aligned:** Students who fail their state test are likely not ready for college. That being said, there are many students who pass their state tests and are *still* not ready to attend or succeed at college. State tests, then, are a necessary but insufficient step to college readiness. It is important to make sure they can meet this bar, and if that is in question, then part or most of the interim assessment should be aligned to the rigor of the state test.

- **College ready-aligned:** The rigor of our assessments determines our commitment to college-readiness. If they aren't aligned, then talk of college-readiness is empty. For high school, there are many assessments already well-defined: Advanced Placement, International Baccalaureate, and SAT. These can be complemented by performance assessments like a well-designed research paper that all students will be required to master. For elementary and middle schools, the task of being college-ready is less well-defined, but the leaders cited in this book aspired for above-grade-level proficiency for all their students. That takes the form of integrating Algebra earlier into the Math curriculum (and assessing accordingly) or setting higher targets for proficiency on reading assessments.

Blazing a Trail: A High School Approach to "College Ready Rigor" On Interim Assessments

In concrete terms, what does it mean to design an assessment with "college-ready rigor"? Although the specific steps may vary depending on the content area involved, there are several common features.

Mike Mann has led Washington Park High School in Newark, NJ, for 20 years, and it has remained one of the highest achieving urban high schools in the nation.[8] When his teachers design their assessments, they start with existing high-rigor materials. They take practice SAT and AP exams. ("It's amazing how much you forget about the rigor of these exams when you haven't taken them in a while!" comments Mike.)

Then they don't assume that curriculum or lesson plans meet that rigor; they adjust the assessments to match. "When I'm thinking about the rigor of SAT questions when I teach, it influences the teaching. It is truly a road map."

- **Curriculum sequence-aligned:** Once you have an assessment that establishes the appropriate level of rigor, then you need to make sure that those assessments are aligned to your curriculum. Namely, in the corresponding 6-8 weeks prior to each assessment does your curriculum teach the standards that will appear on that assessment? If not, teachers will rightfully protest that you're not testing what they're teaching, and that defeats the whole purpose of interim assessments.

Beware: High Quality Instructional Materials do Not Always Equal High Quality Assessments

Despite the increase in high-quality instructional materials in recent years, unfortunately at the time of this writing, most were still lacking in the area of assessment. Their assessments and check for understanding are often well below the rigor of state tests and college readiness. They often lack sufficient writing in ELA and complexity in Math. When that happens, leaders like Michelle Koyama of Colfax Elementary School (more on her in Chapter 8) revise the exit tickets/assessments to elevate and align the target. "We noticed in our ELA curriculum it demanded almost no writing. So, we mapped out exactly what children need to be able to write from fifth grade back to kindergarten, and inserted new tasks and prompts to meet that level of writing." Their ELA scores jumped so significantly that they were performing at the level of the most affluent schools around them.

Don't assume when it comes to your curriculum. Test it. How? Open up your Leverage Leadership App, put in a lesson plan and the materials, and the app will evaluate it against your state test and make the recommended adjustments in seconds.

LL App

Reassess: Interim assessments are not unit tests: they need to keep measuring all that has been learned throughout the year, not just the most recent unit. This is critical because of how difficult it is for children—and adults—to retain learning. Think about your own education. Many of you took Calculus in high school or college. If you took a Calculus final exam today, you likely would not do nearly as well (unless you continue to use that Math). Why? If you don't use it, you lose it.

Core Idea

If you don't use it, you lose it.
Keep reassessing student material yearlong to hold onto the learning.

The latest research in cognitive development only reinforces this statement.[9] If this is the case for us as adults, why do we expect third graders to learn about measurement in September and be able to show mastery in March if they are not asked to do any measurements in the months in between? Reassessing standards throughout the year makes that possible. This principle is just as critical at the high school level. If you are preparing for an AP exam with vast amounts of content, you will need to keep using that content to help you retain it.

A Word On . . . Data-Driven Instruction and Kindergarten

To those who think that data-driven instruction has nothing to do with kindergarten classrooms, you haven't talked to kindergarten teachers! Strong kindergarten teachers are the most data-driven of any: they track student performance on their letters, sounds, shapes, numbers, etc. Though they don't use traditional paper-and-pencil assessments, they are driving instruction with data every day. That is a huge reason why kindergarteners can make such gigantic leaps in learning. Respond to student needs and learning improves. Kindergarten teachers can teach us this lesson as well as anyone!

Developing quality interim and formative assessments that meet these high bars can be a challenge. No longer. Leverage your Leverage Leadership App and AI. Open it up: it will help you generate exit tickets, in-class tasks, quizzes, and interim assessments that are precisely aligned to the rigor of your end-goal assessment.

It will be tailored to your state test or college-ready exam, not something general (this is the risk of curriculum that tries to serve all states equally).

Feasibility Tip

Coping Mechanisms for Imperfect Assessments

In many large school districts, principals and teachers may be required to use district-mandated or curriculum-mandated assessments that don't meet all the criteria mentioned above. Fortunately, we've seen public schools nationwide work around these limitations to build effective data systems. Here are a few of the most common strategies taken:

Common Interim: Are they not every 6–8 weeks?

- Too many assessments too frequently: deprioritize some to focus only on those where deep analysis is possible and most valuable
- Too far apart: place an additional interim assessment in the gap

Transparent: Do teachers not see the interim assessments in advance?

- Give teachers the interim assessments to review at a faculty meeting
- Give teachers a set of proxy questions from your Leverage Leadership App that are tightly aligned to the rigor of the interim assessment

Aligned: Are they not aligned to your state's standards and the rigor of the questions?

- Add questions from your Leverage Leadership App that are more aligned to the difficulty level of your year-end test
- Give teachers sample items and have them design more with their Leverage Leadership App
- Borrow other schools' assessments

Aligned: Are they not aligned to instructional sequence?

- Change sequence to match assessment (or vice versa)

Reassess: Do they not spiral content throughout the year?

- Add spiraled content questions to end of assessment, and use your Leverage Leadership App!

Stop & Do
Leverage Leadership App

Improve your Assessment in five minutes

Open up your Leverage Leadership App and try one of the following—whatever most helps your school:

1. **Improve your interim assessment:** Upload one of your interim assessments and evaluate its alignment to your state test/end goal assessment and get recommended changes to make it stronger.

2. **Improve your daily exit tickets:** Upload your exit ticket and evaluate the rigor of the task compared to the rigor of your end-goal assessment. Receive recommended changes to the exit ticket and the tasks in the lesson that can prepare students for it.

3. **Improve your curriculum tasks and assessments:** Upload the assessments from your curriculum and evaluate their rigor compared to the rigor of your end-goal assessment. Receive recommended changes to the curriculum assessment and the tasks in the lessons that can prepare students for it.

What are your takeaways?

_____

_____

_____

_____

_____

The following table summarizes key criteria for effective assessments, both on a global level and specifically for interim and weekly data collection, respectively.

Data-Driven Instruction
Keys to Effective Assessment

- **COMMON INTERIM:**
  - At least quarterly
  - Common across all teachers of the same grade level
- **TRANSPARENT STARTING POINT:**
  - Teachers see the assessments in advance
  - Assessments define the road map for teaching
- **ALIGNED TO:**
  - State test (format, content, and length)
  - Instructional sequence (curriculum)
  - College-ready requirements
- **REASSESS:**
  - Standards that appear on the first interim assessment appear again on subsequent interim assessments

A Word On . . . "Teaching to The Test"

One frequent objection to data-driven instruction is that a focus on assessment amounts to empty "teaching to the test." In this view, data forces teachers to choose between "real" teaching and irrelevant test preparation. If the assessments a school uses are not rigorous enough or if they are not aligned to what students need to know, then this is a valid critique. However, when interim assessments are well constructed and college-ready, they are an unparalleled resource in driving student learning. If you want students to be able to write a 6-8 page paper stating an original argument, why wouldn't you teach them to do so effectively? In the same way, if students will need to solve a quadratic equation embedded with an area problem at the SAT, shouldn't we prepare our students to succeed?

More pragmatically, in the modern American world performing well on assessments is an unavoidable reality to gain admission to the college of their choice and to succeed in almost every major profession—from fire fighters to doctors. One can argue that society *ought* to work differently, but as educators, we must prepare students to succeed in the real world around them.

The end game is clear: students who are not prepared for high-quality end goal assessments have not learned what they need.

In the end, data-driven instruction is not about teaching to the test; it is about testing the teaching. That makes all the difference.

ANALYSIS: WHAT AND WHY DIDN'T THEY LEARN?

Badminton is a game of speed, explosive power, and deception. For decades, Asian athletes owned the podiums. Then a Spanish left-hander from Huelva rewrote the script. Carolina Marín won the world title in 2014 and 2015 and, to the surprise of many, took Olympic singles gold in Rio in 2016—the first European woman to do so. She later added a third world crown. Her rise reset expectations for what a European shuttler could achieve.[10]

So, how did a player from a non-traditional badminton nation beat the odds? By turning information into advantage. From her teens, Marín and coach Fernando Rivas built an approach that treated training and scouting like a lab: training intensity, match video, and opponent tendencies were logged, tagged, and translated into simple, executable patterns. If a rival serves short to the backhand, expect this reply; if the rally opens with a flick, snap to that counter. Their library of rivals grew season after season, and every cycle they refreshed the clips, the tags, and the counters. She wasn't guessing; she was rehearsing decisions, so the first ball of the match felt like the tenth repetition.[11]

As the tools got better, so did the prep. Before major events they run what Marín calls "virtual matches": AI- and VR-assisted simulations stitched from scouting data. They map a rival's favorite sequences and stress-test counters until the high-percentage choices are clear. The effect is tactical and psychological because she walks on court feeling she already knows the person across the net, which calms her nerves when the score tightens.

Marín's story shows that an upstart from an unlikely country doesn't need superhuman physical gifts to upend favorites. She studied the right data, used it to reshape her plan, and executed it with discipline under pressure. That's how you turn data into advantage and advantage into history-making achievement.

What Marín did is part of a data analytics craze that has swept through every major sport in the world. Swimmers and cyclists study their drag and form to shave milliseconds off their times. All athletes follow tightly prescribed diets that maximize stamina, speed, muscle growth, and recovery. You can't win on talent alone: data drive results.

> ## Core Idea
>
> You cannot win on talent alone.
> Data harness talent to drive results.

The same is true in education. We know that good teaching has a positive impact itself, but there is never enough time in the school day to teach everything we would like. Therein lies the secret: if we want to have more time for teaching, we will need to spend less time on what students already know, and more on what they need.

> ## Core Idea
>
> How do we make more time for learning?
> Spend less time on what students already know
> and more on what they *need*.

Analysis of student work can help you "see" what students need. What follows are the key steps to make this sort of analysis possible.

Immediate

Candace protects time for her team's weekly data meetings more diligently than for any other activity in her schedule. Why? Because data expire quickly. For every day that passes between the time of an assessment and the implementation of a new teaching plan, students are not learning what they need. Marie Culihan, whom you will meet in Chapter 8, is of the same mind. "We will adjust many other parts of our day," says Marie, "but nothing stops our team meetings to look at student work—those are non-negotiable."

As a general guideline, this means reviewing student work as quickly and as efficiently as possible. That means within 24 hours or at maximum one week depending on the length of the assessment. At the end of the chapter, we will address how to make a yearly calendar that incorporates time for analyzing results from interim assessments as well as more regular grade-level team data meetings.

User-Friendly Reports

Before you can analyze, you must have the right data in hand. For starters, we are not talking about year-end data. At that point, the year is over and there is nothing you can do to undo the learning or lack thereof. Great data analysis begins by looking at assessment results—both interim and unit/weekly—to go further into student work. To do so, you need clear and intuitive data reports.

In today's age, we have no lack of data reporting. The key is not the sophistication of your tool, but the simplicity of its use.

Core Idea

The key to effective data reports is not the sophistication of your tool but the simplicity of its use.

Here's one sample of what an effective data report might look like.

Literacy 5-3 Results

Student Name	MULTIPLE CHOICE: TOTAL CORRECT	MULTIPLE CHOICE: % CORRECT	WRITING: AVG. SCORE (OUT OF 4)	1 Main Idea/Theme (RL.5.2)	2 Compare/contrast characters (RL.5.3)	3 Passage Structure (RL.5.5)	4 Figurative Language (RL.5.4)	5 Figurative Language (RL.5.4)	6 Narrative Point of View (RL.5.6)	7 Meaning of vocab/phrases in text (RL.5)	8 Main Idea/Theme (RL.5.2)	9 Write--Compare stories same genre (RL)	10 Prepositions (L.5.1a)	11 Consistent tense (L.5.1d)	12 Perfect tenses (L.5.1b)	13 Too/to/two	14 Pronouns	15 Punctuation (L.5.2)	16 Main Idea/Theme (RL.5.2)	17 Meaning of vocab/phrases in text (RI.5)	18 Main Ideas of a Passage (RI.5.2)
Ashanti	39	98%	92%					a				4									
Shelton	37	93%	83%									4									
Imani	27	68%	75%				c		d	a	d	3									
Lamar	32	80%	67%					a				2						c			
Mary	29	73%	67%				b		a		a	2					a				
Terrell	25	63%	50%	b			b	b	a			2						c			
Jessica	21	53%	58%								d	2	d		d	b		a		b	
Shannon	28	70%	50%					b	a	a		2				d					c
Al-Quan	18	45%	50%	d		c		b			d	2			c	d					c
TOTAL CORRECT PER Q:				18	17	16	10	9	15	19	13	2.8	18	18	13	20	13	15	21	15	19
% CORRECT PER Q:				86%	81%	76%	48%	43%	71%	90%	62%	62%	86%	86%	62%	95%	62%	71%	100%	71%	90%

Repeated 5-1 Standards:	73%
Main Idea/Theme--Lit (1,8,27):	76%
Main Idea/Theme--Info (16,18,38):	92%
Use evidence--Lit (3,6,29,31):	73%
Use evidence--Info (20, 39,42):	68%
Punctuation (15,24,32):	83%
Writing--persuasive (21)	48%

Repeated 5-2 Standards:	75%
Vocab/phrases in context--Lit (7):	90%
Vocab/phrases in context--Info (17,40):	55%
Characters: compare/contrast (2)	81%
Verb tenses (11,12,25,34):	71%
Other Grammar (13,26,33,36, 37):	83%
Writing from multiple texts (43)	67%

	MULT. CHOICE:	WRITING:
RESPEITO	73%	58%

Respeito Performance 5-1 Standards:	60%

Rather than do 50 things, the report keeps it focused on what matters most:

1. **Question level:** How students performed on each question and what wrong answer choices they made. This is incredibly important. It's not enough to know the overall percentage. Were some questions harder than others, and what does that tell us about what broke down? For example, two different texts will likely give different results on the same standard (more on that later).
2. **Skill or standard level:** How students performed on each standard or skill.
3. **Student level:** How well each individual student performed.
4. **Global or whole-class level:** How well the class performed.

To get users absorbing, analyzing, and deciding what to do, include key data points in as few pages as possible. With fewer, carefully selected data points, key takeaways are unmistakable. For clarity and ease of use, present the right data simply. Less is more.

Deep—Teacher-Owned, Test-in-Hand

Once your data are in place, now you can do the actual analysis. Candace, and leaders like her, move beyond the "what" went wrong to "why."

Find the Gap—Math Example

Imagine your students took a seventh-grade Math assessment that included questions #3-5 that we looked at in the Assessment section earlier. In parentheses was the students' mastery on each question:

3. A student earned $24 for mowing three lawns. If she earns the same amount for each lawn, write and solve an equation to find how much she earns per lawn. **(90% mastery)**
4. A plumber charges a flat service fee of $45 plus $25 per hour of work. Write an equation for the total cost C in terms of hours h, and find how many hours she worked if the total bill was $145. **(80% mastery)**
5. A moving company charges a one-time equipment fee of $40, plus $25 for each hour of labor. Last weekend, Maya and her friend hired the company for a short job. The total bill came to $190. Two workers completed the job, and each worked the same number of hours. How many hours did each worker work? **(30% mastery)**

What analysis can you already start to do without even seeing student work? In questions #3 and #4, the student demonstrates strong mastery of single-variable linear equations both in one-step and multi-step problems: they correctly isolate the variable, perform operations in sequence, and interpret the meaning of h in context. Clearly, what they are lacking in #5 is the difference from the other two.

Go a little deeper and look at student written work for each question. Here are two representative samples of the type of work most students produced:

STUDENT WORK SAMPLES	
Question #4:	**Question #3:**
$C = 45 + 25h$	$40 + 25h = c$
$145 = 45 + 25h$	$40 + 25h = 190$
$145 - 45 = 100$	$25h = 190 - 40$
$100 = 25h$	$25h = 150$
$100 \div 25 = h$	$\dfrac{25h}{25} = \dfrac{150}{25}$
$h = 4 \text{ hours}$	$h = 6 \text{ hours}$

Where did students go wrong? It wasn't in the foundations of linear equations; it is understanding what the variable represents compared to what the question is asking for. In this case, the variable h in #3 represents a repeated quantity: the combined hours of two workers. So, you're not solving for h; you're solving for ½h.

This is the power of a well-designed assessment: by varying question rigor, we open the hood on student error and get more clarity. We can see what they have and what they're missing. That will allow us to focus our efforts on what they need.

Core Idea

In analysis, start with what they have, then notice what they're missing.

Find the Gap—Literacy Example

One of the biggest errors I see in schools is superficial analysis of literacy assessments. The Science of Reading has greatly helped teachers spot and remediate errors in fluency, decoding, and the building blocks of Reading. But what happens when they have proficiency in those and still struggle with comprehension?

Too often, schools resort to reteaching a short list of standard skills: making inferences, arguments, finding evidence, finding figurative language, etc. Yet why does reteaching those same skills every year not translate to mastery of inference the following year? The challenge lies in the way we think about comprehension.

Let's learn by example. A group of seventh grade students took an assessment on a passage from Mildred Taylor's *Roll of Thunder, Hear my Cry*, set in the time of sharecropping in the South. In the scene in question, we learn that Papa has been working multiple jobs. The students had to answer the following prompt:

- "What do the details in the story reveal about Papa? Use two details to support your response."

The passage ends with this section:

> I [Papa's daughter Cassie] asked him once why he had to go away, why the land was so important. He took my hand and said in his quiet way: "Look out there, Cassie girl. All that belongs to you. You ain't never had to live on nobody's place but your own and long as I live and the family survives, you'll never have to. That's important. You may not understand that now, but one day you will. Then you'll see."

Here was a student response that was representative of the most frequent gap in the class (Note: this is a real student response on a timed digital assessment, so I have left in the typos and grammatical errors):

> The details in the story reveal that papa is caring and hard working for family. One detail for this is, "Look out there Cassie girl. All that belongs to you. you ain't ever had to live on nobody's place but your own and long as I live and the family survives you'll never have to. That's important you may not understand that now but one day you will and you'll see". Another detail is papa set out looking for work going as far north as Memphis and as far as south as the delta country." That's what show how papa is hard working

Of course, there is work we can do with the student's writing quality. But let's focus for now on his comprehension of the text. Where did it break down?

A superficial answer would look at the standards assessed (in this state's case, "identify a character's perspective" and "determine a central idea with key details from the text") and simply state that students don't have mastery of either. Another would be to say that this text is complex, and they don't have enough knowledge to access it ("They don't read at grade level so this it too much of a stretch for them").

Jessica Mullins, principal of Trevista at Horace Mann School in Denver, takes a different approach (more on her in Chapter 2). She starts with a basic framework to look at student responses to reading—we introduced these in *Love & Literacy*[12]:

RACE AND ANEZZ	
Frameworks for Teaching and Analyzing Student Writing	
Elementary School—RACE	**Upper Grades—ANEZZ**
R—**R**estate the question **A**—Make a solid **A**rgument that makes an inference about the text **C**—**C**ite key evidence to support the argument **E**—**E**xplain how that evidence supports the argument	**A**—Make a solid **A**rgument that makes an inference about the text **N**—**N**ame the technique the author uses to make that argument **E**—Cite key **E**vidence to support that argument **Z**—**Z**oom in on that evidence to unpack and analyze the word choice/author's technique **Z**—**Z**oom out to explain how that evidence contributes to the argument

Using that framework, when she evaluates student comprehension (in writing and in discourse), she asks a series of questions in a very specific order:

1. **Do they have a solid argument (A)?**
   - If yes: can they justify it with solid evidence and explanation?
   - If limited:
     - Is the breakdown in their selection of evidence or how they unpack that evidence?
     - Is the breakdown in their understanding of the basic gist of the text or in the deeper meaning of it?

2. **Do they select good evidence? (C)**
   - If no: what about the complexity of the text is preventing them from identifying it?

3. **Can they explain their evidence to support the argument (E)?**
   - If no: what about the evidence (word selection, difficulty) are they struggling to unpack?

What does Jessica's process reveal? Find the answer in the student response: Argument first. Evidence second. Explanation third. Then the text complexity will unlock the answer.

> ## Core Idea
>
> Find the answer in the student response:
> Argument first.
> Evidence second.
> Explanation third.
> Then the text complexity will unlock the answer.

What makes Jessica's analysis remarkable is that it is laser-focused on the real outcome: Did students deeply comprehend the argument of the text? She doesn't get lost in teaching inference in isolation, or work on unpacking metaphors without students ever understanding what value that adds to the text. It always starts with the argument. And when you find where the breakdown occurs, you'll find the answer as to why in the text complexity itself. In reading, the text defines the rigor. Each text whispers how to teach it. When students struggle, let the text tell you why.

> ## Core Idea
>
> Each text whispers how to teach it.
> When students struggle, let the text tell you why.

The ACT established this argument nearly 20 years ago when they proved that the biggest differentiator in performance for each student on the ACT was not the difficulty of the question (e.g., inference vs. key details vs. symbolism). Rather, it was the complexity of the text. Students performed notably higher on all standards with a less complex text and notably worse on all standards with a more complex one.[13] Yet teaching standards independent of text complexity rules in most literacy classrooms.

How can we think differently and improve literacy results? Teach comprehension one complex text at a time. (For a deeper dive on the latest in analyzing and acting on literacy results, stay tuned for my next book!)

Before you go on, try it: analyze your data in a new way:

———————————————⬤———————————————

Stop & Do
Leverage Leadership App

Improve your Analysis in Five minutes

Open up your Leverage Leadership App and try one of the following—whatever most helps your school:

1. **Analyze a daily exit ticket:** Upload your students' exit tickets and ask for help analyzing the gap. It will guide you through using your understanding of the standard and your end-goal assessment.

2. **Analyze student work from the latest assessment:** Upload your students' work from the latest assessment and ask for help analyzing the gap. It will guide you through using your understanding of the standard and your end-goal assessment.

What are your takeaways?

_____

_____

_____

_____

_____

_____

ACTION: TEACHING TO MASTERY

All the quality assessments and deep analysis are meaningless if we don't act. Until we teach differently, learning won't change. At the same time, action without proper analysis is meaningless: you will be spinning your wheels.

> ## Core Idea
>
> Assessments and analysis are meaningless if we don't act.
> Yet action without proper analysis is just
> spinning your wheels.

So, what does effective reteaching—and teaching in general—look like to achieve mastery?

Over the course of 25 years, I have had the privilege of observing the highest achieving schools and teachers across the globe. That experience has revealed a clear set of teaching practices that consistently close learning gaps for students:

- Activate knowledge
- Model
- Guide discourse
- Monitor and spiral to mastery

Let's unpack these practices in detail.

Activate/Build Knowledge

When students don't master a concept the first time, our instinct is often to reteach the same content again, just slower or louder. But what expert teachers know is that effective reteaching doesn't start with delivery; instead, it starts with activation (or building) of knowledge. Before students can make inferences, they need to retrieve and reconnect what they already know. Activating or building knowledge strengthens neural pathways. In every subject—from math to music to biology—what we remember depends on how often and how meaningfully we recall it.

> ## Core Idea
>
> Activating knowledge activates the brain: you make connections between what you already know and what you're about to learn.

Activating or building knowledge is the bridge between skill and understanding. Teaching a strategy without connecting it to knowledge is like teaching driving without a car—students might know the motions but have nothing to move forward with.

> ## Core Idea
> Teaching strategies without schema is like teaching driving without a car.

We can spend a lifetime building knowledge for students who don't have it. But what can we do in the moment, even with major knowledge gaps?

1. **Narrow the focus** to the knowledge they need the most for this task. What knowledge is *most* essential for grappling with the text and my lesson/unit goals?

2. **Activate or drop the knowledge.** One key tip: don't give away the answer to the text. Just give them knowledge. For example, when teaching Mildred Taylor's *Roll of Thunder, Hear my Cry* don't tell them that Papa doesn't want to be a sharecropper because it will be indentured servitude. Just let them learn what sharecropping is. Then push them to figure out how this applies to Papa's desire.

When teachers deliberately build and activate schema, they help students "see further," as Newton put it, standing on the shoulders of what they already know to reach higher-order thinking. Whether reteaching how to analyze a character, interpret a data set, or apply a scientific principle, the same rule applies: knowledge first, strategy second. (For a more in-depth look at this topic, you can read *Make History* or *Love & Literacy*.)

Modeling vs. Discourse

After activating knowledge, most other strategies boil down to two approaches: modeling or guided discourse (with many variations within each). Either the teacher shows the students what to do, or the teacher guides students to do the work to figure it out. The best teachers use both methods, matching them to the needs of their students and the strengths of their teaching. Here is a quick summary of some of the pros and cons for each approach:

Modeling Vs. Guided Discourse

TEACHING METHOD	PROS	CONS
Modeling	• Easier to plan • If students don't have a model of success to refer to, they likely won't be able to replicate success • Clarity: there are clear bright lines around what students must do	• Can be too procedural as opposed to conceptual • Dependent upon students learning passively at first
Guided Discourse	• Stickier, since students learn more actively and do more of the thinking • Easier to dig deeper on a conceptual level	• Harder to plan as it's dependent on excellent questions and ability to manage the discourse • Dependent on some students being close enough to push remaining students the rest of the way • Can result in only the most advanced students understanding

Let's dive into the details of how reteaching functions on the ground, beginning with the easier of the two—modeling.

Modeling

On the surface, modeling is simple: teachers show the students what to do. The challenge is how to distinguish between a lecture and an actual model. Ashley Oliver teaches at

PS 307 Pioneer Academy in Queens, NY with the coaching of principal extraordinaire Cecilia Jackson. Ashley shows us what this looks like:

 WATCH Clip 3: Oliver—Reteach Modeling, Part I (Teaching Clip)

 WATCH Clip 4: Oliver—Reteach Modeling, Part II (Teaching Clip)

Stop & Jot

What does Ashley do to model the thinking for her students?

_____

_____

_____

_____

_____

Ashley took a complex skill—how to determine the main idea by finding the best evidence—and made it simple. But she also made sure the students were set up to maximally benefit from the model. Here are the keys:

Clear Listening/Note-Taking Task: Ashley gives students a listening task that fosters active listening. Then she debriefs the model, asking:

- "What did I do in my model?"

- "What are the key things to remember when you are doing the same in your own work?"

Model the Thinking Questions, not just the Procedure: What makes Ashley's model different than many is that she models the thinking it takes to solve the problem, not just a rote procedure. She does so by naming the questions she asks herself when modeling. Some of these are universal prompts ("What is this question asking me to do?" "What do I already know about this?" "How can I check my work?"). Other questions are unique to that context. ("So what type of evidence am I looking for?"). Students will remember a thinking process, not a list of steps. So, follow Ashley's lead and demonstrate replicable thinking steps that students can follow. Students will then learn how to think, not just mimic.

Core Idea

Teach them how to think, not just mimic.

End with You Do: Of course, a model is only valuable if students then get the opportunity to apply it.

Guided Discourse

Guided discourse is often seen as the magic in the classroom, when students engage in rigorous dialogue and reach deep, thoughtful conclusions. Yet there are risks to manage. As one teacher shared with me, discourse can be like a squirrel—you never know quite where it is headed and it can run up the wrong tree really quickly! So how you do get that squirrel of discourse running up the proper tree?

Dienabou Magassa shows us an example of how to do this. Dienabou worked at Baychester Middle School in Queens, NY. In the video clip here, you'll see part of what makes her so successful. The students are grappling with a key question in Math: does the value of a number change if a zero is included in the decimal? They have the following examples to spark the thinking: 3.106 and 3.160. Watch what Dienabou does to drive discussion:

  WATCH Clip 5: Magassa—Guided Discourse (Teaching Clip)

Stop & Jot

How does Dienabou guide her students to generate the answer themselves?

Write First, Talk Second: Before beginning discourse, Dienabou has students complete a task. That allows her to monitor, collect data, and anticipate where the conversation will go. It will also give her the opportunity to determine which students have strong answers or which are struggling so she can call on them at key moments during the discussion. Too often, teachers start with discussion: let 100% participate before you do so!

Show-Call: Dienabou makes a very simple move at the beginning of the discourse that changes everything. Instead of talking, she simply displays two samples of student work. Think about the power of this action: she reduced her language significantly, and she shifted the thinking back to the students. Doug Lemov calls this Show-Call.[14] You can do this with exemplar student responses, incorrect responses, or in this case, with both.

Turn and Talk, then Poll the Room: Rather than begin with large-group discussion, Dienabou starts with a Turn and Talk. This action sounds simple, but it is often overlooked. Yet Turn and Talks maximize the number of students who are sharing during discussion. It lets everyone work it out verbally with a peer before sharing to the large group. Dienabou then takes it one step further by polling the room to see where they stand before starting the discussion. In this way, she has an immediate idea of where students are. This allows her to decide how to manage the conversation.

Strategic Questioning: Once the class comes together for a large-group discussion, Dienabou uses the data she collected from the writing task and classroom poll to call on students based on their learning need. When most people have gotten to the right answer, Dienabou can call on a student who initially had the wrong answer to check for understanding to make sure they know why. If most of the class is still struggling, she can call on someone who had the right answer initially to justify their response. Strategic questioning allows Dienabou to reduce the likelihood of haphazard conversation and get students grappling with the key learning challenge.

End with You Do: Just as with modeling, guided discourse doesn't get solidified until students get the opportunity to try it again on their own.

A Word on . . . Special Needs Students And DDI

I've had the chance to interact with and learn from the highest-achieving special education teachers, and to a person they tell me: data-driven instruction is at the heart of what they do. When you serve children with specific learning needs, you identify their personal learning gaps and design teaching strategies to match. There is no other choice: without being data-driven, your children won't learn!

Natascha de la Torre, an incredibly successful SPED instructor at Vailsburg Elementary School in Newark, New Jersey, says data-driven instruction is one of the most important tools she uses to help special needs students meet learning goals. "You have to know where you want every student in your class to be but also to understand each individual student's learning profile," Natascha says. "That means you need to identify a realistic place you might get that student to first. Being data-driven lets you build a trajectory that will get them to that larger goal eventually. It might take some of my students longer to meet those goals, but we're not going to lower the bar."

Here are some of the tips special educators like Natascha have shared with me to pass on to you and your special education teachers:

First line of action: Grab the low-hanging fruit first.
Often the challenge of analyzing interim assessment data for a student with special needs can be that there are too many questions "in the red"—that is, where they were not proficient. When that happens, start with the low-hanging fruit:

- Sort classroom data by students' scores: look for the questions that only the struggling students are getting wrong. These are likely the easiest access points, and other questions will likely be addressed by the general education teacher in the large group setting. Natascha points out this helps students of all learning abilities because it underscores standards that need to be retaught to *everyone*, not just special needs students.

- From there follow the same steps of analysis as for any other student:
  o What are all the steps the students need to take to answer these questions correctly?
  o Which of these steps need to be made more explicit to the students?
  o What sort of practice do the students need to master this standard—heavy repetition of computational skills? Following a multi-step protocol?

Second line of action: Provide in-class support during reteaching

For special needs students who take classes with their general education peers, the best thing to do is support the lead teacher during reteaching:

- What are the standards that will be reviewed or retaught for the whole class?

- Are the struggling students' misunderstandings different than those of the rest of the students on these standards?

- What additional support or steps will struggling students need when these standards are being reviewed?

In short, as Natascha's colleague Michelle Rolfert puts it, "The only difference between the general education setting and the special education setting is the need to reassess more frequently and with differentiated assignments. The process is the same."

Academic Monitoring and Follow up

When a school leader or teacher asks me for the highest value, in-classroom action to improve student learning, without hesitation I say academic monitoring. You can have the best classroom culture in the world or the finest model or guided discourse, but what you do during independent practice is the biggest difference. We explore this deeply in *Get Better Faster 2.0* (see Phase 2).[15] To see this in action, check out elementary teacher Melissa Erberti from PS 226 in the Bronx, NY:

 WATCH Clip 6: Erberti—Academic Monitoring (Teaching Clip)

Melissa highlights the key to student improvement: you cannot correct what you don't detect.

If you want to immediately impact student achievement, follow Melissa's lead: she gave individual feedback to every student at least three times in just 15 minutes of independent practice. That's more feedback than many students get in a month. When you do this repeatedly, you slowly chip away at misunderstanding and work to mastery.

Candace knew this early on: a single successful reteaching lesson didn't seal the deal for her students. "Reteaching and reassessing is so important." Reteaching is a marathon, not a sprint. Monitoring reveals if the students learned what the teacher taught—and success requires reteaching and reassessing over and over again.

Core Idea

Reteaching is a marathon, not a sprint.

ACTION: COACHING TO MASTERY, PART 1: WEEKLY DATA MEETINGS

What is the highest leverage 30 minutes for a school leader? That is a loaded question, but let's give it some consideration. Consider a principal who is committed to observing class instructions as often as possible. If the principal observed every teacher in his or her school for 15 minutes a week, she would be among the most diligent school leaders in the country. Yet even at this breakneck pace, how much instruction would she actually see? Do the math:

- Typical teaching load per teacher: **5 classes/day, 50 minutes each**
- Total minutes of instruction per week: 5 classes/day × 50 minutes × 5 days/week = **1,250 minutes**
- One classroom observation per week per teacher: **15 minutes**
- 15 minutes/1,200 minutes total instruction = **1.2% observation of instruction**

For all her attentiveness, this principle is watching her students through a peephole. Even if leaders identify the most critical 1% with these observations, they would still need to make broad assumptions about what students learned the other 99% of the time.

Now consider a leader who has rolled out data-driven instruction. On one interim assessment alone, that leader can gauge *six to eight full weeks of teaching*. Maybe that assessment doesn't capture 100% of the standards taught in that period, but it can certainly capture 80% of them. In one meeting, the leader changed the percentage of instruction she observes from 1% to a game-changing 80%:

Observation Alone:

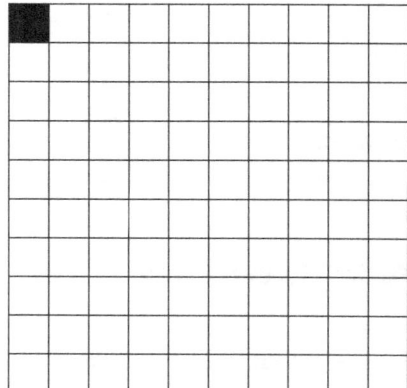

Interim Assessment Analysis Meeting:

Core Idea

Data analysis meetings shift the focus
from observing 1% of student learning to 80%.
That makes all the difference.

So, what do effective data meetings look like? Candace follows a simple, replicable protocol that all her grade-level teams use. We made mention of it in the Introduction: See It. Name It. Do It.

- **See It:** See the exemplar and the gap
- **Name It:** Name the key gap in conceptual understanding for the students
- **Do It:** Plan how to reteach the content with modeling or guided discourse, practice, and build a follow-up plan

To learn how these steps apply to a leader's work in practice, we'll follow Candace's school through one of her data meetings. Read on to understand what actions Candace takes to make this meeting successful.

Pre-Work

Muhammad Ali once said, "The fight is won or lost far away from witnesses—behind the lines, in the gym, and out there on the road, long before I dance under those lights."[16]

Nowhere is this more the case than data meetings. Candace does not schedule weekly data meetings and show up hoping they succeed; instead, her preparations prior to the meeting are what guarantee their impact. Follow her lead to set up effective meetings:

- **Prepare for the meeting:** To ensure the meeting is effective and efficient, Candace doesn't simply assume good analysis; she makes sure of it. She and her instructional leaders look at student work in advance to identify gaps and develop preliminary action plants. This allows them to support the teachers when their analysis is superficial or their action plan won't close the gap. This work used to take a long time but no longer. Open up the Leverage Leadership App, upload a sample of student work, and you can do the following in minutes:

  - Review or write the ideal interpretation of the standard being addressed

  - Identify the gap in student understanding

  - Plan the key part of an effective reteach plan to address that gap

LL App

- **Room and Materials Ready:** One of the most striking things about the most effective data meetings is how smoothly they run. That is due in no small part to having the room set up with all the materials. Here is a quick go-to list that leaders like Candace use to set up their meetings:

  - Timer

  - Copy of the standard and exemplar response

- Chart paper and/or whiteboard to take notes
- Upcoming lesson plans and any materials needed to plan a reteach lesson
- A sample of high/medium/low student work—typical errors that are representative (this will save hours of sorting student work during the meeting and let teachers focus on the analysis itself!)

The importance of preparation cannot be understated: you are super-charging the meeting and stripping away time that would be lost for non-essential actions. In this way, you have 30–40 minutes of deep conversation, rather than just 10–15: that makes a huge difference over time.

A Word on . . . Content Expertise

One of the most challenging aspects of preparing for data meetings—and participating in them—is having a level of content expertise that allows you to dive into the assessments to determine the errors. This can be a daunting task for third-grade Math, but it definitely rears its head as you get into higher level content. For a high school instructional leader, it is next to impossible to have enough content expertise to deeply analyze AP-level Chemistry, English, History, Calculus, Spanish and more!

So, what do leaders do when they must coach outside of their own content expertise? Lean on other experts to help them.

Stephanie Amaya (more on her in Chapter 6), stretched herself when she moved from being an elementary principal to leading a large comprehensive HS in Dallas, Texas. "I leaned on my best teachers for their expertise, but we also created a culture that said, 'You might know the content, but you can still learn better pedagogy."

HS Principal Taro Shigenobu (Chapter 2) takes it one step further: He uses the Leverage Leadership App to bring the experts to him. "When I need to, I use AI to learn the standard. If I just try to learn one standard at a time for each meeting I lead, it is not quite as daunting. And I'm just trying to set the "floor" for the rigor of our meeting: the teacher can always exceed me!"

Each time you engage in the content by looking at student work or planning a unit, by nature you gain more understanding. Little by little you'll be on your way to supporting your teachers across all content areas.

Try it out! Open the App and it will guide you step-by-step.

LL App

See It and Name It

With the preparation locked in, Candace is ready to lead meetings of impact. Watch how quickly Candace dives into the work of the content itself:

 WATCH Clip 7: Young—See It (Exemplar)—Weekly Data Meeting

Stop & Jot

What actions does Candace take to start the data meeting successfully? Jot down what you notice below.

_____

_____

_____

_____

_____

See the Success: Candace doesn't start with the gap or the challenge. She starts with their success. This isn't an act—this is an intentional decision to always be on the lookout for when student learning improves. And she asks her teachers to reflect on their gains with such warmth that it allows the teachers to celebrate and feel energized to tackle the next problem. Your first five minutes sets the tone for the rest of the meeting, and Candace doesn't leave that to chance.

> ### Core Idea
>
> You never get a second chance to make a first impression.
> The tone for any meeting is set in the first five minutes.

See the Exemplar: The next tempting place to start a data meeting is looking for the gap in student work. Candace doesn't do that: instead, she pre-selects a key question to focus on, and they dive in by reviewing the standard and the exemplar response. Why? Looking at the wrong answers first is like rushing to the fire without bringing water to extinguish it. You need the exemplar response to give you the pathway.

> ### Core Idea
>
> Start from the exemplar.
> If not, you will be rushing to the fire without water to extinguish it.

You'll notice that Candace mentions a Know-Show Chart: a simple way to put all the key information about a standard and task in one place. It answers the fundamental question: "What does a student need to know and be able to do to master this standard?" Here is an example:

Third Grade Math	
Know	**Show**
• Addition and subtraction are inverse operations, meaning you can use one to check the other. • Subtraction represents the difference between two values or the missing addend in addition. • Moving to the left in place value represents ten times the value. • You can regroup numbers across place values as long as the total remains the same.	• Write both equations (e.g., use subtraction to check addition). • Convert subtraction into addition to find the missing number (e.g., 175 + ___ = 423). • Show evidence of one or more algorithms: line up numbers vertically so the place values correspond in each column, or group by tens and ones, etc. • Use regrouping notation—cross out digits or add small numerals to show the exchanged tens/hundreds.

Third Grade Math	
Know	**Show**
• When a digit is zero, you must regroup across multiple place values to create the needed value while keeping the total the same. • The commutative property of addition is $a + b = b + a$; it means that changing the order of addends doesn't change the sum.	• Show multi-step regrouping correctly across zeros (borrowing from hundreds to tens to ones). • Write equations in different orders to verify equality (e.g., $175 + 423 = 423 + 175$). • Check work by using the inverse operation with the answer.

The "know" represents the conceptual understanding: if students get it right and you ask them why, what do you want them to say? The "show" represents what you want to see on student's work.

The beauty of reviewing the standard and exemplar side-by-side with such a chart is that the standard can give you academic language to describe the student thinking needed to answer the question.

What Candace does in this meeting isn't rocket science, and she didn't become a master of on-the-spot thinking. Rather, she used a set of prompts that are applicable to nearly any assessment item at any grade level:

- "What were the keys to an ideal/exemplar answer?"
- "How does the exemplar response connect to the standard?"
- "How does your student exemplar compare to the teacher exemplar? What is the gap or does it offer something yours does not?"
- "Do students have different paths/evidence to demonstrate mastery of the standard?"

Step back and note the value of what Candace just did. "By starting with the exemplar, we can more readily see what to teach to close the gap," Candace shares.

Let's see this in another context—Literacy. Watch this video of Michelle Coleman, Director of Instruction at Amethod Public Schools in California. Observe as she leads a data meeting with her middle school Literacy teacher. With an unpacked exemplar in hand, Michelle and her teacher are now equipped to get to the heart of the matter: what are the gaps between the exemplar student response and the student responses that don't reflect mastery?

WATCH Clip 8: Coleman—See It (Exemplar and Gap)—
Weekly Data Meeting

Stop & Jot

What actions does Michelle take to guide her teacher to identify the gap in Literacy?

_____

_____

_____

_____

_____

See the Gap and Name It: Here we see the impact of a Know-Show Chart that unpacks the exemplar: the teachers can use it as a reference to identify the gaps in the rest of the student work. Seeing and naming the gap in this way makes the data meeting powerful. Not only do the teachers know what to target, they've done so in a collaborative environment that cultivates trust. In this context, discovering what needs to be retaught in a classroom isn't about pointing fingers at teaching gone "wrong." It's about seeing what students need with shared clarity, so you can reach solutions together. Here Candace does the same:

 WATCH Clip 9: Young—See It (Gap)—Weekly
Data Meeting

Naming the gap seals the deal. Writing down the student error and the conceptual misunderstanding evident in that error locks in *what* went wrong, which will allow the teachers to quickly pivot to *how* to fix it.

Core Idea

You don't lock in the learning until you seal it.
Naming *what* went wrong makes it easier to plan *how* to fix it.

Do It

With solid analysis, the teachers are ready to shift their focus to reteaching. Watch what Candace and Michelle do next:

 WATCH Clip 2: Young—Do It (Plan)—Weekly Data Meeting
WATCH Clip 10: Coleman—Do It (Plan)—Weekly Data Meeting

Stop & Jot

What actions do Candace and Michelle take to get their teachers to plan the reteach?

_____

_____

_____

_____

_____

_____

Plan the Reteach: What Candace and Michelle guide the teams to do—plan the reteach—seems pretty standard. Yet most teams of teachers never get that far when analyzing student work. How all leaders does so is what makes their leadership so effective. Giving teachers time first to plan independently actually saves time: they have already articulated their ideas before they speak! But the real magic is having them "spar" with another reteach plan: that pushes them to excellence so much faster. You need to perfect a reteach plan before you practice: if not, you'll just practice doing it wrong.

Core Idea

Perfect the plan before you practice.
If not, you'll just practice the wrong way to reteach.

Candace and Michelle use some key prompts that could be used in nearly any data meeting:

- "Should we use modeling or guided discourse?" "Why?"
- "Take _____ minutes and write your script. I will do the same so we can spar."
- "Let's compare our reteach plans. What do you notice? What can we pull from each to make the strongest plan?"

At this point, both Candace's and Michelle's teachers are ready to put it all together. Watch an example from Michelle:

 WATCH Clip 11: Coleman—Do It (Practice)—
Weekly Data Meeting

Stop & Jot

What actions does Michelle take to facilitate effective practice? Jot down what you notice below.

_____

_____

_____

_____

_____

Practice: Note how Michelle and her teacher practice: as routine as any other part of the meeting. Rehearsing in this way may feel awkward at first, but develop it as an expectation with your teachers, and it will quickly become more comfortable for them (and for you!). Build a culture of practice, and practice will happen and it will change your school.

"Early on, sometimes my teachers would attempt a reteach, but really they'd just be teaching louder," Candace recalls with a laugh. "So, we'd have to go back and practice that and we would have teachers role playing their reteach for each other." That approach made all the difference. For Michelle, it is the same: practice makes perfect, making it more likely for the teacher to succeed.

Once you've practiced, it's time to lock it in. Let's visit the meeting of another leader, Alicia Iwasko from Blanton Elementary School in Dallas, TX. Watch how Alicia closes out her meeting:

 WATCH Clip 12: Iwasko—Do It (Follow up)—Weekly Data Meeting

Follow-up: Alicia asks her teachers to list all the action items at the end of the weekly data meeting and to schedule the follow up. And there is a clear target to reach. "While our end goal is 100%," shared Candace, "sometimes that number is intimidating, so we set a target of 85% to allow teachers to exceed their goal."

Think of the effectiveness of what you just witnessed. In 30 minutes, Candace's, Michelle's, and Alicia's teaching teams carefully analyzed student work and came up with a concrete reteach plan for a challenging standard. Now multiply that impact by the regular meetings that their teachers have at every grade level across the entire year. Not only do these meetings impact the assessment items that they directly tackle; they also build the habits of mind for teachers to repeat this process every day as students learn in their classroom. Candace has effectively shifted the focus from teaching to learning, and by doing so, she has raised expectations for everyone in school. Her results tell it all.

On the following pages, we've consolidated all the best practices of Weekly Data Meetings into a precise guide that you can use to lead data meetings yourself.

Weekly Data Meetings

Leading Teachers to Analyze Student Work

Prepare Before the meeting	Prepare
	Have your resources in hand:
	• Student work: student exemplar and representative sample of work that (meets standard, almost there and further off—including from students with disabilities and second language learners).
	• Lesson materials: upcoming lesson plan(s), reteaching one-pager
	Plan the meeting:
	• **Do the work:** unpack standard, ID the gap(s) in student understanding; script the reteach plan(s)
	• **Lock in participants:** core teachers that teach/support (general education, special education, and ELL)
	• **Preview protocol with teachers:** assign roles, novice teachers speak first, veteran teachers add on and clarify, leader provides additional clarity at end, chart, preview the need for concision from more verbose team members, use of a timer, creation of note taking template
See It 12 min	**See Past Success, See the Exemplar, and See and Analyze the Gap**
	See the Success:
	• "Last week we planned to reteach _____ and we went from ___ % proficient to ___%. Nice job!"
	• "What actions did you take to reach this goal?"
	See an Exemplar (8 min):
	• Narrow the focus: "Today, I want to dive into [specific standard] and the following assessment item."
	• Unpack the standard/text:
	◦ Humanities: Analyze the text and task alongside the standard
	◦ STEM: Interpret the standard(s)

- "Take 1 min: in your own words, what do students need to know/and be able to do to master this task and text?"
- Chart it: Know and Show (OR use a previous Know-Show Chart)
- Go last: add anything that is missing
- Unpack the teacher's written exemplar:
  - "Take 1–2 min to review the exemplar: What were the keys to an ideal answer?"
  - "Is there anything you would add to our Know-Show Chart?"
- Analyze a student exemplar:
  - "Take 1 min: How does your student exemplar compare to the teacher exemplar? Is there a gap?"
  - "Do students have different paths/evidence to demonstrate mastery of the standard?"
  - "Is there anything you would add to our Know-Show Chart?"

See the Gap (5 min):
- Look at a representative sample of un-mastered student work:
  - "Take 2 minutes: What are the key gaps between the rest of our student work and the exemplar?"
  - "Look back at our chart: Using the language of the standard and exemplar, what are the key misconceptions for our students?"
  - (When multiple teachers present) All teachers determine the gap for their set of student work

Name It 2 min	Stamp the key conceptual ("know") and procedural ("show") misunderstanding

Punch it—Stamp the Conceptual and Procedural Understanding:
- Identify the highest leverage gap:
  - Conceptual (know): "If they get this right and you ask them why, what do you want them to say?"
  - Procedural ("show"): annotating text, showing work, line-by-line computation, etc.
- Highlight the key parts of the Know-Show Chart that represent the gap

Do It 20–45 min	Plan the Reteach, Practice, and Follow Up
	Plan the Reteach for the Trending Gap (8–10 min):
	• Select the reteach structure:
	◦ "Will this be a mini-lesson for a full lesson reteach?"
	◦ "Do we need to activate any knowledge first?"
	◦ "Should we use modeling or guided discourse?" "Why?"
	■ Prompt to use the reteaching one-pager if they need guidance
	• Select the materials and exemplar response:
	◦ Select the task and text
	◦ Confirm (if needed) what knowledge to activate or teach
	◦ "What is the ideal answer we want to see that will show we've closed the gap?"
	◦ (If needed—follow-up question): "What is the 'why' that students should be able to articulate?"
	• Plan the reteach:
	◦ "Take _____ min and write your script. I will do the same so we can spar."
	■ **If a model:** write the think aloud and questions
	■ **If guided discourse:** select student work for Show-Call, write prompts
	■ Plan how to activate knowledge
	◦ Spar: "Let's compare our reteach plans. What do you notice? What can we pull from each to make the strongest plan?" (Revise the plan)
	• Plan the independent practice:
	◦ "What will you monitor to see if they are doing this correctly? What laps will you name?"
	Practice the Gap (remaining time):
	• "Let's practice."
	◦ **If a model:** practice modeling the thinking, precision of language, and checking for understanding

Do It 20–45 min (cont'd)	<ul><li>○ **If guided discourse:** practice Show-Call, prompting students, and stamping the understanding</li><li>○ **If monitoring:** practice the laps, annotations, and prompts when students are stuck</li></ul><ul><li>(If a struggle) "I'm going to model the teaching for you. [Teach.] What do you notice?"</li><li>Repeat until the practice is successful. Check for understanding: "What made this more effective?"</li><li>Lock it in: "How did our practice meet or enhance what we planned for the reteach?"</li></ul>**Follow Up (last 2 min):**<ul><li>Set the follow-up plan: when to teach, when to reassess, when to revisit this data</li><ul><li>○ (When multiple reteach plans) Finalize which students will get which reteach plans</li><li>○ Observe implementation within 24 hours; teacher sends reassessment data to leader</li><li>○ Spiral: Identify multiple moments when teacher can continue to assess and track mastery: Do Now questions, homework, modified independent practice</li></ul><li>Move to the lowest scoring work:</li><ul><li>○ "What students do we need to pull for tutoring? What do we need to remediate or revisit?"</li></ul></ul>

Try it Yourself!

The best way to gain expertise at Weekly Data Meetings is to start leading them! Ready? Select a set of student work from one of your classrooms, and from that pick a few mastered, a few near mastery, and a few unmastered. Then click on our Leverage Leadership App.

Stop & Do
Leverage Leadership App

Plan your Weekly Data Meeting

Gather your student work, the standard, and any Know-Show Charts or exemplars (if you have already built them).

Open your Leverage Leadership App and click "Plan a Weekly Data Meeting." In a few minutes, you'll have a plan.

What are your takeaways?

_____

_____

_____

_____

_____

Print out the script to your meeting, revise it to meet your teachers' and students' needs, and go for it. In no time, you'll have launched data-driven instruction in your school.

ACTION: COACHING TO MASTERY, PART 2: MONITORING THE LEARNING

Weekly Data Meetings are a critical driver. When you apply the same principles to your classroom observations, you'll change the game by transforming feedback into measurable growth.

Leaders like Taro Shigenobu (more in Chapter 2) show us what this looks like. Watch this video of what Taro does when preparing to observe a teacher and when actually observing:

 WATCH Clip 13: Shigenobu—Monitor the Learning

What is powerful is not just what Taro does, but what he doesn't do. Taro doesn't start with the teacher; he starts with the students. What objective are they trying to master today based on previous data? What is their current master at this point in the class, and what are their gaps?

Before Taro even looks at the teacher, he determines the level of student mastery. Students first. Teacher second.

Core Idea

Students first. Teachers second.
Start from the student work to determine the learning gap,
then look at the teaching actions that are producing it.

That order matters. Observing through the lens of student mastery ensures that our coaching targets what students actually need, not what teachers happened to plan. We move from coaching pedagogy to coaching learning.

This approach completely changes what Taro can do next. Watch the next part of this observation:

 WATCH Clip 14: Shigenbobu—Monitor the Learning

Because Taro and his instructional leaders took the time to identify the student learning gap, their coaching improves. They don't simply try to improve the teaching; they address the learning at the same time. Taro's criteria are clear: coach the teacher on what will improve the learning. And not just for tomorrow—for today.

This approach requires one mindset shift above all others: my coaching is not effective unless the learning improves. And it involves creating a culture of feedback in the classroom (more on that in Chapter 3).

Taro and leaders like him across the globe take the following steps to monitor the learning:

Monitor the Learning

1. **Start from the end goal.**

   - What is the most important thing for students to master today?
   - Where in the lesson should that mastery appear?

2. **Observe the students first.**

   - What percentage have pen to paper or are actively working?
   - Do they have good habits? (annotations, showing their work, using notebooks, etc.).
   - What are the gaps in their answers? What are they missing?

3. **Observe the teacher next.**

   - What teacher actions are contributing to the student gaps?
   - What is the highest leverage teacher move to change the trajectory of the learning?

4. **Coach in real time.**

   - What immediate feedback or prompt can improve student learning *now*?
   - What can you coach versus what you need to model?
   - How will you debrief this moment later to solidify teacher growth?

In the end, monitoring the learning isn't about supervision; it's about transformation. When leaders and teachers alike coach the learning while observing, they don't just improve instruction. They get better results right there, in the moment, where it matters most.

Findings from the Field
Shift the Paradigm

"Monitoring the Learning shifted the paradigm for us. In the old way, we'd observe from the back of the room, send an email, and follow up later in a feedback meeting. Now, we are actively coaching in the moment, using universal prompts for the teacher and the coach of the teacher. Get staff invested in a culture of feedback, and then work with your leadership team to be consistent in their implementation. It has skyrocketed achievement."

—Taro Shigenobu, principal, Henderson, NC

Monitoring the Learning
Coaching a Teacher Side by Side to Improve the Learning

Prepare Leader actions before observing classroom	Prepare
	Tools in hand: • Simple tools to collect student work across all courses (e.g.,—Google Drive) • Resources in hand: Get Better Faster Sequence of Action Steps **Prepare:** • Start from the end goal: Review recent data to find the most important student learning objective 　○ Determine the most important task of the lesson and create the exemplar • Anticipate the student gap—where students may struggle

	<ul><li>Anticipate the teacher gap—where teachers may struggle<ul><li>(If available in advance) Review the lesson plan—identify if wrong tasks are prioritized</li><li>Prepare your real-time feedback aligned to the teacher gap to the productive struggle in the lesson</li></ul></li></ul>
See It. Name It. Do It. Cycles of Implementation while Observing	**Co-Monitor**

Before Monitoring:

- Start from the end goal:
  - "What are you looking for in student thinking/student papers? What will it sound like for students to be correct/answer why?"
  - "What prompts will you use if you don't see it?"
  - "Where are you going to collect data?"
- Narrate your support: "I'm going to monitor with you and we will debrief what we are seeing."

During Monitoring:

- Monitor student work:
  - Developing teachers: Monitor alongside them (look at student work jointly)
  - More proficient teachers: Split up the room and monitor separately to spot the trend faster
- ID the error:
  - "What is the level of mastery?"
  - "What are you noticing?"
  - "What is the pattern/gap in student work?"

- Plan to respond to error:
  - "What's your response to data? Why?"
    - Use RTD resources to guide teachers to select right option based on level of mastery
  - Strategically call on students:
    - "What student work will you Show-Call?" "What students will you call on?" "What will you chart?"

Coach the Teacher and Fix the Learning:

- Observe and deliver RTF; model where needed
- Quick debrief of affirmation and impact with the teacher and/or next steps

Repeat

Stamp it

Debrief
After the observation

Stamp it:

- Stamp student gap:
  - "Looking at our exemplar, what was the end goal?"
  - "Let's separate exit tickets into mastered or not mastered." "What is the level of mastery?"
  - "Does the level of mastery match our prediction? Why or why not?"
  - "Let's move to unmastered work, are there any trends?"
- Stamp the teacher action step:
  - "How can we adjust our teaching next class/ tomorrow to close these student errors?"
  - Model any fix or practice closing the gap

All of the work needed for successful Data Driven Instruction can be distilled into three basic actions that profoundly transform a school and the quality of student learning: assess, analyze, act. Yet so many obstacles can get in the way of teachers and leaders remaining focused on this approach. What distinguishes leaders like Candace is their use of systems that lock in these actions. Let's look at what those are.

MAKING IT WORK: HOW IT FITS INTO A LEADER'S SCHEDULE

The data meetings we just watched were impressive, but even the best meeting won't matter if it only happens once a year. The second key to making data-driven instruction work is a calendar that locks the process in.

Yearly Calendar—Data-Driven Instruction

When Principal Yanela Cruz was named to lead the turnaround of Libertas Academy Middle School in Springfield, Massachusetts, she had her hands full. After re-establishing student culture (you'll see her again in Chapter 5!), she set her sights on data-driven instruction. "I knew that consistency—our ability to maintain this year-round—would either make us or break us." So, she led her leadership team to plan all the data systems to make this work. That entailed scheduling all key tasks and then building the rest of their calendar. Here is a sample template that is built on experience in thousands of schools, laying out all the pre-work and implementation work that will set you up to succeed. You can use the Leverage Leadership App to take it and adjust to your context. You'll have a clear map of what to do and when to do it:

Data-Driven Instruction Monthly Map

Key Tasks for the Year

(NOTE: 1 represents the 1st week of the month, 2 is the 2nd week of the month, and so on)

Month	Task
June	☐ 1—Develop Interim Assessment Calendar (IAs, analysis, reteach, PD)
	☐ 1—(If needed) Acquire/revise/develop interim assessments

July (Summer tasks)	☐ 1—(If new leader) Grade school using the DDI implementation rubric to identify where the school stands and where you need to be before the school year begins
	☐ 1—(If needed) Change curriculum scope and sequences to match interim assessments that will be used (or vice versa)
	☐ 1—Identify who will help you complete the assessment/curriculum adjustment process to be ready for launch by the beginning of the school year
August	☐ 3—Present DDI PD session to new teachers (use materials from *Get Better Faster* and *Driven by Data*)
	☐ 4—First Week of School
September	☐ 2—Have the first round of interim assessments (or the closest proxy) finalized
	☐ 2—1st interim assessments (or the closest proxy) have already been seen by the teachers (Transparency) so that they can plan for mastery
	☐ 4—Develop plan to determine how test scoring and analysis will be completed
October	☐ 1—Teachers predict performance on interim assessment #1
	○ Mark each question: "confident" (sure that the students will get it right), "not sure," and "no way" (students will definitely get it wrong)
	☐ 2—Interim Assessment #1
	☐ 2—Deliver PD to school's instructional leaders in DDI analysis and leading analysis meetings (use *Get Better Faster* and *Driven by Data* for PD agenda, materials, and resources)
	☐ 3—Have Teacher Analysis and Action Plan templates ready
	☐ 3—Teachers produce Assessment Analysis Instructional Plans

	☐ 3—Instructional Leaders run test-in-hand Analysis Meetings with Teachers
	
	    ○ Compare performance to what the teacher predicted: highlight areas of discrepancy (i.e., teacher over/under predicted how well the students were going to do on certain test questions)
	
	    ○ Follow one-pager: Leading Effective Analysis Meetings
	
	☐ 3—Principal observes analysis meetings, giving feedback to instructional leaders about their facilitation
	
	☐ 4—Staff PD:
	
	    ○ Run Results Meeting to plan to reteach challenging standards Teachers add rigor to their lessons using "Data-driven Best Practices for Increasing Rigor"

November	☐ 1—Second assessment is in the hands of the teachers so they can plan to teach for mastery ☐ 2—Review lesson plans: is there evidence of implementation of teacher action plans from the assessment analysis meeting? ☐ 2—Observe classes: is there evidence of implementation of teacher action plans and changed teaching practices? ☐ 2—Evaluate School on DDI Rubric ☐ 3—Teachers predict performance on 2nd interim assessment ○ Mark each question: "confident" (sure that the students will get it right), "not sure," and "no way" (students will definitely get it wrong)
December	☐ 1—Interim Assessment #2 ☐ 2—Teachers complete data entry, analysis, and action plan ☐ 2—Principal leads, observes, or models analysis meetings for instructional leaders ☐ 2—Teachers complete Assessment Analysis Instructional Plans ☐ 3—Staff PD: Run Results Meeting to plan to reteach challenging standards

January	☐ 1—Third assessment is in the hands of the teachers to plan for mastery
February	☐ 1—(If needed) Follow-up PD for school leaders to improve analysis meetings
	☐ 1—Interim Assessment #3
	☐ 2—Teachers complete Assessment Analysis Instructional Plans
	☐ 2—Data Analysis and Analysis Meetings
	☐ 3—Staff PD: Run Results Meeting to plan to reteach challenging standards
March	☐ 4—Interim Assessment #4
April	☐ 1—Teachers complete Assessment Analysis Instructional Plans
	☐ 1—IA Analysis Meetings
	☐ 2—Staff PD: Run Results Meeting to plan to reteach challenging standards
May	☐ 1—State Tests
	☐ 2—State Tests
June	☐ 3—Final Performance Tasks
	☐ 4—Last week of School

Stop & Do
Leverage Leadership App

Build your Assessment Calendar

Open up your Leverage Leadership App and select DDI. Pull up a full-year assessment calendar. Then adjust it to meet the needs of your school and state.

LL App

What are your takeaways?

_____

_____

_____

_____

_____

_____

Weekly Schedule—Week of Interim Assessments

With the yearly calendar in place, you can lock in an effective week of interim assessments. This sample high school schedule includes what to do during the weeks of interim assessments. (You can find this example as well as elementary and middle school samples in the Leverage Leadership App.)

Interim Assessment Week Schedule—Sample

ASST WEEK	MON	TUES	WED	THURS	FRI
MORNING:	Literacy Interim Assessment*	Math Interim Assessment	Science Interim Assessment	History Interim Assessment	Spanish and Art Interim Assessment
PREP PERIODS/ AFTERNOON:	Literacy Teachers grade assts	Math/Literacy teachers grade assts	Everyone grades assts	**Faculty Mtg:** Cancel: give time to fill out analysis templates and Action Plans	**½ Day PD (or 2nd wk)**:** EITHER: Results Meetings by grade level/ department OR: Ind. Creation of Action Plans

WEEK POST-ASST	MON	TUES	WED	THURS	FRI
CLASSES:	Reteach	Reteach	Reteach	Reteach	Reteach
PREP PERIODS:	1-on-1 Analysis Meetings: Literacy	1-on-1 Analysis Meetings: Math/Science	1-on-1 Analysis Meetings: Other Subjects		**½ Day PD (or 1st wk)****: See above

* Literacy assessments come first because they normally involve essay grading that takes longer.
** ½ day PD sessions are scheduled for the week of the assessments or the week after. This allows time to complete analysis and action plans and to offer targeted PD to meet the student learning needs.

Weekly Schedule—Rest of the Year

The real magic for Candace is consistent regularly scheduled data meetings throughout the year as a part of the standing grade-level team meetings. She calls it her "5-day cycle": prepare to teach, analyze, and reteach to mastery.

Scheduling Weekly Data Meetings

REGULAR WEEK	MON	TUES	WED	THURS	FRI
TEACHERS:	Prep Period: Grade-level Weekly Data Meetings	Teach new standards and spiral	Reteach Key Standard	Teach new standards and spiral	Teach new standards and spiral
LEADERSHIP TEAM:	Lead weekly data meetings (one leader per meeting)	Leadership Team Mtg: ID patterns from meetings and what to observe	Observe reteaching	Observe reteaching	

TURNAROUND—DDI IS THE STRATEGY

As noted in our introduction, building a strong, data-driven foundation is one of the "super-levers" for schools looking for dramatic transformation. What are the first steps a leader can take to put this into action in a school that is struggling?

In every other chapter, you'll find unique mechanisms and shortcuts to work through a challenging situation. In this chapter, however, data-driven instruction *is* the turnaround strategy. Katie Harshman (you'll meet her in Chapter 4!) says, "Data-driven instruction drives *everything* we do." This is the lever that will jumpstart student learning, right alongside student culture. Your task is quite direct: take this monthly action plan and adjust it to meet your school's yearly calendar. Each one of the action steps listed needs to happen, but they can happen at the time that works for you within the framework given here. The best additional advice leaders like Candace offer is to *remove* as many other initiatives/projects as possible to keep yourself singularly focused on making DDI work. Too often we take on more than we can handle, and nowhere is this more the case than in turnaround situations. Keep it simple: use this chapter as your preeminent guide.

In the Leverage Leadership App, you have all the tools, ready for you to adapt them to your school's context. Just click here to get started:

LL App

CONCLUSION

When Candace recalls Northeast's journey from where it used to be to where it is now, she shares: "It's all about integrity. If I believe in the power of data meetings, I have to be willing to do the work along with the team. Now there's no stopping us. We won't stop until every child is learning." And her staff feels the same way.

As mentioned in *Driven by Data 2.0*, when properly implemented, data-driven instruction does not require teacher buy-in: It creates it. With Candace at the helm, teachers used the time available to them in a way that turned around the educational experience of every child at Northeast. They didn't do it by magic: they did it by finding out what their students needed and giving it to them unfailingly. That's the power of data-driven instruction.

Action Steps for Principals

Data-Driven Instruction

LEVER	DATA-DRIVEN INSTRUCTION—KEY ACTIONS IN SEQUENCE
	Plan

DDI	**Assessments and Curriculum—Align the Rigor**
	
	1. **Lock in quality interim assessments**
	  • Identify the end-goal assessment (state test, college entrance exam, college assessment) that exemplifies what successful students should know and be able to do.
	  • ID essential content and rigor that students must master for success on end-goal assessment.
	  • Acquire or develop effective IAs that are aligned to end-goal assessments.
	  • Develop a common IA calendar that identifies when IAs will take place, who/what will be assessed, and when IA data analysis meetings will take place.
	
	2. **Lock in high-quality lesson plans/curriculum materials with assessment that align to the interim assessments**
	  • Adjust the unit/weekly/daily assessments to align to the rigor and content of the interim assessments
	  • [See lever of "Planning" for details on lesson plans curriculum]
	
	3. **Narrow your focus—identify grade levels and content areas of focus based on last year's data and current context**
	  • Pick the grade levels and content areas that most need focus for increasing achievement using the following criteria:
	    ◦ End-goal and IA assessment data at the grade-level and teacher level
	    ◦ Areas that have key shifts in curriculum or testing
	    ◦ Areas where you have expertise and lack expertise with the teachers or leadership team

DDI
(cont'd)
	Data Meetings—Tools and Structures for Weekly Data/Interim Assessment MTGS
	
	4. **Establish essential data meeting structures that result in evidence-based action planning**
	
	   • Create meeting schedule to conduct data meetings to analyze IA data (six weeks) and to conduct Weekly Data Meetings (WDM)).
	
	   • Establish consistent protocols and pre-work expectations for effective data meetings (e.g., IA analysis meeting protocol, WDM protocol).
	
	   • Develop a system to regularly collect representative student work (e.g., exit tickets or spiral review from students of varying proficiency) to use as evidence to identify trends in student learning.
	
	5. **Create effective principal monitoring tools for all post-assessment action plans**
	
	   • Develop an action plan tracker that identifies teacher reteach goals, timeline, and focus area
	
	   • Create systems to have access to assessments and/or DDI action plan when observing
	
	   • Create observation schedules to observe teachers in reteaching implementation

Roll Out	

	PD on Data Driven Instruction:
	
	6. **Roll out PD for data-driven instruction:**
	
	   • Assessment: the power of the assessment items and writing exemplars.
	
	   • Analysis: set clear expectations and practice exemplar IA and student work analysis.
	
	   • Action: create six-week action plans (IA) or targeted reteach plans (WDM).

DDI (cont'd)	**Analyze for Trends**

7. **Conduct a deep analysis of the data to identify schoolwide and teacher specific trends**
   - Find the overall trend
     - For IAs: Identify schoolwide patterns in the data: outlier teachers and students (below mastery and advanced) and key standards that need focus.
     - For WDMs: Review the student work to select the highest leverage standards/question to focus on for analysis.
     - Design a reteach the closes the gap.
   - ID the key conceptual understanding and error for a given standard/task
     - Determine what students should be able to do/say to demonstrate mastery of the standard
     - Identify the key gap between the ideal response and student work: both the key procedural errors and conceptual misunderstandings
     - Determine the highest leverage action steps to take to close the gap

Data Meetings—Lead Effective Weekly Data and IA Analysis Meetings with Teachers

8. **Prepare:**
   - Narrow your focus: pick the assessment item and student work in advance that highlight key errors
   - Prepare the exemplar and write your meeting script to ensure an effective, efficient meeting

9. **See It:**
   - Start with the standard(s)/text: unpack the key parts of the standard (and text for Humanities) that align to the students error to identify what students must know (conceptual understanding) and do/show (procedural understanding) to demonstrate mastery |

DDI (cont'd)	• Unpack the teacher/student exemplars to ID how they demonstrate mastery of the standard
	• Use the anchor chart of the unpacked standard/exemplar to identify the conceptual and procedural gap
	  ○ Conceptual (know): "If they get this right and you ask why, what do you want them to say?"
	  ○ Procedural ("show"): e.g. annotating text, showing work, line-by-line computation, etc.
	
	10. **Name It:**
	  • Punch it: Succinctly name the key procedural errors and conceptual misunderstandings
	
	11. **Do It:**
	  • Perfect the plan before you practice.
	    ○ Plan the structure of the reteach: activate knowledge, independent practice, modeling, and/or guided discourse.
	    ○ Select the task and the exemplar response.
	    ○ Plan the reteach individually: "Take five minutes to write your script. I will do the same."
	    ○ Spar: "Let's compare our reteach plans. What can we pull from each other to make the strongest plan?"
	  • Practice the gap.
	    ○ ID the most essential elements of the reteach for the teacher to practice, especially the parts that will be hardest to master.
	    ○ Prompt the teacher to "go live" and practice the prompts that will be used during the reteach.
	  • Build an effective follow-up plan.
	    ○ Close each meeting with a measurable goal and action steps to meet it: when to reteach, when to re-assess, and when to revisit this data.
	    ○ Embed the action plan into upcoming lessons and unit plans.
	ID when observations will take place to see plan in action and how it will be assessed.

DDI (cont'd)

12. **Monitor the Learning—actively monitor implementation in the classroom**
    - Observe the end goal:
        - Evaluate if the lesson plan objective and exit ticket align to rigor of the interim assessment and to what students most need based on the data
        - Evaluate the opening Routines—look for targeted reteach aligned to the end goal
            - Targeted Do Now review—only the problems that need focus
            - Activate needed knowledge and skills
    - Observe student work:
        - Level 1: pen-to-paper (how many students are doing the work?)
        - Level 2: annotations ((how many students are showing good habits—annotating text, marking up questions, line-by-line computation, etc.?)
        - Level 3: correct answers (what students have it correct and what is the gap?)
    - Observe the teaching:
        - What about the teaching is causing the gap in student work?
        - ID the highest leverage action step for the teacher
    - Coach the teaching to fix the learning
        - Give real-time feedback to the teacher to improve the learning
        - [See Real-time feedback section in Observation and Feedback for details]
13. **Monitor the implementation of action plans outside the classroom**
    - Observe weekly data meetings of other instructional leaders (live or via video)
        - ID the patterns across meetings and the key areas of growth for the leader's facilitation.

DDI (cont'd)	• Track implementation of six-week action plans and student outcomes following reteach
	
	   ◦ Have teacher post lesson plans and/or 6-week action plans in the classroom to be able to observe both the plan and the execution to identify gaps.
	
	14. **Adjust leader schedule to respond to weekly data**
	
	   • Adjust classroom observations and meeting schedule at the end of every week to respond to data collected throughout the week

IMPLEMENTATION RUBRIC

Data-Driven Instruction and Assessment

The rubric is intended to be used to assess the present state of data-driven instruction and assessment in a school. The rubric specifically targets interim assessments and the key drivers leading to increased student achievement.

   4 = Exemplary implementation; 3 = Proficient implementation; 2 = Beginning implementation; 1 = No implementation

Data-Driven Culture	
1. **Active Leadership Team:** Instructional leaders consistently lead data meetings and monitor student work/learning trends across the school, adjusting their weekly schedule to prioritize key subjects/teachers and follow up effectively	/4
2. **Implementation Calendar:** Begin school year with a detailed calendar that includes time for assessment creation/adaptation, interim assessment analysis, weekly data meetings, and reteaching (flexible enough to accommodate district mandates/changes)	/4
3. **Introductory Professional Development:** Introduce teachers and leaders to data-driven instruction; understand how assessments define rigor, how to analyze student work, and how to adapt instruction	/4

4. **Ongoing Professional Development:** PD calendar is aligned with data-driven instructional plan and includes student work analysis, action planning and learning how to teach content		/4
5. **Build by Borrowing:** Identify and implement best practices from high-achieving teachers and schools: visit schools/classrooms, share and disseminate resources/strategies		/4

Assessments	Lit.	Math
1. **Common Interim** Assessments 4–6 times/year	/4	/4
2. **Transparent Starting Point:** teachers see the assessments at the beginning of each cycle; assessments define the road map for teaching	/4	/4
3. **Aligned to state tests _and_ college readiness**	/4	/4
4. **Aligned to instructional sequence** of clearly defined grade level and content expectations	/4	/4
5. **Reassess** previously taught standards	/4	/4

Analysis	
1. **Immediate:** turnaround of assessment results (ideally 48 hrs)	/4 /4
2. **Simple—user-friendly, succinct data reports include:** _item-level_ analysis, _standards-level_ analysis and _bottom line_ results	/4
3. **Teacher-owned:** teacher analyzes own student work supported by instructional leaders	/4
4. **Test and student work in hand:** start from the exemplar and identify the gaps	/4
5. **Deep:** move beyond _what_ students got wrong and answers _why_: identify key procedural and conceptual misunderstandings	

Action	
1. **Reteach:** teachers effectively use the appropriate strategy to close student gaps: activate knowledge, academically monitor, guide discourse (e.g., Show-Call) and/or model	/4
2. **Six-week action plans:** execute plans that include whole-class instruction, small groups, tutorials, and before/after-school supports	/4

3. **Ongoing assessment:** regularly check for progress on key standards: academic monitoring of independent work, questioning, and in-class assessments to ensure student progress between interim assessments	/4
4. **Engaged Students:** know the end goal, how they did, and what actions to improve	/4
5. **Follow-up/Accountability:** instructional leaders review lesson and unit plans and give observation feedback driven by the action plan and student learning needs	/4
	TOTAL: /100

Stop Here

Take a moment and evaluate your school on the Data-Driven Instruction Implementation Rubric. Then follow the steps below:

If your School is Below a 70 on the DDI Rubric:

As mentioned in the introduction, data-driven instruction is the super-lever without which none of the other instructional levers work effectively. **If you don't think your school is proficient on this DDI rubric (a score above 70), then this chapter should remain your primary focus for instruction. Skip ahead to Student Culture—Chapter 5.** While you can implement the other instructional levers as well, don't launch anything that will prohibit your ability to implement DDI and Student Culture proficiently. *Driven by Data* is a great additional resource as it includes all the professional development materials and tools you need to launch DDI effectively in your school.

If your School is Above a 70 on the DDI Rubric and Student Culture is locked in:

Option 1—Choose Planning (Chapter 2) or Observation and **Feedback (Chapter 3):** As the next most important levers after data-driven instruction and student culture, Planning or Observation and Feedback would be the next best levers to implement..

Option 2—Read the chapters in order—Planning, Observation and Feedback, and PD (Chapters 2–4) These three levers complete the coaching cycle to create a robust instructional plan for your entire staff to move from good to great.[17]

Pulling the Lever

Action Planning Worksheet for DATA-DRIVEN INSTRUCTION

Self-Assessment

- Assess your school cn the Implementation Rubric for Data-Driven Instruction and Assessment. What is your score? ___/100
- What items on the Implementation Rubric are your biggest areas for improvement?

_____

_____

_____

_____

Planning for Action

- What tools from this book will you use to develop data-driven instruction at your school? Check all that you will use (you can find all in the LL App):

___ **Weekly Data Meetings One-Pager**

___ **Exemplar Know-Show Charts**

___ **Tool to Evaluate the Rigor/Alignment of our Assessments/Exit Tickets**

___ **Monitoring the Learning One-Pager**

___ **Assessment Results Spreadsheet**

___ **Teacher Action Plan**

___ **Reteaching one-pager**

___ **Action—Follow-up Accountability Measures One-Pager**

___ **Interim Assessment School Calendar**

___ **Implementation Rubric for DDI**

___ **Monthly Map for DDI**

Note: Additional Data-Driven Instruction PD materials can be found in Driven by Data 2.0.

- What are your next steps for launching data-driven instruction?

Action:	Date:

Chapter 2

Planning

One-on-One: Planning with a Purpose

The sun is shining through the window of Taro Shigenobu's office at Henderson Collegiate High School in Henderson, North Carolina. His AP Environmental Science teacher is sitting alongside him, and they have their unit guide and lesson plans out in front of them.

"Now let's take it live." His teacher nods, and takes out the plan she built during the meeting. "Ok, eyes on me. We only scored 55% on this question because we are forgetting to include why urban areas have more storm runoff than rural areas. Let's look at this answer: how can we take it to the next level? Turn and talk."

For the next 10 minutes, Taro and his teacher rehearse the key moment of discourse in the class. At the end, Taro smiles, "Wow. Great job—really cool how you handled extra layers of complexity!" The teacher pumps her fist in the air and smiles.

 WATCH Clip 15: Shigenobu—Do It (Practice)—
Weekly Planning Meeting

In recent years, the importance of instructional planning has elevated the national discourse on teaching. High-Quality Instructional Materials (HQIMs) are sweeping through the United States, and other countries have similar initiatives. Yet despite all the promise that higher quality materials seem to offer, student achievement has not improved very much.[1] What's the missing link? How do we get teachers to use those plans; in short—how do we plan to teach.

If data-driven instruction is about plotting the route to rigor and closing gaps when you find them, effective lesson planning is about anticipating the gaps and preventing them from occurring.

> ## Core Idea
>
> Data-driven instruction is about plotting the route to rigor and closing gaps. Planning is about anticipating gaps and preventing them from occurring.

As such, planning doesn't just help schools up from the bottom: it also helps you soar to new heights. When Taro Shigenobu first became high school principal at Henderson Collegiate, he knew he had to get culture and data-driven instruction right ("I cannot focus on rigor without them"). Then instructional planning took the school to the next level. By 2025, Henderson Collegiate was outperforming the state of North Carolina by 33%, was the highest performing school in the tri-county area, and was a National Title 1 Distinguished School.

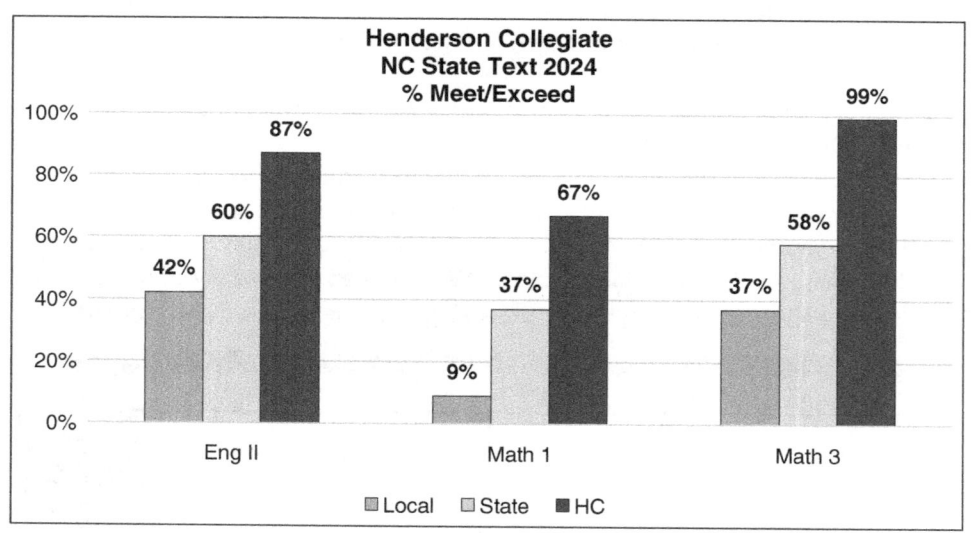

This chapter will show you how to leverage effective planning by looking at it in four sections:

- **Unit plans:** Craft or internalize/adjust unit plans to be data-driven and aligned to the level of rigor you wish your students to reach

- **Lesson plans:** Build or adjust existing lesson plans day-to-day to effectively drive student learning

- **Coaching planning:** Guide your teachers to master the skills that will make them effective planners on their own and effective teachers of the content

- **Monitoring planning:** Observe lessons in action to find out which parts of your plans are working and which aren't

EFFECTIVE UNIT AND LESSON PLANS

In the last decade, more and more schools and districts have moved toward standardized curriculum, often those officially designated as High-Quality Instruction Materials (HQIMs). So, how do we leverage these materials and tailor them to accelerate the learning?

Let's unpack how to do that.

Plan Backward from Assessment

If standards are meaningless until we define how to assess them (core idea from Chapter 1), then assessments are the starting point for instructional planning.

Too often, however, curriculum planning does not follow this guidance. HQIMs have generic assessment prompts that often don't match the demands of each state, let alone college-ready assessments (and at the time of this writing, HQIM evaluation tools are not even including it in their measure of "quality"). This is the top pitfall of planning, and it can sabotage a curriculum plan. Without alignment on the rigor of the assessment, teaching will either undershoot what the end-goal assessment demands, or every teacher will interpret the curriculum to different levels of rigor. Both create vast disparities in children's experience with the content.

Michelle Koyama shared this with us in Chapter 1 (Findings from the Field). Her literacy scores at Colfax Elementary School climbed considerably once they made the decision to rebuild the writing requirements of the mandated curriculum to align to the state assessment. "Before, our children just weren't being asked to write often, and what writing happened was beneath the rigor they needed." Build your assessment and curriculum hand in hand, then plan what you need to teach to get there.

Not sure whether your curriculum's built-in assessments are aligned to your state test? Test it out.

Stop & Do
Leverage Leadership App

Analyze Quality of Your Unit Assessments/Tasks

Open up the Leverage Leadership App.

Type in a few of the assessment tasks for the upcoming unit in your curriculum. The App will give you feedback on their alignment to your state test and the changes you can make to align it further.

What are the key gaps right now in the alignment between my own school's curriculum and our assessments? What actions can we take to close those gaps?

_____

_____

_____

_____

_____

This is why Taro always starts from the assessments: they are the sunlight that can break through the clouds of imperfect curriculum.

Core Idea

Lock in your assessments first:
They are the sunlight that can break through the clouds of imperfect curriculum.

These assessments help you plan the necessary focus of each lesson. Take a look at the objectives, lesson tasks, and the exit ticket, which is a final task to end class. Lesson plans lack focus unless the objective, tasks, and exit ticket are aligned.

> ## Core Idea
> Lesson plans lack focus unless the objective, tasks, and exit ticket are aligned.

Adequate Time for Independent Practice

The best assessment in the world means little if students don't get the chance to practice it. For example, you can measure much of the impact of a literacy curriculum based on the frequency of time that students spend reading. But lessons and curriculum can become bogged down with everything but that, which leaves teachers little chance to identify the errors students make while learning and to help them along the way.

Want a simple guideline? Make sure that at least 10 minutes of every hour-long lesson is devoted to independent practice.

Content and Skill

In the Analysis section of Chapter 1, we showed an example of Literacy analysis that demonstrated that students need knowledge and skill to unpack a complex text. The same is true of every subject. While the current debate might swing the pendulum in one direction or another,[2] the reality is that you will always need both.

As a real-world example, doctors can memorize thousands of details about every type of illness or disease, but if they cannot pull all of that together to accurately diagnose and effectively treat their patients, they are not effective. So, what are we to do?

School leaders like Taro have figured out, as is often the case in education, the best option is the combination: you need content *and* skill to achieve mastery.

> ## Core Idea
> You need content and skill to reach mastery.

While this idea seems simple on the surface, how to apply it varies by the content you are teaching. In observing and learning from college professors and the most effective K-12 educators across the country, we've come up with a simple table to describe the key differences in needs of some of the core content areas. As you read this table, how does your school do in the implementation of content and skill?

Content and Skill		
Key Needs in Core Subjects		
Subject	Keys to Content	Keys to Skill/Analysis:
Math	**Mathematical fluency:** Build proficiency at solving efficiently to free up mental space for application (e.g., addition, multiplication tables, isolating variables in linear equations)	**Application:** Solve complex word problems that integrate various standards into one problem as would happen in both abstract math and the real world (e.g., Find the value of x for a rectangle that has an area of 6 square feet with sides of length 2x-1 and x)
English	**Background knowledge/ schema:** Create and utilize background knowledge and vocabulary to be able to access increasingly complex texts **Building blocks:** Lots of time for actual reading and mastering the building blocks (fluency, decoding, etc.)	**Reading for meaning and analysis:** Learn key reading and writing skills to be able to unpack meaning of any text and analyze it critically
Science	**Terms = concept:** Understand and properly use scientific terms with precision: their use represents understanding	**Application and enhanced understanding:** Use scientific method and knowledge of terms to generate additional understanding and analyze new scenarios

Subject	Keys to Content	Keys to Skill/Analysis:
History	**Context of yesterday, not today:** Internalize key knowledge of each historical era of study: key dates, events, trends, movements, etc.	**Historical thinking:** Apply the knowledge of yesterday to evaluate and analyze historical sources
Foreign Language	**Vocabulary and grammar:** Learn key vocabulary words and grammar/conjugation structures	**Interpretive/Communicative:** Understand the spoken and written word and communicate in speech and writing

Think about the usefulness of this table to help educators on both sides of the spectrum. For example, a Math teacher might be excellent teaching inquiry-based lessons that focus on conceptual understanding of the math, but she might not give her students enough independent practice to nail down mathematical fluency. For future math, that fluency will be essential or they won't have the mental space to learn the new concept. Or think of your History teacher. He might be excellent at more traditional instruction of history and get his students to internalize large amounts of key knowledge from a particular era. Yet those students might not be able to analyze Abraham Lincoln's Gettysburg address if they don't practice historical thinking skills to unpack the deeper meaning.

In general, match the plans to the nature of your subject to meet the needs of your students.

Core Idea

Match the plans to the nature of your subject to meet the needs of your students.

Stop & Jot

When I think of all the core subjects and teachers in my school, where do we have a lack of balance between the content and skills mentioned above?

_____

_____

_____

_____

Modeling or Guided Discourse

The final piece of the planning is how to teach the new material. The heart of every lesson is how students learn something new. As we discussed in data-driven instruction, most of that teaching can be put into one of two categories: modeling or guided discourse (see Chapter 1 and the section on Action). As a quick reminder, here are the keys to each one:

- Modeling:
  - Clear listening/note-taking task
  - Model the thinking questions, not just the procedure
- Guided Discourse:
  - Write first, talk second
  - Show-call
  - Turn and talk, then poll the room
  - Strategic questioning

Make it Memorable and Meaningful

How many times has someone taught you something, and a few months later you cannot remember how to do it? How often have you attended a presentation and no matter how entertaining, a few weeks later you couldn't recall much of what you learned?

This is our experience generally because our brain struggles to retain isolated pieces of information. If it happens to us as adults, it is easy to imagine that the same thing happens to children. Multiply this by children often learning five or six different subjects on a given day from different teachers, and we wonder why retention is so difficult!

So, what do Taro and educators like him do about this? Make curriculum memorable—and meaningful.

Give Students the "Why": Allow students to understand why they are learning this material and how it helps them understand the world.

Make the Learning Sticky: According to top neuroscientists in the field of information retention, we cannot remember what we learn unless we can link it to other knowledge we remember.[3] You can make the learning stick by hooking new ideas to what students already know and then planning so that each lesson reinforces and extends their knowledge.

A Word On . . .
Rigor and Relevance

In far too many instances, educators can feel like they must choose between high academic expectations and making content inspiring and relevant to the current world of our students.

Jal Mehta and Sarah Fine are researchers that focus on questions of deeper learning,[4] and when Jal has observed high schools, he has lamented how many schools think they are pushing for deeper learning with creative hands-on projects when really they end up lowering the bar.

This leads us to have AP courses that are rich in rigor—but only for the elite—and other classes that try to engage but don't demand depth or rigor of content. The highest achieving schools I have observed see this as a false dichotomy: you can have both rigor and relevance.

Let's take a few examples. Imagine the following task in a middle school science class:

"Design a poster showing your favorite planet and explain why you like it best." This task might seem engaging—it invites creativity and color—but it doesn't build or assess any conceptual understanding of astronomy or planetary systems. The creative hook is there, but the cognitive demand is not.

Now imagine instead: "Design a model for a planet that could support human life. Use what you know about gravity, atmosphere, and distance from the sun to justify your design." This task still allows for creativity and choice, but now students must apply core scientific principles to defend their reasoning. The rigor stays high because students must transfer and synthesize their learning to a new context.

The same principle applies to history. Consider this simple prompt: "Pretend you are living during the Industrial Revolution. Write a diary entry about what your day might be like."

This activity may encourage empathy, but it stops short of analysis. Students can write detailed and imaginative entries without ever demonstrating historical understanding.

With a small shift, the task can demand real thinking: "You have been asked to attend a mediation between the Leeds Cloth Woolen Workers and Leeds Cloth Merchants. Defend one of the groups with an argument for or against industrialization, using evidence from primary sources."

Now the creative framework remains, but the task is anchored in argument, evidence, and historical reasoning. It's sticky *and* rigorous.

Relevance without rigor is entertainment. Rigor without relevance is abstraction. The best lessons do both.

Lesson Planning

Keys to Effective Planning

1. **Plan backward from assessment:** align objectives, tasks, and daily exit tickets to the rigor of the end goal assessment
2. **Adequate time for independent practice** (ideally at least 10 minutes per lesson)
3. **Both content and skill**
4. **Modeling or Guided Discourse**
5. **Make it memorable**

Stop & Do
Leverage Leadership App

Analyze Quality of Your Lesson Plans

Open up the Leverage Leadership App.

LL App

Take one of your lesson plans or unit plans and evaluate it, making the changes to match what students need.

Key Takeaways:

_____

_____

_____

_____

Now you've had a chance to get a more intimate understanding of the unit and lesson plan forms. The next two sections of this chapter will show how leaders like Taro set both these structures up in their schools: first through coaching around lesson planning, and then through monitoring.

COACHING FOR EFFECTIVE PLANNING: WEEKLY PLANNING MEETINGS

How do successful leaders like Taro coach for effective planning in their schools? I have observed schools in action and talked with other leaders in the field of curriculum implementation, and a new prominent idea is slowly emerging. While mapping out the curriculum for the year is important (if your curriculum doesn't already do that for you), the fastest and highest leverage way for a teacher to get better at their content is perfecting a single lesson on a consistent basis.

I asked Steve Leinwand, author and former president of the National Council of Supervisors of Mathematics, what has been the most effective method to develop Math teachers? Without hesitation, Steve replied, "Plan a lesson together. You'd be amazed at what it does to unlock understanding and teacher skill."[5] (You can glean more of his insights in a longer segment in *Get Better Faster 2.0*).

Coaching teachers how to create and deliver a strong lesson on Monday, for example, has a ripple effect. Those skills transfer to a better lesson on Tuesday even if Tuesday's lesson is not as tightly planned. Raise the ceiling on lesson quality, and you inevitably raise the floor. Or another way to think about that: Start high and keep climbing. Start low and keep scrambling.

> ## Core Idea
>
> Raise the ceiling of lesson quality, and you inevitably raise the floor.
> Start high and keep climbing. Start low and keep scrambling.

How can you lead Planning Meetings like this? Follow the guidance of Taro and others with the same framework: See It. Name It. Do It. With a few twists. Let's see what it looks like.

See It

Jessica Mullins is the principal of Trevista at Horace Mann Elementary School in Denver, CO. Her school didn't just close the COVID-19 learning gap: instead, they reversed it: 20+ gains in ELA achievement from 2019 to 2025 for her school that was once one of the lowest achieving.[6]

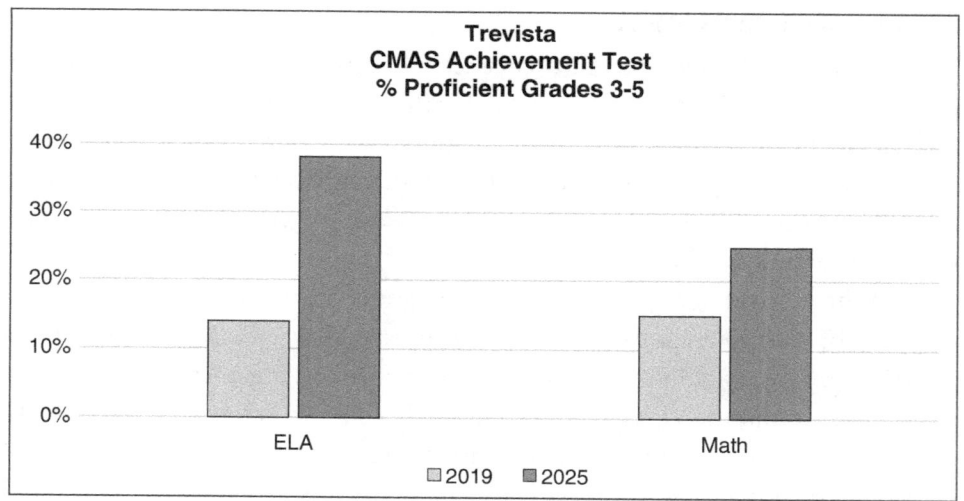

In this video clip, Jessica is working with her third-grade teacher on her Literacy lesson. They have been reading about Julius Caesar and are about to read the key passage when the people turned on Caesar because he was a threat to the Republic. Jessica starts the meeting the same way as a Weekly Data Meeting by seeing the success of past meetings. Watch what happens next.

WATCH Clip 16: Mullins—See It (Exemplar)—Weekly
Data Meeting

See the Exemplar: Before they dive into the lesson itself, she asks a key question: why is this lesson important in the overall unit? Too often, we skip that step. When we do, teachers tend to see lessons as isolated events rather than as part of a larger learning arc. By asking why, you move teachers from thinking about the day's objective to thinking about the unit's purpose—how this lesson builds the foundation for what comes next.

Core Idea

By asking why, you move teachers from thinking about the day's objective to thinking about the unit's purpose.

Jessica then asks her teacher to unpack the text: what is an exemplar response and what will make the text challenging? Notice how she uses the RACE framework (see Chapter 1) to break down the complexity of the text into a Know-Show Chart:

Know	Show

Standard:
 	
• A (Argument): Understand the character's motivation to determine the theme
• C (Cite evidence): Cite key evidence to support that argument
• E (Explain): Explain how that evidence supports the argument
 	
Vocab/Content/Background Knowledge:
 	
• Republic and Senate; Rome's fear of kings, dictator, Rubicon
 	
Text Structure:
 	
• n/a
	• **A (Argument):**
	  ◦ He was killed because he destroyed the republic.
	• **C (Cite evidence):**
	  ◦ Defying the senate and crossing the Rubicon
	  ◦ Starting a civil war
	  ◦ Declaring himself dictator for life
	  ◦ Changing things without approval from the senate
	• **E (Explain how evidence supports argument):**
	  ◦ Rubicon (went against the senate)
	  ◦ Civil war (Romans killed each other, which causes people to hate those who led it, like Caesar)
	  ◦ Dictator for life (means no freedom and end of republic they valued)
	  ◦ Change things without the senate approval (ditto)

Note the power of this approach: Jessica is breaking down the complexity of the text into bite-sized chunks: what success looks like in student responses and which knowledge and skills will get students there. And that's where the magic happens—when lessons are designed so students engage in the right kind of challenge. Growth lives in the productive struggle that skillful teachers create.

> ## Core Idea
>
> The magic of growth lies in productive struggle.

We don't want lessons where students find it too easy. Nor do we want them drowning. And how do we make the struggle productive if the lessons are too challenging? Jessica doesn't lower the rigor; she simply adjusts the lesson plans to give them access.

- **Focus.** Select the tasks that will provide the most important struggle for this objective/unit
- **Activate.** Plan what skills and knowledge need to be activated to access the task
- **Adjust.** Adjust the timing of the lesson to give enough time for the students to grapple with the content that will have the biggest impact.

In just a few minutes, Jessica homed in on what matters most: how the students need to grapple with their learning and what the teacher can do to support them when that happens.

> ## Core Idea
>
> Home in on what matters most: how students need to grapple with their learning and what the teacher can do when that happens.

Now watch what Jessica does next:

WATCH Clip 17: Mullins—See It (Model)—Weekly Planning Meeting

See the Model: Jessica doesn't just talk about the lesson, she steps up and models it. The teacher gets a clear guide of how to teach the key part of the lesson. In a few minutes, the teacher has clarity not only of *what* they want to teach but *how* to teach it.

Name It

Jessica follows the model with a debrief and then naming a precise action step for the teacher. (We'll dive more into the value of this in Chapter 3.)

Do It

Once they have seen a model, Jessica and her teacher follow the Weekly Data Meeting format: develop the plan and practice taking it live. Taro does the same. Take a look at these two examples—one from high school STEM and one from elementary school Literacy.

WATCH Clip 15: Shigenobu—Do It (Practice)—Weekly Planning Meeting
WATCH Clip 18: Mullins—Do It (Practice)—Weekly Planning Meeting

What Jessica does is the same principle you'll see throughout the book. They don't just talk about the lesson plans; they practice teaching them. That way they can make mistakes and correct them before they ever step foot in the classroom.

There is something else very powerful about Jessica's and Taro's approach to coaching planning: it looks remarkably similar to a Weekly Data Meeting. That makes it easy for a leader to learn to switch between them as the need arises. In essence, a Weekly Data Meeting starts from student work; a Planning Meeting starts from the lesson plan.

Core Idea

Weekly Data Meetings start from student work.
Weekly Planning Meetings start from the lesson plan.

One closes a gap that exists in student learning; the other tries to anticipate and eliminate the gap before it occurs.

Stop & Do

Leverage Leadership App

Prepare a Weekly Planning Meeting

Does preparing for planning meetings feel daunting, especially when you haven't taught that content or the teacher has more expertise than you? No worries. Open the Leverage Leadership App. Pick a lesson plan, and you are on your way to learning the content to preparing to coach.

Open up the Leverage Leadership App.

Prep the Weekly Planning Meeting.

Key Takeaways:

_____

_____

_____

_____

_____

Here is the precise one-pager for leading these meetings yourself:

Weekly Planning Meetings

Planning to Teach Daily Lessons

Prepare
Before the meeting
Plan for the Essential Lesson

Start from the end goal—the essential standard/objective of the week and day:

- Identify the most essential enduring understanding students have to master this week/unit
- Narrow the focus to the key lesson of this week (where students will have productive struggle)
  - Humanities: ID the most difficult passage/text that will unlock understanding/analysis
  - STEM: ID the most essential task they need to get right to achieve mastery
- ID the ideal answer(s) you are looking for and listening for in that lesson

Plan the meeting:

- Anticipate the student gaps rooted in recent student work
- Identify the teacher action step from recent observations
- Determine resources (coherence guides, videos, readings) to develop teacher knowledge
- Prepare a model and practice aligned to the teacher action step and the student gap

See It
15 minutes
See It—Develop Content Expertise

See the Success: Ground success in student work and achievement as a result of teacher actions

- "Last week, we set a goal of _____ and now we see that students are able to _____."
- "Nice work! What made the difference?" or "What was the impact on student learning?"

See the Exemplar:

- Narrow the focus: "Today, we are going to focus on lesson ____."
- Ask why: "When looking at the arc of the unit, why does this lesson or text matter?"
- Unpack the key understanding of the lesson:
  - Solve it: "Let's solve the most rigorous task of this lesson. What are the possible exemplar responses? Let's solve ___ using multiple representations."
  - See It: "What must students know and show to demonstrate mastery?" (Know-Show Chart)
    - Humanities: argument, evidence, inference, background knowledge, author's intent
    - STEM: Enduring understandings and key concepts that impact multiple upcoming lessons
    - "If they get this right and you ask them why, what do you want them to say?"
  - (If needed) Leverage resources to deepen knowledge of the key understandings

See the Gap:

- **Narrow the focus:** "What are the 2–3 key tasks that will produce productive struggle?"
- **Anticipate:** "Based on student data, what are the student gaps: where will they struggle with these tasks?"
- **Activate:** "What knowledge do we need to activate in the launch so that they can access the task/text?"
  - Adjust the Do Now/oral review/opening activities to activate needed knowledge and/or skills
  - ID and leverage resources: word walls, previous notes in notebooks, knowledge organizers, etc.
- **Adjust:** Revise the lesson to focus on what matters most:
  - "What should we cut and/or adjust timing from the lesson to have enough time for these 2–3 tasks?" or
  - "How do we level up this lesson plan so that they are able to do the rigorous task?"

(If Needed) See the Model:

- Frame—tell them what to look for:
  - "I'll model one part of the lesson for you. As I model, consider: What am I thinking? and What do I say and do?"
- Model—model the thinking, not just the actions:
  - Model the part of the lesson that is key for the productive struggle, then focus on teacher action step
  - "*Pause.* What do students need? Hmm. . .They're missing __. So, I'm going to [teacher action]. *Action.*"
- Debrief:
  - "What did you see me say and do in the model?"
  - "What is the difference between the model and what you are currently doing?" "What is the impact?"

Name It

3 minutes

Punch It: Name the Teacher Action Step

Name the action step:

- "Based on what we discussed today, what do you think your action step should be?"
- "What are the key steps to take to implement this action step?"

Punch it:

- "So your action step today is _____"—state clearly and concisely:
  - <u>what</u> the teacher will work on (e.g., universal prompts during discourse)
  - <u>how</u> the teacher will execute (e.g., 1. Revoice a limited response using a neutral tone, 2. Ask 2–3 students to "agree, disagree, or build" onto student's response, and 3. Prompt a student who initially had a limited response to stamp the understanding)
- Have teacher restate the action step; then write it down

Do It
20–45 minutes
Practice the Teaching to Make the Learning Productive

Plan:

- Select the key part of the lesson to practice aligned to the teacher action step
  - "Based on what you are working on right now, what would be the best part of the lesson to practice?"
- Plan what to say:
  - "Take ___ minutes and write what you will say/prompt. I will do the same so we can spar."
    - Management action steps: Focus on delivery of instructions/what to do during key moments
    - Monitoring: Plan what you will look for when students are working independently (e.g., your laps) and plan the prompts you will use if they are struggling
    - Discourse: Plan the prompts and/or what/how to Show-Call student work
  - Spar: "Let's compare our plans. What can we pull from each to make the strongest plan?"

Practice:

- "Let's practice."
  - **If management/engagement:** Focus on what to do; directions and teacher action step
  - **If monitoring:** Practice telling students what you are looking for (i.e., laps), monitoring annotations/answers to find patterns, and prompting when students are stuck
  - **If guided discourse:** Practice Show-Call, prompting students, and stamping their understanding
- (If a struggle) "I'm going to model the teaching for you. [Teach.] What do you notice?"
- Repeat until the practice is successful. CFU: "What made this more effective?"

- Lock it in:
  - "How did our practice meet or enhance what we planned?"
  - "Would you add anything to our lesson plan based on the practice? Let's add it now."

Follow up:

- Reflect:
  - "What are your takeaways about teaching this lesson?"
  - "Which question on the exit tickets will tell us if students mastered the key understanding for today?"
  - "What percent of students should master this based on our plan and where students currently are?"
- Plan for real-time feedback:
  - "When will you be taking this lesson live with your students?"
  - Agree on a predetermined cue for next observation: "When I come in, I will observe for ___. If I see you struggling I will [give you a cue]."
- Set dates—both teacher and leader write them down:
  - Observation: when you'll observe live or need teacher to film
  - Next meeting and if/when a weekly data meeting for this lesson will occur

MONITORING PLANNING

In Chapter 1, we talked extensively about monitoring the learning and its impact. Monitor the learning, not just the process. Student first; teacher second.

The same applies for monitoring planning. Evaluating the quality of lesson plans while observing will always be the highest leverage move because then you can verify if the lesson plan is being followed. Monitoring paper/digital lesson plans without seeing instruction is like studying a football team's game plan but not watching the actual game. You won't know what happened!

Core Idea

Monitor the lesson while observing the instruction.
Watch the actual game, not just the game plan.

We presented an overall framework for monitoring the learning in Chapter 1. Here are the questions that directly tie to the planning process:

Monitoring Planning

A Guide to Reviewing Lessons

Action	If Not. . .
1. **Look at the objective and the end-goal assessment:** Does the objective align to the rigor of the state or AP exam?	• Determine an assessment to test learning of this objective that would set the rigor appropriately high (see Chapter 1). • With assessment in hand, move on to #2.
2. **Look at the Exit Ticket:** Does it meet the bar for rigor set by the assessment for that objective?	• Revise the Exit Ticket and then continue to #3.
3. **Look at the whole week's strand of lessons:** Do the other lessons in the sequence meet the bar for rigor?	• Complete this process for the whole week's strand of lessons.
4. **Look at the independent practice:** Does it prepare students to succeed on the Exit Ticket, and is there sufficient time?	• Revise the independent practice and/or the timing of it and then continue to #5.
5. **Finally, look at the strategies the teacher plans to use to teach the material:** Is the teaching strategy conducive to the students learning what they need to succeed on independent practice?	• Revise the lesson accordingly.
6. **Now you can observe the teaching!**	• See Chapter 1—Monitor the Learning—and Chapter 3—Observation and Feedback— for more guidance!

Stop & Do
Leverage Leadership App

It is faster than ever to evaluate the quality of a lesson plan. Open up the app your-self. Let your teachers do it as well! You'll get immediate recommendations to align the rigor to that of your state test/college-ready assessment and adjustments to the lesson itself. You'll see an immediate impact.

LL App

TURNAROUND—WHAT TO DO FIRST

In a school in which teachers are not engaged in this depth of curriculum and lesson planning, leaders need to decide where to begin. The context of your school will dictate your choice.

For Schools with Mandated Curriculum

The most common context for public schools is that you have a district curricular pac-ing guide that you must follow, but it doesn't address the depth of each lesson plan and the quality of the learning objectives. If this is your context, making sure the data-driven instruction model (Chapter 1) is in place is *always* the most effective step to accompany a pacing guide. If DDI is locked in, then you can focus on developing teachers' capac-ity to develop and lead effective lessons via the Weekly Planning Meeting: it is such a natural next step! Follow the guide to leading these meetings (you can even rotate them with Weekly Data Meetings) and you'll start to see the results. When leaders carefully work with teachers on their plans, they will more consistently identify potential pitfalls and increase the quantity of effective teaching.

For Schools with Curriculum Planning Autonomy

Having curriculum planning autonomy gives leaders more options: plan their own curriculum/lessons or borrow from others. With the rise of AI, inventing lesson plans from scratch has never been easier, and when teachers participate in the process, it will increase their investment. The key is to map out all the assessments and work products for each unit at the beginning of the year—creating a skeletal curriculum plan—and then dive into the weekly planning the rest of the year. Remember: make sure to plan backwards from your end-goal assessment to get the rigor high enough.

For most leaders in turnaround, that is overly daunting in Year 1. It is often best to acquire quality curriculum plans from another school and devote your efforts to supporting teachers in the daily lesson planning.

CONCLUSION

Corliss James is the principal of Leadership Prep School in Memphis, Tennessee. When she first started coaching planning, teachers were resistant. "They felt like we were just adding more requirements to what they had to do." Change happened when Corliss and members of her leadership team started planning meetings side by side with teachers. Slowly, one practice session at a time, teachers saw the value in the quality of their teaching. "Lead by example and do the work," she shares. Then the culture—and the quality of lessons—will start to shine.

Action Steps for Principals

Planning

LEVER	PLANNING—KEY ACTIONS IN SEQUENCE
	Plan

	Curriculum—Unit Plans Aligned to Assessment:
	
	1. **Identify or design high quality unit plans that align to the end-goal assessments**
	
	  • Identify, design, or adjust exemplar unit plans to meet the following criteria:
	
	    ◦ aligned to your end-goal assessment (see "Data-Driven Instruction")
	
	    ◦ address both content and skills specific to that subject
	
	    ◦ adequate time for independent practice
	
	    ◦ appropriate activation of knowledge
	
	    ◦ quality models and discourse that are memorable and meaningful
	
	Lesson Plans
	
	2. **Plan effective lesson plans:**
	
	  • Design, identify or adjust exemplar lesson plans to meet the following criteria: data-driven objective, aligned exit ticket, activated knowledge, adequate time for practice, effective guided discourse or modeling
	
	Planning Tools and Structures:
	
	3. **Establish essential unit/lesson planning structures that result in consistent lesson plan quality**
	
	  • Establish essential curriculum planning structures and templates for year-long plans, unit plans, and weekly and daily lesson plans
	
	  • Establish effective protocols for creation or adjustment of unit and lesson plans (when plans will be submitted, who will review them, etc.)

LEVER: Planning

	• Identify key cornerstone lessons (lessons that present the highest leverage standards of the week/unit) to prioritize for planning meetings and data meetings throughout the school year
	4. Establish essential Weekly Planning Meeting structures
	• Create meeting schedule to conduct data meetings to analyze IA data (6 weeks) and to conduct WDMs.
	• Establish consistent protocols and pre-work expectations for effective data meetings (eg. IA analysis meeting protocol, WDM protocol).
Planning (cont'd)	**Data Meetings—Tools and Structures for Weekly Data/ Interim Assessment MTGS**
	5. Establish essential data meeting structures that result in evidence-based action planning
	• Create meeting schedule to conduct data meetings to analyze IA data (6 weeks) and to conduct WDMs.
	• Establish consistent protocols and pre-work expectations for effective data meetings (eg. IA analysis meeting protocol, WDM protocol).
	• Develop a system to regularly collect representative student work (e.g., exit tickets or spiral review from students of varying proficiency) to use as evidence to identify trends in student learning.

	Execute

Planning (cont'd)	**Lead Effective Weekly Planning Meeting**
	
	6. **See It—see the end goal** (identify the key understandings of the lesson):
	   • Go deep—Solve the most rigorous task of the lesson or of the week/unit and debrief:
	      ◦ (If needed) Leverage resources to deepen understanding of the global idea
	      ◦ Prompt for precision—"What are the most essential understandings students must master?"
	   • Narrow to today—ID the key understandings of this lesson:
	      ◦ "Looking at this lesson, what ideal answer are looking for in their writing/class discussion?"
	
	7. **See It—see the gap** (adjust the lesson):
	   • Focus—select the 2–3 tasks that students must grapple with to ensure mastery (productive struggle)
	   • Anticipate student gaps—determine where they will struggle with the tasks
	   • Activate knowledge—chart the key knowledge that students will need to know (e.g., vocab, terms, events)
	   • Adjust: cut and/or adjust the timing of the lesson to give most time to the most important
	
	8. **See It—model:**
	   • Frame: Name what the teacher should focus on
	   • Model: Lead an effective model of the teaching aligned to the teacher's action step.
	   • Slow down to model the thinking:
	      ◦ Create meta-moments to reveal your thinking: "Hmm. I can see that the student is almost there. I'm going to use my Stretch It question."

	◦ Create bright lines between meta-moments and teacher-mode: shift tone and body language with crisp cues: "Pause." "Action."
	• Use a visual resource: Post the word wall to activate knowledge as well as imperfect responses
	9. Name It—name the teacher's high leverage action step
	• Name the highest leverage teacher action step to implement while teaching this lesson: both what the teacher should do and how to do so (using the Get Better Faster Sequence as a guide)
	10. Do It—plan and practice the lesson
	• Perfect the plan before practicing
	◦ Use the planning time to script an exemplar for your teacher to spar with
Planning (cont'd)	◦ Ask "Let's compare. What do you notice?"
	• Practice:
	◦ Give real-time feedback to strengthen the practice; jump in and model again if teachers struggle
	11. Follow up—both teacher and leader write them down:
	• Reflect and write down: "What are your key takeaways from our meeting today?" (both about the content itself and the teaching)
	• Lock in tasks:
	◦ Completed Materials: when teacher will complete revised lesson plan/materials.
	◦ Revisions to future plans: "Where can this [action step] be applied next week/month?"
	◦ Observation: when you'll observe the teacher
	▫ "When would be best time to observe your implementation of this?"

○ (When valuable) Self-video: when you'll tape teacher to debrief in future meeting

Monitor and Follow-up

12. **Observe teaching to identify schoolwide and teacher-specific trends:**

- Create and use a rubric and set a schedule for review lesson plan execution; embed as a part of your observation schedule (See "Observation and Feedback")

- When observing, evaluate the quality and alignment of the key components of the plan

  ○ Objective aligned to the end-goal/interim assessment

  ○ Exit ticket aligned to the end-goal/interim assessment

  ○ Sequence: lesson fits in a logical sequence of lessons that is building to student mastery

  ○ Activate knowledge: lessons activate or build needed knowledge to give students access

  ○ Independent practice: adequate time for students to practice the new content/skill

  ○ Modeling or guided discourse: effective instruction aligned to student learning needs

- ID the pattern of error across a set of lesson plans, HW, or class materials to create a grade/schoolwide goal/action step for improving rigor.

13. **Follow up to achieve 90% implementation**

- Conduct audits of lesson/unit plans and build plan for improvement

- ID individual teachers who have not mastered or are not building effective lesson plans and plan additional follow-up (modeling, focused planning, extra support).

Planning (cont'd)

Pulling the Lever

Action Planning Worksheet for PLANNING

Self-Assessment

- How frequently are your teachers getting feedback about their lesson and curriculum plans? ____/year or ____/month

- What percentage of your teachers' lesson and curriculum plans are well aligned with interim assessment data? ____ %

- What percentage of the activities students do in class would you say are well aligned with lesson objectives and classroom assessments? ____ %

- Refer back to the top school leader action steps for data-driven instruction and planning. What are the top three action steps you could implement immediately to improve planning at your school?

  _____

  _____

  _____

  _____

Planning for Action

- What tools from this book will you use to improve planning at your school? Check all that you will use (you can find all in the LL App):

  ____ **Planning Meeting One-Pager**

  ____ **Exemplar Know-Show Charts**

  ____ **Tool for Evaluating and Adjusting the Rigor/Alignment of Your Lesson Plans**

  ____ **Planning Meeting Rubric**

- What are your next steps for improving lesson/curriculum planning?

Action:	Date:

Chapter 3

Observation and Feedback

Face-to-Face to Move The Needle

It's a Monday afternoon at Minnequa Elementary School, and you can hear the energized discourse coming from the classroom across the hall from Katie's office. Principal Katie Harshman has already observed that class in the morning (and many others), but she is just getting started.

Sitting by her side is one of her teachers, leaning forward as she reflects on her own progress in creating more discussion time in her classroom. Katie builds on that success.

"Do you remember the focus of our Faculty PD last week?" she asks.

"Of course," replies her teacher. "We were focused on the discourse cycle."

"Right!" affirms Katie. "We are going to zoom in on this a little bit, and I'm going to model for you using universal prompts while teaching your lesson from this Wednesday. As you watch my model, I want you to pay attention to just three things: how do I push the thinking back on our scholars, and what's the purpose and impact of these actions. Ready?"

The teacher nods expectantly, her lesson plan in hand to follow along. "For the role play scene, I'll ask you to play the role of a student with the incorrect answer and another with the correct answer. Here we go."

Katie pulls out the mathematical task for that lesson: an exercise that asks students whether 1/4 + 1/4 + 1/4 + 1/4 is equal to two halves. "Is this question true?"

The teacher plays the role of the incorrect student adeptly: "There is no way that 4 pieces can be the same as 2. They are not the same." Katie pauses and role plays addressing the whole class: "Agree or disagree?" The role play continues, as Katie models prompting students, her teaching observing intently.

WATCH Clip 19: Harshman—See It (Model)—
Feedback Meeting

When Katie Harshman arrived at Minnequa Elementary School back in 2017, the school had spent nine consecutive years with the label of a "turnaround" school. With 95% free-reduced lunch students, Minnequa had some of the lowest results in Pueblo and in the entire state of Colorado, with fewer than 10% of students proficient in ELA and Math. Teacher morale was understandably low, with many just going through the motions.

Fast forward to 2025, and Minnequa not only closed the COVID-19 learning gap—it obliterated it. They made 40 point gains in every subject and grade level to be one of the highest achieving schools in their district and well above the statewide average.

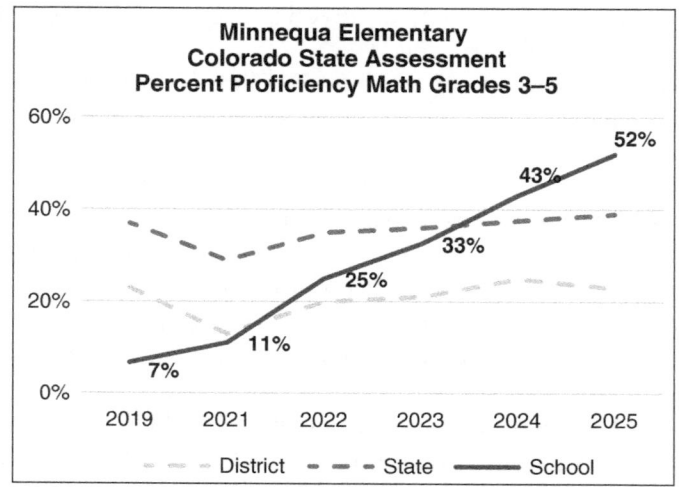

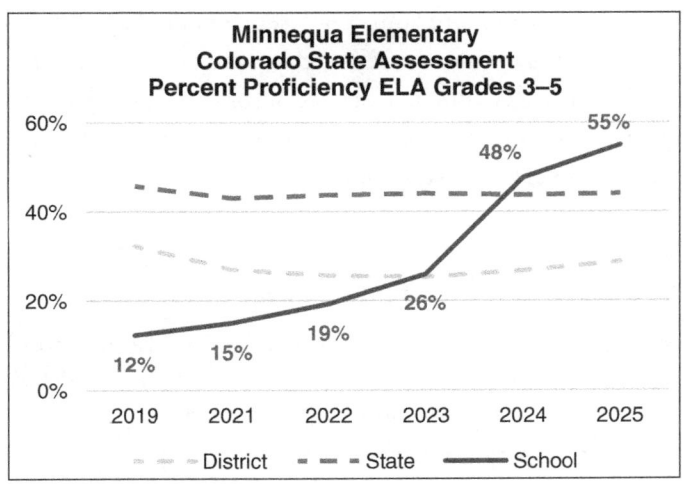

Minnequa Elementary
Colorado State Assessment
Percent Proficiency ELA Grades 3–5

55%

48%

26%

19%

15%

12%

2019 2021 2022 2023 2024 2025

- - - District   - - - State   ——— School

How did that happen? Katie didn't hire all new staff—she just invested in the ones she had. She started with the super-levers of Data-Driven Instruction (Chapter 1) and Student Culture (more on that in Chapter 5), but after that it was all about face-to-face feedback. "Culture created stability, and data-driven instruction built momentum," recalled Katie. "But coaching—consistent observation and feedback—changed the entire game."

Why was coaching so powerful? "In the end," Katie shares, "if you and your teachers aren't getting better each day, neither will your students. Either we coach, or we leave learning to chance."

Put another way, Katie didn't use her feedback to evaluate teachers—she used it to develop them in the most effective way possible. By delivering coaching instead of evaluation, she made her teachers better at teaching faster.[1]

Core Idea

The real purpose of observation and feedback is not to evaluate teachers, but to develop them.

Walk the halls of the best schools in the world, and an indisputable pattern emerges: the difference between a good school and a great school is not seen in the strongest teachers (there are strong teachers in nearly every school). Instead, when the difference between your strongest teacher and your weakest one is small, you've got a great school. If your strongest teacher is an island, then the rest are also isolated from the resources that could make them better. But if teachers across the campus learn and replicate what's working in the strongest teachers' classrooms, you've built a bridge between those classrooms, and everyone's students will thrive.

Core Idea

If your strongest teacher is an island, the rest will be stranded as well. Coach every teacher, and you've built bridges between those islands; then all students will thrive.

One of the most crucial questions any school leader faces is this: How can you close the gap between your best teachers and your up-and-coming talent?

This chapter shows you how to bridge the performance gap in the same way Katie did. We'll break the process down into these four key adjustments to the way you observe and coach:

- Observe more frequently and consistently
- Identify the right action step for each teacher
- Give teachers effective feedback
- Monitor and follow up

Core Idea—Keys To Observation And Feedback

- **Observe Frequently and Consistently:** Lock in frequent and regular observations
- **Identify the Key Action Step:** Identify the top areas for growth
- **Give Effective Feedback:** Give direct face-to-face feedback that practices specific action steps for improvement
- **Monitor and Follow-up:** Develop systems to monitor teacher development and follow up accordingly

---

Let's dive in.

OBSERVE MORE FREQUENTLY

Imagine you have a new passion—anything from weightlifting to playing bass guitar to dancing—and you are training every day to compete in a national competition. You are looking for the best coach to help you get better. Imagine that one of the coaches you find tells you, "I'll come watch you once or twice this year, and then I'll send you written feedback." Unless you have no alternative, you would say no immediately.

If we would reject such periodic coaching for our passions, why do we accept intermittent coaching as the norm when it comes to teaching? Coaching is no less essential in teaching than in any other profession. As Robert J. Marzano, Tony Frontier, and David Livingston showed in their seminal text *Effective Supervision*, "Teachers need input from sources other than themselves."[2] Yet according to their survey of the largest K-12 systems in the United States, the median new teacher is only observed twice a year, with the median veteran teacher being observed only once every two years.[3] And while more frequent observation is on the rise in some circles, many of the most progressive educational initiatives in the country still only require or recommend two or three observations per teacher per year.[4]

Seeing a teacher once or twice a year isn't coaching—it's evaluation. Effective coaching requires ongoing observation, not drive-by evaluations. Just as no soccer coach would watch only a few minutes of two games a season and expect improvement, effective instructional coaching requires a steady, sustained gaze, not a sporadic one. It's all about frequency and consistency.

That's why leaders like Katie follow a core commitment: 15-minute observations combined with 15–30 minute feedback meetings in the same week. Even if she only accomplishes this every other week, do the math: Katie's teachers are getting as much feedback in one year as most do in *twenty*.

Core Idea

By receiving biweekly observations and feedback, a teacher gets as much development in one year as most receive in twenty.

Getting to this frequency of observation is the first key to bridging the gap between your strongest teachers and your struggling ones. After all, you can't build a bridge to an island you can't see. (Even with this frequency, we acknowledge that these regular observations may still only allow you to see 3% of instruction compared to the 80% that data reveal as Chapter 1 on Data-Driven Instruction highlighted. Yet when combined with DDI, these observations can be the difference between illuminating the gaps in teachers' craft or coaching them to close them.)

The first question, then, is this: how can a leader make the time to observe teachers weekly or bi-weekly? Part of the key, to be certain, is re-allocating your time so you spend less of it on work that doesn't impact student learning as meaningfully—something we'll show how to do in more detail in Chapter 8 on Finding the Time. But you can also make regular observation and feedback more feasible simply by optimizing the efficiency of your observations. Three strategies for doing so are worth addressing here: share the work among multiple qualified leaders, schedule observations strategically, and make your preparation for feedback meetings more efficient.

Share the Work: Distribute Across Your Leadership Team

If you're thinking it is incredibly difficult for a single leader to observe every teacher in a school every week, you're right (unless that school is small). What a single leader *can* do, however, is observe up to 12 teachers per week, or 24 teachers every other week. And fortunately for students across the nation, most schools have a teacher-to-leader ratio that makes it possible to instate weekly or bi-weekly observations when you split them up among multiple leaders.

As a result of giving workshops all over the United States, we've found about 90% of schools have a leader-to-teacher ratio of 24:1 or less, and an increasingly large number are getting to 12:1 ratios. We've also seen again and again that 12:1 is the golden ratio to get to weekly observations.

Want to see if that would work at your school? Let's do the math.

———————————●———————————

Weekly Observation Feasibility Worksheet

Complete the following steps to determine if you can feasibly observe every teacher every week at your school.

1. **Add up all of the teachers at your school:** _____ teachers
2. **Add up all of the leaders at your school, including any assistant principals, coaches, deans, etc.:** _____ leaders

3. **Divide the number of teachers in your school by the number of leaders:**
_____ : _____ ratio of teachers to leaders

Results

- **If your ratio of teachers to leaders is 12:1 or fewer:** Congratulations! You have the resources you need to observe every teacher in your school once a week.

- **If your ratio is 24:1** or fewer: Congratulations! You have the resources to observe every teacher in your school every other week.

If You Want to Improve your Ratio (you are greater than 24:1 or want to get to 12:1):

- **Count again:** are you sure you've accounted for *every* adult in your school who could fulfill a leadership position?

- **Expand your leadership bench:** consider ways you could maximize the expertise on your campus such as giving some teachers part-time instructional leadership roles. For example, a full-time teacher could coach one other teacher if you reduced a few other responsibilities like lunchroom duties.

The last bullet is important; get creative about the ways you delegate the work of leadership on your campus if 12:1 initially appears out of reach! Take some time to reflect on this as we move forward and return to this page when you begin building your schedule in Chapter 8.

Schedule Strategically

Katie knew that the key to observing regularly was making it a habit. "If I didn't leave my office on Monday to observe, I knew I would become complacent and not leave the office the rest of the week, either." So, she made it a point to observe all her teachers Monday morning (brief observations, but long enough where she could find a trend and coach). Then she scheduled her feedback meetings to happen that same afternoon or the next day. "That way, I had to maximize my prep time and didn't take the work home with me. Why wait when I can turn around the feedback while still fresh?" Katie then spent the rest of the week simply doubling down on that feedback—short and sweet real-time feedback for any additional observations (more on real-time feedback later in this chapter).

What makes Katie's actions remarkable is how replicable they are. You don't need unlimited time; instead you just need to maximize the time you have. Here are three key tips to follow Katie's lead:

1. **Lock in feedback meetings:** Schedule your weekly feedback meeting with each teacher *before* you plan when to observe them, and you'll have a built-in accountability tool for completing your observation because you need to observe to know what action step to deliver during the feedback meeting. "Before I locked in feedback meetings, I wasn't really developing teachers to be great at what they do," reflects Candace Young, whom you met in Chapter 1. "I have to see what they need to make sure they don't give up." Few things are as powerful motivators as knowing a teacher will be waiting in your office expecting that you'll have feedback for them!

2. **Shorter Visits in Blocks:** In contrast to the traditional, hour-long block, Katie only observes for roughly 10–15 minutes per teacher. "Blocking" your observations— that is, observing multiple teachers back-to-back— reduces inefficiencies in travelling between rooms and transitioning between tasks. Just like Katie observed all her teachers Monday morning, you can schedule three or four (or more!) brief observations back-to-back to gain extra time. So long as leaders are strategic about what they are looking for, a brief observation is sufficient for thorough and direct feedback. Indeed, significantly longer observations are often inefficient, especially when they come at the expense of observing far fewer teachers.

3. **Adjust your schedule week-to-week:** Champions of frequent observation don't lock in one schedule—they master the art of strategic flexibility, building opportunities to adjust observations in response to teacher needs. Katie keeps a tracker of her observations and looks at the patterns across her teachers. If a certain group/ grade level/department is struggling, she will shift her focus for the week to close gaps more effectively. Alternatively, Candace Young (Chapter 1) makes sure to observe the reteach lessons that were generated in the Weekly Data Meetings. Any number of approaches like these may be fruitful. The key is having a locked-in time when you will make adjustments for the week—your leadership team meeting, or a set day of the week (e.g., Sunday afternoon when you make your schedule for the week). If not, you run the risk of simply not observing.

Making It Happen:

Your first reaction might be to think this is not all possible in a school leader's day. Let's show how by doing the math:

- Typical Teacher-to-Leader load (when all leaders are counted): 12 teachers/leader
- One classroom observation per week: 15 min
- Total minutes of observation per week: 12 teachers x 15 min = 180 min = 3 hrs
- One feedback/planning meeting: 30 min
- Total minutes of feedback/planning meetings: 12 teachers x 30 mins = 6 hrs
- Total hours devoted to teacher observation and feedback: 9 hrs
- Percentage of a leader's time (assuming 7-4 school day): 20%

Think to yourself: this only requires 20%. You can make that happen!

Marie Culihan is the principal of Albany School of the Humanities (more about her in Chapter 8). Here's how her schedule makes it all possible:

Marie Culihan's Schedule

Observations and Meetings (Feedback and Planning)

DAILY SCHEDULE:					
	MONDAY	**TUESDAY**	**WEDNESDAY**	**THURSDAY**	**FRIDAY**
6:30 7 AM					
:30					
8 AM					
:30	Whole School Walkthrough		2nd Gr Walkthroughs	5th Grade CPT	
9 AM					
:30	4th Grade CPT	Wissman Wkly Mtg			
10 AM					

(Continued)

:30	1st Grade CPT				
11 AM	1st Grade CPT		4th Gr Walkthroughs		
:30			3rd Gr Walkthroughs		Feedback Meetings
12 PM				1st Gr Walkthroughs	Feedback Meetings
:30	K Walkthroughs			Feedback Meetings	
1 PM	Feedback Meetings			Feedback Meetings	
:30	SPED Visits				
2 PM					
:30					
3 PM					
:30					
4 PM					
:30					
5 PM					

As you can see, committing to observation and feedback does require a substantial time investment but not an unreasonable one. You still have plenty of time for everything else. In Chapter 8 (Finding the Time), we'll dive even more deeply into more strategies to keep non-instructional items from interfering with your ability to observe teachers.

Once you have developed a schedule like this one, you are one step closer to making dramatic improvements in teacher development. The next step is the know-how to observe effectively.

IDENTIFY THE RIGHT ACTION STEP

Like many experienced educators, Katie doesn't miss much when she observes a class. She immediately sees dozens of areas for improvement. We certainly have plenty of guidance on all the teacher actions that get teachers better, from *Get Better Faster* to books like Doug Lemov's *Teach Like a Champion* and Jon Saphier's aptly-named *The Skillful Teacher*. These books have already answered this question in rich taxonomies that cover everything from the proper posture to the best questioning strategies that make students think. For a diligent leader with access to these resources, the real problem is not identifying areas of growth; it's: "Where do I start?" In a book on teaching that is hundreds of pages long, where do we turn first to transform pages into practice?

Characteristics of Effective Action Steps

Over the past 20 years, I have worked with educators to answer a critical question: what do the most successful leaders do to develop their teachers most quickly—especially their newest ones? That began a multi-year, on-site project to identify and codify those practices. One of the first big "a ha" moments was when we looked at the type of feedback these leaders were giving their teachers. Here are some examples of the action steps they used in their feedback meetings.

Sample Teacher Action Steps from Top Leaders

- **What to Do:** Use economy of language when giving directions:
  - Chunk your directions: give them one-by-one in sequential order
  - Make them bite-sized (e.g., three to five words) and observable
  - Check for understanding on complex instructions.

- **Guide Discourse 101:** Launch the discourse cycle around the productive struggle:
  - Everybody writes or Show-Calls (post student work for students to analyze—exemplars, non-exemplars, or both)
  - Turn and talk
  - Cold call, then volleyball (multiple students speak before teacher)
  - Prompt for and praise basic Habits of Discussion to strengthen conversation and listening skills (build, evaluate, agree/disagree, etc.)
  - Stamp the key understanding: "What are the keys to remember?"

Take a moment to review these action steps. What do they all have in common?

Name It
Sample Action Steps for Teachers

What characteristics do these action steps have in common? Write your response below.

_____

_____

_____

_____

_____

_____

_____

You probably noted many characteristics in common, one of which was the size of them. You might expect that the quickest way to develop teachers would be to give them more feedback at once, but in fact, the opposite is true. Teachers grow most quickly when leaders narrow their focus to the highest-leverage focus area and deliver that feedback in the form of the most specific, granular action steps possible.

In his excellent book *The Talent Code*, Daniel Coyle explains why this is the case. Traveling to talent hotbeds all over the world, he discovered that bite-sized actions fueled the growth of excellence in nearly every field. At Moscow's Spartak Tennis Club, he found tennis players who spent hours upon hours correcting their racquet swing to the last movement before they practiced actually hitting tennis balls. At New York's Meadowmount School of Music, he found orchestras that practiced music at a snail's pace, getting each note exactly right in isolation before they tried hitting them at tempo.[5] Why does this work? Because if you master your grip on the racquet earlier, there's less to fix later. Building the right foundation from the start—down to the very last detail— builds deeper expertise faster in the long run. The smaller and more precise the action step, the quicker the growth.

> ## Core Idea
> The smaller and more precise the action step, the quicker the growth.
> Be bite-sized, not book-sized.

It's the opposite of a several-hundred-page tome on teaching. Effective action steps are bite-sized—small enough to be chewed, swallowed, and digested in one sitting.

So what else makes a great action step? Here are four criteria that work together for maximum impact:

1. **Highest-leverage.** Will this help the teacher to develop most quickly and effectively? Is it connected to a larger PD goal?

2. **Sequenced.** Each action step builds on the preceding ones.

3. **Measurable.** The action step is what the teacher can practice: it names the "what" (e.g., use economy of language) and the "how" (e.g., give crisp instructions with as few words as possible [e.g. three-word directions], and check for understanding)

4. **Bite-sized.** If your teacher can't make the change in a week, the action step isn't small enough!

Keys to Great Action Steps

Great action steps are:

- **Highest leverage.** Will this help the teacher to develop most quickly and effectively? Is it connected to a larger PD goal?

- **Sequenced.** Each action step builds on the preceding ones.

- **Measurable.** The action step is what the teacher can practice: it names the "what" and the "how."

- **Bite-sized.** If your teacher can't make the change in a week, the action step isn't small enough!

Narrowing action steps to what is highest leverage and measurable changes your whole mindset about feedback—it's the mental equivalent of shifting the zoom lens on your camera from macro to micro. But this mental exercise takes a lot of work because you must zoom in on the most important part! How can you develop the skill of writing bite-sized action steps when you coach so many teachers and have so little time?

Over the past 20 years, we have developed a set of high-leverage action steps for teaching— tested in the classrooms of teachers worldwide. We've collected feedback to continually revise and sharpen the action steps to make them work for any teacher. We discovered that there was a commonality not only to the nature of the action steps these leaders were delivering to their teachers, but also to the *order* in which those action steps were delivered. Great action steps go granular, but the most effective action steps build on each other logically. They prioritize the most crucial skills of great teaching, carefully keeping their focus specific while addressing classroom management and the rigor of instruction in tandem.

The result? The Get Better Faster Scope and Sequence. This guide can save time for those leaders who strive to follow in their footsteps.

Read on to see the sequence! As you read, put a star next to any action step that stands out as something you could implement into your daily coaching practice, perhaps something you see your teachers stumble over often, or something that you haven't thought about for years. Place two stars beside anything that strikes you as especially important to implement in your school right away. (If a step reminds you of a particular teacher you work with, consider putting that teacher's initials next to it!)

Get Better Faster Scope and Sequence

Top Action Steps Used by Instructional Leaders to Launch a Teacher's Development

Phase 1	Management Trajectory	Rigor Trajectory
Phase 1: Pre-Teaching (Summer PD)	**Develop Essential Routines & Procedures** 1. **Routines & Procedures 101:** Design and Roll out • Plan & practice critical routines and procedures moment-by-moment: ○ Explain what each routine means and what it will look like	**Develop Content Expertise & Lesson Plans** 1. **Develop Understanding of the Content:** • Analyze end-goal assessments: identify the most rigorous end-goal assessment (AP items, SAT, state test, etc.) and name what students need to know and show to complete the tasks

Phase 1	Management Trajectory	Rigor Trajectory

	o Write what teachers and students do at each step and what will happen with students who don't get it right at first
	
	• Plan & practice the roll out: how to introduce routine for the first time:
	
	  ᵒ Plan the "I Do": how you will model the routine
	
	  c Plan the practice and what you will do when students don't get it right the first time
	
	2. **Confident Presence:** Stand and speak with purpose
	
	• Confident stance: when giving instructions, stop moving and strike a formal pose
	
	• Warm-demander register: when giving instructions, use a warm but firm register, including tone and word choice
	
	Note: Many other topics can be introduced during August training. What are listed above are the topics that should be addressed to reach proficiency. Other topics to introduce—even if the teachers will not yet master them—could be:
	
	• *What to Do*
	
	• *See your Students*
	
	• *Narrate the Positive*
		• Develop/internalize unit plans: Sequence the big ideas of the content into a logical progression/story
		
		  o Identify and name the key concepts/enduring understandings
		
		  o Describe the relationships between the concepts within the grade span and across preceding and upcoming grades
		
		2. **Develop Effective Lesson Plans 101:** Build the foundation of an effective lesson rooted in what students need to learn:
		
		• Write precise learning objectives that are:
		
		  o Data-driven (rooted in what students need to learn based on end-goal assessments & analysis of assessment results)
		
		  o Centered on enduring understandings of the unit
		
		• Plan a launch: Use of Do Now, oral review, etc.
		
		• Create/identify key tasks for students that lead to the most important conceptual understanding of the lesson

Phase 1	Management Trajectory	Rigor Trajectory

	• *Individual Student Correction*
	• *Do It Again: have students do routines again if not done correctly*
		• Plan the basic structure of the lesson (e.g., direction instruction, inquiry)
		• Design an exit ticket (brief end assessment) aligned to the objective
		
		3. **Internalize Existing Lesson Plans:** Make existing plans your own
		• Identify the moment of most productive struggle in the lesson—articulate what students need to know/be able to do to master it
		• Internalize & rehearse key parts of the lesson
		• Build time stamps into the lesson plan
		• Adjust the lesson plan to target the knowledge/skills students need
		
		4. **Write an Exemplar: Set the bar for excellence**
		• Script out ideal written responses you want students to produce throughout the arc of the lesson
		  ○ Humanities: includes key evidence, inferences, arguments
		  ○ STEM: if they get this right and you ask them why, what do you want them to say?

Phase 2	Management Trajectory	Rigor Trajectory
Phase 2 (Days 1-30)	**Roll Out and Monitor Routines**	**Roll out Academic Routines:**

Management Trajectory

Roll Out and Monitor Routines

3. **What to Do:** Use economy of language when giving directions:
   - Chunk your directions: give them one-by-one in sequential order
   - Make them bite-sized (e.g., 3-5 words) and observable
   - Check for understanding on complex instructions.

4. **See your Students:** Know when students are engaged or unengaged
   - Make eye contact: look at all students for on-task engagement:
     - Choose 3-4 focus areas (places where you have students who often get off task) to look toward consistently
   - Circulate the room with purpose (break the plane):
     - Move among the desks and around the perimeter
     - Stand at the corners: identify three spots on perimeter of the room to which you can circulate to stand and monitor student work
     - Move away from the student who is speaking to monitor the whole room.

Rigor Trajectory

Roll out Academic Routines:

5. **Independent Practice:** Set up daily routines that build opportunities for students to practice independently
   - Write first, talk second: give students writing tasks to complete prior to class discussion, so that every student answers independently before hearing his or her peers' contributions
   - Implement a daily entry prompt (Do Now) to either introduce the day's objective or review material from the previous day
   - Use an Exit Ticket (brief final task) to assess end-of-class mastery

6. **Academic Monitoring 101:** Check students' independent work to determine whether they're learning and what feedback is needed
   - Create and implement a monitoring pathway:
     - Name the gap: Announce what you will be looking for and how you will code work/give feedback as you circulate
     - Monitor the fastest writers first to gather trends, then the students who need more support

Phase 2	Management Trajectory	Rigor Trajectory

	5. **Routines & Procedures 201:** Revise and perfect them
	
	• Revise any routine that needs more attention to detail or is inefficient, emphasizing what students and teachers are doing at each moment
	
	• Do It Again: have students do the routine again if initially incorrect
	
	Build Trust and Rapport
	
	6. **Narrate the Positive**
	
	• Warm welcome: make eye contact, smile, and greet students
	
	• Narrate what students do well, not what they do wrong
	
	    ◦ "Table two is ready, their books are open, and all are reading."
	
	    ◦ "I like how Javon has anticipated a counter-argument to strengthen his thesis."
	
	• Praise intellect, not just behavior—reinforce students getting smarter:
	
	    ◦ Affirm the effort, not just the outcome: "Your diligence on revising your thesis really paid off here."
		• "Pen in hand": Give written feedback to student work
		
		    ◦ Compare answers to the exemplar: what are they missing?
		
		    ◦ Give quick feedback (star, circle, pre-established code)
		
		    ◦ Cue students to revise answers using minimal verbal intervention (affirm the effort, name error, ask to fix it)
		
		• Gather data while monitoring and prepare to respond:
		
		    ◦ Track student responses: ideal, almost there, further off
		
		    ◦ Determine how to respond: stop the class for a quick fix, activate knowledge, model or discourse
		
		7. **Guide Discourse 101:** Launch the discourse cycle around the productive struggle:
		
		• Everybody writes or Show-Calls (post student work for students to analyze—exemplars, non-exemplars or both)
		
		• Turn and talk

Phase 2	Management Trajectory	Rigor Trajectory

	• While narrating the positive, look at student(s) who are off task
	
	7. **Make authentic connections:**
	  • Memorize student names & use them each time you call on them
	  • Make self-to-student connection when they share a struggle, interest, or passion ("I struggled when. . ." or "I love that, too!")
	   ◦ Show genuine concern: keep a track of important details and dates for each student to follow up with them; check in with them after class when something is off
		• Cold call, then volleyball (multiple students speak before teacher)
		
		• Prompt for and praise basic habits of discussion to strengthen conversation and listening skills (build, evaluate, agree/disagree, etc.)
		
		  Stamp the key understanding: "What are the keys to remember?"

Phase 3	Management Trajectory	Rigor Trajectory

Phase 3
(Days 31-60)
	Engage Every Student:
	8. **Whole-Class Reset**
	  • Implement a planned whole class reset to re-establish student expectations when a class routine has slowly weakened over previous classes
		Activate Knowledge and Model:
		8. **Activate Knowledge:** Prompt students to access their knowledge
		  • Point students to resources (word wall, notes, texts)
		  • "What do we know about __?"

Phase 3	Management Trajectory	Rigor Trajectory

	○ "I've noticed that only 40% of us are writing end notes. These are important because they demonstrate your understanding of the text as a whole. Today, I'll be looking for end notes in all your annotations."
	
	• Implement an "in-the-moment reset" when a class veers off task during the class period
	
	  ○ Example: Stop teaching. Confident stance. Clear What to Do: "Pencils down. Eyes on me in 3-2-1. Thank you: that's what Harvard looks like." Pick up tone & energy again.
	
	9. **Engage All Students:** Make sure all students participate:
	
	• Cold Call: record which students participate in each class; cold call those who don't to ensure everyone participates.
	
	• Pre-call/warm call: let a student who needs more time know you're calling him/her next
	
	• Turn & Talk: implement briefly (15–60 second) and frequently
		• Use a knowledge organizer (cheat sheet)—all key points on 1-2 pages
		
		• Retrieve knowledge by applying it—give a simple task (organize events in chronological order, quick math fluency, etc.)
		
		• "Drop" knowledge:
		
		  ○ Give them knowledge in the middle of the lesson when it will unlock understanding (stating definition of a vocab word that cannot be understood with context, etc.)
		
		9. **Model:** Model for students the thinking behind the doing
		
		• Narrow the focus to the thinking students are struggling with
		
		• Give students a clear listening/note-taking task that fosters active listening:
		
		• Model the thinking, not just the procedure:
		
		  ○ Model replicable thinking steps that students can follow (e.g., "Hmm. . . . So, what is this prompt asking me to do?" OR "So what do I already know about this time period?")

Phase 3	Management Trajectory	Rigor Trajectory
	<ul><li>Intentionally alternate among multiple methods in class discussion: cold calling, all hands, & turn and talks</li><li>Provide supports to students with pre-identified needs<ul><li>Executive functioning (checklist, written steps, timer, etc.)</li><li>Social supports (e.g. communication strategies, strategies for resolving conflict)</li><li>Stress (e.g. strategies for naming and managing)</li></ul></li></ul>10. **Individual Student Corrections**<ul><li>Anticipate unengaged student behavior and rehearse the next two things you will do when that behavior occurs. Redirect students using the least invasive intervention necessary:<ul><li>Proximity</li><li>Eye contact</li><li>Use a non-verbal</li><li>Say student's name quickly</li><li>Small consequence Engage in "close the loop" conversations with students to process what happened and improve for next time.</li></ul></li></ul>	<ul><li>Vary your tone and cadence from the normal teacher voice to highlight the thinking skills</li><li>Make your thinking visible (anchor chart, annotations)</li></ul><ul><li>Check for understanding after the model:<ul><li>Debrief the model by asking students to identify the thinking skills</li><li>Stamp the key points/steps to make sure you draw out the aspects you students to focus on</li><li>Give students additional "at-bats" to practice independently</li></ul></li></ul>

Phase 4	Management Trajectory	Rigor Trajectory

Phase 4 (Days 61-90)	**Increase the Energy of the Classroom:**
	
	11. **Build the Momentum**
	  • Give the students a simple challenge to complete a task:
	  • Example: "Now I know you're only fourth graders, but I have a fifth-grade problem that I bet you could master!"
	  • Warm energy: speak faster, walk faster, vary your voice, and smile
	
	12. **Pacing:** Create the illusion of speed so students feel constantly engaged
	  • Use a hand-held timer to stick to the times stamps in the lesson & give students an audio cue that it's time to move on
	  • Increase rate of questioning: no more than 2 seconds between when a student responds and a teacher picks back up instruction
	  • Use countdowns to work the clock ("do that in 5..4..3..2..1")
	  • Use Call and Response for key words
		Deepen Discourse:
		
		10. **Universal Prompts:** Push the thinking back on the students through universal prompts that can be used at any point:
		  • Revoice: Prompt students to paraphrase others' reasoning
		    ◦ "If I hear you correctly, you seem to say X. Is that right?"
		    ◦ "Are you really saying [paraphrase or re-work their argument to see if they still defend it]?"
		  • Press for reasoning: Prompt students to elaborate or justify their answer with evidence
		    ◦ "Tell me more." "Why/why not?"
		    ◦ "How do you know?" "Prove it." "Why is that important?"
		
		11. **Strategically Call on Students** based on learning needs
		  • Create a sequence of students to call on based on the rigor of each prompt and a review of student work (first ask a student who is struggling, then one who is partially there, then almost there, etc.)

Phase 4	Management Trajectory	Rigor Trajectory

	13. **Engaged Small Group Work:** Maximize the learning for every student during group work:
	
	• Deliver explicit step-by-step instructions for group work:
	
	    ◦ Make the group tasks visible/easily observable (a handout to fill in, notes to take, product to build, etc.)
	
	    ◦ Create a role for every person (with each group no larger than the number of roles needed to accomplish the tasks at hand).
	
	    ◦ Give timed instructions, with benchmarks for where the group should be after each time window
	
	• Monitor the visual evidence of group progress
	
	    ◦ Check in on each group every 5–10 minutes to monitor progress
	
	• Verbally enforce individual & group accountability:
	
	    ◦ "You are five minutes behind; get back on track."
	
	    ◦ "Lorena: focus."
		• Launch discourse by calling on a student with a limited answer
		
		• Call on students whose responses are closer to the exemplar when the class is struggling
		
		• Call on student with originally limited response to stamp new understanding
		
		12. **Stretch it:** Prompt to push for depth and conceptual understanding
		
		• Problematize: Create tension
		
		    ◦ Name the debate: "Some of you say X. Some of you say Y. What do you think?"
		
		    ◦ Provoke debate: "[Name] would say [counter argument]. How would you respond?"
		
		    ◦ Play devil's advocate: "I disagree. I actually think. . . ." or "Who can play devil's advocate?"
		
		    ◦ Feign ignorance: "I don't understand. I was thinking. . . ."
		
		• Sophisticate: add complexity

Phase 4	Management Trajectory	Rigor Trajectory
		○ Apply within different or new context/perspective: "Consider 2x +5y = 4. Does our rule still apply?" ○ Give a hypothetical: "What if. . . ." ○ Consider alternatives: "What's another way to interpret this?" Generalize: "So what's the emerging rule we could apply to all problems like this one?"

This guide doesn't claim to cover *all* action steps that can be given to a teacher; it doesn't need to. Rather, it focuses on the sequence of actions that get teachers to a level of proficiency where they can fly to even greater heights, particularly in their content expertise. But if we can get all teachers in our schools to that level, we'll truly have built a land of excellence rather than isolated islands!

(The book *Get Better Faster 2.0* unpacks these action steps—and the coaching steps to train a teacher to perform each of them masterfully—in much greater detail. Refer to it for a month-by-month guide to coaching your teachers.)

Where Do I Start? Choosing an Action Step When Observing

While it's a powerful tool to have the *Get Better Faster* Scope and Sequence in hand, the next challenge is identifying which one to use when observing a teacher. The following case studies give you practice in doing just that.

Try the following two case studies of what a coach might observe in a teacher's classroom. As you read, keep the *Get Better Faster* Scope and Sequence handy. (Remember: you can download a print-friendly version of the scope and sequence right from the LL App.) Which action step would you give each teacher if you observed them in class?

Observation and Feedback Case Study
ID the Action Step

Scenario 1:
You enter Ms. Santiago's third-grade classroom during independent reading. As you check out the lesson plan, students are reading an appropriate text and the prompt is aligned to the end goal. The opening routines are smooth—students move quickly to their seats, open their books, and begin reading silently. The atmosphere is calm and focused and Ms. Santiago is circulating to lean in with students as they read.

After a few minutes, you notice three students in the back whispering to one another. Whenever Ms. Santiago passes by, they pretend to be reading, but they go back to whispering as soon as she moves on. Ms. Santiago notices this behavior each time she looks up (and she appears to be checking regularly), and each time she says while looking around the room, "Let's make sure we're all reading!" The three students quiet briefly but then start whispering again. She repeats, "Eyes on your books, everyone."

The pattern continues and students generally stay on task, but a few repeat offenders keep breaking focus. Ms. Santiago keeps giving general reminders to the class as she circulates around the room.

Based on this information, what action step would you give this teacher?

_____

_____

_____

Scenario 2:
You step into Mr. Delgado's ninth-grade history class. Students are reading the primary source document "Letter from a Birmingham Jail" by Martin Luther King, Jr. The task is well aligned to the interim assessment and quite rigorous. As you observe, you can see that all of the students are engaged and have written substantive answers in their notebooks answering the prompt, "What was the purpose of this letter?" They are underlining key parts of the text and taking time to write their responses.

Mr. Delgado is circulating the room, and as he comes close to you in the back of the room, he comments, "Everyone is missing the fact that King was writing this to evangelical Christian pastors who have been generally sympathetic to the cause but disagree with King on his decision to break segregation laws. I'm going to have to address this." He walks to the front of the room.

"Hold on, class!" he says, calling them to attention. "I modeled for you last week how to make sure to figure out the audience of the text, but all of you are missing that. This was written to evangelical Christian pastors, and he's trying to persuade them why nonviolent demonstration is so important. Let's write that down." He writes that sentence on the whiteboard. "Be sure to include that in your essay." Students begin adding that to the next part of their essay.

As you look over the shoulder of a student to see the assignment, you see that the source line reveals some of this information, but students had skipped over it.

"Ok, class: let's come back together." The students clearly understand this direction and pause writing to look up at Mr. Delgado. "Turn to your partner. Compare your answers: what do you think? How would you revise your response?" Students immediately begin talking with each other as you leave the classroom.

Based on this information, what action step would you give this teacher?

_____

_____

_____

---

[1] _The source line in the document, which was written at the very top of the page, was as follows: "Letter from a Birmingham Jail," 1963. Birmingham City Jail. Recipient: Eight evangelical clergymen who called his breaking of laws "unwise and untimely."_

Scenario 1 Answer: Let's look closely at Scenario 1. The key is to look for the root cause. The class begins smoothly: routines are strong, transitions are quick, and most students are engaged. As a coach, you ask yourself this: has she already mastered giving clear directions? Yes. Are expectations clear to the class? For most of the students. Is the breakdown happening because students don't know what to do or because a few of them are not _doing_ it? The answers to these questions suggest this teacher has mastered several earlier management skills: Do Now routines, What to Do directions, and Positive Narration. The off-task behavior doesn't spread widely—it stays with a few students who continue whispering despite general reminders. The issue isn't that the class doesn't know expectations; it's that the teacher's feedback is too general to correct the few students who need it most.

That leads you down the management "waterfall" to a more precise skill:

- **Individual Student Corrections** — Anticipate unengaged student behavior and rehearse the next two things you will do when that behavior occurs. Redirect students using the least invasive intervention necessary:

  ○ Proximity

  ○ Eye contact

  ○ Use a non-verbal

- ◦ Say student's name quickly
- ◦ Small consequence
  (Get Better Faster Sequence—Management #10)
- Example: Walk more closely to Joanna to see if that is sufficient for her to get on task. If not, make eye contact with Joanna and nonverbally signal by opening your hands to indicate opening her book to read. If she doesn't respond, prompt: "Joanna, eyes on your book, please—thank you."

Scenario 2 Answer: Let's take a closer look at Scenario 2. The teacher launches students into a high-level task—analyzing a primary source text. The lesson begins with purpose, but students struggle almost immediately. Is this a classroom management issue? It doesn't appear to be—students aren't off task until they don't understand the text. So, their confusion isn't about the format or directions (those are clear); it's about the content.

- Is it a questioning issue? Not yet—we haven't reached that stage of the lesson.
- Where did the struggle begin? The moment students were asked to grapple with complex material they didn't yet have the tools to access.

When you trace the "rigor waterfall," you realize the root cause lies above questioning or text-dependent analysis; instead, it's in the teacher's **entry point** into the lesson. Before analyzing a challenging text, students need to **activate their prior knowledge** so they can connect new information to what they already know.

- **Activate Knowledge** — Before reading or discussion, prompt students to recall and connect prior learning or experiences that relate to the new content. (Get Better Faster Sequence—Rigor #8)
- Example: "Before we read, let's think back to my model from yesterday. What are the key things we should do to understand the purpose of a document? Refer to your notes if you need to."

When we asked Marie Culihan (you saw her Observation and Planning Meeting Schedule under Make it Happen above) how she moved her school from good to great, she reflected on her use of the Get Better Faster Scope and Sequence and a simple mantra: "Stick to the waterfall." Start at the top of the sequence and work your way down until you hit the first major growth area this teacher needs.

Core Idea

When you choose an action step for a teacher, think waterfall.
Start at the top of the Scope and Sequence,
and stop when you hit the first major growth area.

"The Scope and Sequence is a lifeline in the choppy seas of a classroom with 50 things happening at once," says Kathleen Sullivan, former principal and managing director of the Leverage Leadership Institute. "Do I see evidence of this? Yes so move down to the next step. When you no longer see evidence of it, you are at your destination. It emboldens you as a coach to shut out the din of everything else in the class and focus on getting your teacher better one step at a time."

Findings from the Field
Want to Get Better? Co-Observe with Another Leader

It's not easy to "stick to the waterfall" when you're first learning to identify action steps. One of the fastest ways to build this muscle is to do it side-by-side with a coach while walking your school.

When I work with an instructional leader, we visit a classroom together. I start by observing quietly and deciding for myself what I believe the highest leverage action step is. (And, yes, I always have the Get Better Faster sequence in hand. Even if I wrote it, I never trust memory alone. The guide keeps me focused and concise.)

Then I turn to the coach and walk through the Monitoring the Learning protocol we shared in Chapter 1. Rather than telling them what I saw, I start probing their thinking:

- "Look around the room: what are you seeing from the students?"
- "What is the gap for students?"
- "What is the gap for the teacher that's causing this?"
- "Looking back at your Get Better Faster sequence, what do you think the action step is?"

I don't say anything until I understand how they reason. If I jump in too soon, I can't see where their gap is:

- Do they recognize the gap in student learning?
- Do they see the struggles in the classroom but can't pinpoint the specific skill?
- Do they focus on a lower-leverage issue instead of the root cause that will improve the learning?

By prompting first, I can diagnose the leader's thinking, not just the teacher's. Then I model the reasoning, sharpen their analysis, or guide them through a live example. And the best part? We can do it all over again in the very next classroom. In 30 minutes, the leader gets better.

Once you've developed the skill of pinpointing the right action step, the next challenge is delivering feedback that helps the teacher master it quickly. Let's look at what separates feedback that informs from feedback that transforms.

DELIVER EFFECTIVE FEEDBACK

Imagine you do everything we've already discussed in this chapter: you make sure every teacher in your school is being observed at least once a week, and you and your fellow leaders hone your skill at identifying the right bite-sized action step at the right time. Then you use ChatGPT to generate a feedback report and leave it on the teacher's desk, feedback delivered in just a few minutes. Isn't that the value of AI? Actually, no. That's the pitfall.

Perhaps the most talented and motivated teachers will be able to translate written feedback into discrete action steps and train themselves to become expert at teaching, but most of us don't master skills by reading about what we need to do. Powerful coaching that improves teaching requires face-to-face interaction; that's a non-negotiable requirement proven over and over again by leaders everywhere. (Think about it: Occasionally, there are gifted athletes who can teach themselves to play a sport at the highest level on their own. But the rest of us will fly much higher with a skillful coach by our side.)

By saving time and adding quality to preparation, AI can and should support your coaching, but it is nowhere close to replacing it.

> ## Core Idea
>
> AI can and should enhance human coaching, but it won't replace it.

Here are the top five errors to avoid in giving feedback.

> ## The Top Five Errors to Avoid
>
> **Error 1: Inform, rather than transform:** Use AI to write out effective feedback and email it to the teacher (or write a lengthy evaluation yourself)—that drives change as effectively as anything.
>
> - **Top-tier Truth: Face-to-face makes the difference.** The rise of AI has caused many leaders to think that the best AI application is to have tools observe the teacher and generate written feedback to hand to them. This is the same error as the myth of lengthy written evaluations. The reason why this error persists nationwide among school leaders is that there is a subset of teachers for whom AI-generated or lengthy written evaluations are effective (just like there is a small group of learners for whom lengthy lectures are most effective). This creates the dangerous conclusion that all teachers develop well from lengthy evaluations. Yet as AI has advanced in every field, what has risen to the top is the need for face-to-face interaction: for community, connection, and results.[6]
>
> **Error 2: More is better.**
>
> - **Top-tier Truth: Less is more.** Many leaders fall prey to the temptation to deliver feedback on every aspect of the lesson. While that is a useful tool to demonstrate your instructional expertise, it won't change practice nearly as effectively. As we can learn from coaches in every field, bite-sized feedback on just one or two areas delivers the most effective improvement.[7]
>
> **Error 3: Just tell them; they'll get it.**
>
> - **Top-tier Truth: If they don't do the thinking, they won't internalize it.** In classroom instruction, highly effective teachers push the students to do the thinking. If teachers eclipse this thinking by providing conclusions or answers too quickly, students will disengage. Feedback is not any different: if teachers don't participate in the process of thinking about their teaching, they will be less likely to internalize the feedback. This is metacognition applied to teacher development: having teachers think about their teaching improves their performance.

Error 4: State the concrete action step. Then the teacher will act.

- **Top-tier Truth: Practice makes perfect.** If a surgeon simply tells residents how to perform an operation, they will be less effective than if the resident practices with the surgeon's guidance. Teaching is the same: practicing implementation of the feedback *with the leader* is at the heart of speeding up the improvement cycle. It also allows teachers to make mistakes before they're in front of the students again.

Error 5: Teachers can implement feedback at any time.

- **Top-tier Truth: Nail down the timing.** Having a concrete timeline in which feedback will be implemented serves two purposes: it clarifies expectations for implementation (what and when) and exposes action steps that cannot be accomplished in a week. That sets the teacher up for success and the coach up for timely re-evaluation.

What is the alternative to these errors? To lock in success for your school, coach your teachers like Katie does. See It. Name It. Do It. Here's how.

See It

Rick Romain (whom you met in the Introduction) is leading a feedback meeting for his teacher on academic monitoring. Let's watch it piece-by-piece to see his coaching. What does Rick do to launch his feedback meeting?

    WATCH Clip 20: Romain—See It (Model)— Feedback Meeting

Stop & Jot

How does Rick launch his feedback meeting? What are all the steps he takes in coaching his teacher? Jot down what you notice below.

_____

_____

_____

_____

What Rick does is quite powerful and replicable. Let's break it down.

See the Success: Just as we saw in Weekly Data Meetings and Planning Meetings, Rick begins coaching with a positive message. Right away, Rick builds confidence and that engenders trust and a willingness to accept new guidance and feedback. But Rick's actions go beyond that. Rick uses affirmation (specific praise) and an invitation to think (with a simple follow-up question "What was the impact of that on their practice?") to help his teacher see that she is improving! When your teachers see and own their success—especially when it's linked to previous meetings—you create a culture where feedback matters to them. Teachers then want more because they experience the value first hand.

See the Model: Then Rick's work really takes off. He calls on his teacher to recall how something she's practiced before in PD feels when it's done well ("What are the keys to academic monitoring?"). Next, he shows a video that gives his teacher the chance to break down a master teacher's concrete actions around academic monitoring, asking her, "What is this teacher doing when she makes her laps?" Through all these steps, Rick does what words alone cannot do: he gets the teacher to see what excellence looks like.

There is so much power in this mantra, which is why "See It" permeates every chap-

> ## Core Idea
>
> If you want teachers to get it, get them to see it.
> To see it is to believe it.

ter of this book! Without a clear model, there is no pathway to success. Moreover, if Rick simply told his teacher what exemplar teaching looks like in so many words, she wouldn't get as clear an image of what she needs to do and she might not take Rick's word for it. Show a model, however, and the teacher will see right away why the action is so powerful.

See the Gap: Once the teacher has seen the exemplar, Rick gets her to identify the gap in her own teaching and now it is easy to do so. He simply steers their conversation about what made the model teacher so successful to the logical next question: "When you think back to your independent practice today, what is the biggest gap between what you did today and what you just saw _____ do?" The teacher can articulate that gap right away. When you get teachers it see it, their pathway becomes clear.

Name It

Let's watch another example, this one from Marie Culihan, principal of Albany School of the Humanities (more on her in Chapter 8). Watch how she starts the same way as Rick and what she does next:

WATCH Clip 21: Culihan—See It. Name It— Feedback Meeting

Stop & Jot

What does Marie do to ensure her teacher knows the action step? Jot down what you notice below.

_____

_____

_____

_____

_____

_____

After seeing the model Marie asks her teacher to name the action step. Just as in the case of seeing the model, it's more powerful if the teacher can get there herself. But Marie doesn't stop there: she then restates the action step in formal language. Why? This ensures they have a common language of exactly what they are working on and can refer to it throughout this meeting and beyond. Here are some prompts that accomplish this:

Prompt Teacher to Name the Action Step:

- "Based on what we discussed today, what do you think your action step should be?"
Punch it: Lock in the action step by stating it clearly and concisely, or "punching" it:

- "So, your action step today is ____":
  - *what* the teacher will work on (what-to-do directions, etc.)
  - *how* the teacher will execute it (e.g., "1. Stand still, 2. Give a what-to-do direction in less than five words, and 3. See if all students are following.").

- Have teacher restate the action step; then write it down.

Naming the action step seems basic and might feel unnecessary. Yet we don't lock it in until we name it clearly and concisely. You leave them with a single instruction that tells them both *what* to do and *how* to do it: an indispensable tool as they set out to put this new skill to use.

Core Idea

You don't lock in the learning until you stamp it.
Transformative action steps name the *what* and the *how*.

Do It

If the meeting ended there, most of your work will be for naught. What happens next is what converts an effective meeting to a transformative one:

 WATCH Clip 22: Culihan—Do It (Plan and Practice)— Feedback Meeting

Stop & Jot

How does Marie ensure that her teacher will have a successful practice? Jot down what you notice below.

_____

_____

_____

_____

_____

Here Marie brings to life the core principle of this entire book: for coaching to be effective, it needs to center around practice. Tennis players don't get better at swinging their racquets without doing it, and teachers won't get better at teaching without doing it, either. But if you want your practice to be successful you have to plan it, and plan it well.

> ## Core Idea
>
> Perfect the plan before you practice.
> You cannot practice well unless you know what you're looking for.

Marie takes many steps to make this planning as perfect as possible, and by doing so she sets her teacher up for success when she practices. First, she has the teacher plan on her own while Marie completes the same process so that they can spar. "What are your key takeaways?" Marie asks when they've compared notes. Informed by Marie's responses, the teacher can now revise her original plan to make it even stronger.

With planning squared away, leaders like Rick, Marie, and Katie are ready to dive into the high-quality practice we saw them engage in at the beginning of this chapter. Take another look to see how they do it.

 RE-WATCH Clip 23: Harshman—Do It (Practice)— Feedback Meeting

Stop & Jot

What final steps does Katie take to get her teacher to master the action step? Jot down what you notice below.

_____

_____

_____

_____

Think about the power of what you saw in this meeting. Katie didn't just talk about teaching with her teacher: they acted upon it. And they didn't just practice; instead, they practiced until they got it right.

> ## Core Idea
>
> What you practice is what you value.

When something truly matters to us, we make time for it. If we care about our faith, we gather in community to pray, reflect, or serve. If we care about our health, we move our bodies—running, lifting, or walking with a friend. Teaching is no different. If we value it, we will practice it.

Yet for most of us that was not the norm in education when we were teachers. No one asked me to rehearse before a lesson (if I did so, it was in front of the mirror in my home). But Katie shows us why the best schools schedule practice on purpose. They don't leave growth to chance; they systematize it. Teachers rehearse lessons, role-play feedback conversations, and refine questioning techniques together until excellence becomes habit.

Core Idea

The best schools practice until excellence becomes habit.

To understand the impact, imagine what would have happened without getting teachers to practice. They might have been excited about what they learned in the feedback meeting, but the first time they'd try it would be in front of kids. In essence, we're asking him to experiment with getting better without having tried it out first! Using precise practice, Rick, Marie, and Katie dramatically accelerate their teachers' development and confidence by greatly increasing the likelihood that they will be successful when they teach the next period. These leaders make practice optimally effective in four key ways.

Practice Effectively:

- **Practice the gap:** Katie creates a direct simulation of what they have already agreed the teacher needs to do to close the gap.. The teacher practices what matters most for his/her development.

- **Practice perfect:** Practice isn't just about having at-bats; it's about getting better. So, leaders like Katie give their teachers feedback during the practice so they can build muscle memory of success, not failure.

- **Add complexity piece-by-piece:** If you're working with a newer teacher or on a more complex action step, start the practice simply, then add complexity only after the teacher has mastered the basics: "Let's try that again, but this time I will be [student x who is slightly more challenging]."

- **Lock it in and re-name the action step:** Katie wraps up practice by asking her teachers, "How did your practice align with what we saw in our exemplar?" That lets teachers process their growth on a metacognitive level, leaving them with utter clarity about what they're doing differently by the end of this practice session.

Follow up: Katie concludes the meeting by identifying precisely how she will follow up, in this case, observing later that day. Here are a number of follow-up actions that you can take in your own meetings:

- **Set dates**: both teacher and leader write them down.
  - Completed Materials: when the teacher will complete revised lesson plan/materials. "When I review your plans, I'll look for __."
  - Leader Observation: when you'll observe the teacher. "When would be best time to observe your implementation of this?" or "I'll come in tomorrow and look for this technique."
- **Plan for real-time feedback:** Agree on a predetermined real-time feedback cue aligned to action step for next observation: "When I come in, I will _____" (See box below for more guidance on real-time feedback)

Stop & Do
Leverage Leadership App

Prepare an Observation Feedback Meeting

Open the Leverage Leadership App. Pick an action step from the Get Better Faster Sequence of action steps, and you will have a plan for your feedback meeting in the style you want.

LL App

Prep the Observation Feedback Meeting.

Key Takeaways:

_____

_____

_____

_____

_____

See It. Name It. Do It. You have the tools at your fingertips to lead effective feedback meetings. To make it even easier, we've consolidated all that information in one place below. In the Leverage Leadership App, you'll find this in a printer-friendly version that will give you a two-sided "one-pager" for easy reference:

Giving Effective Feedback
See It. Name It. Do It.

Prepare During observation	Prepare
	• Have your tools in hand:
	◦ Get Better Faster Scope and Sequence, teacher lesson plan, video tool, observation tracker
	• Select the highest leverage, measurable, bite-sized action step
	• Plan your feedback while observing:
	◦ Fill out planning template
	◦ Prepare a model for the teacher (video, exemplar resource, or your own live model, etc.)
See It 2–8 mins	**See It: Success, Model, and Gap**
	See the success:
	• "We set a goal last week of _____ and I noticed how you [met goal] by [state concrete positive actions teacher took.]."
	• "What made that successful? What was the impact of [that positive action]?"

See the model:

- Narrow the focus: "Today, I want to dive into [specific element of lesson, action step area]."
- Prompt the teacher to name the exemplar:
  - "What are the keys/criteria for success to _____ [action step/skill]? What is the purpose?"
  - "What did you ideally want to see/hear when _____?"
  - "What was your objective/goal for _____ [activity/lesson]? What did the students have to do to meet this goal/objective?"
  - Connect to PD: "Think back to the PD on _____; what were the keys required for _____?"
  - Read a one-pager or prompting guide: "What are the essential elements of _____?"
- (If unable to name the exemplar) Show a model—choose one:
  - Show video of effective teaching: "What actions did the teacher take to do _____?"
  - Model: "What do you notice about how I _____?" "What is the impact and purpose?"
  - Debrief real-time feedback: "When I gave real-time feedback, what did I say? What did I do? What was the impact of the real-time feedback?"

See the gap:

- "What is the gap between [the model/exemplar] and class today? What keys were missing?"
- "What was the challenge in implementing [technique/content] effectively during the lesson?"
- (If unable to name the gap) Present the evidence:
  - Present time-stamped video from observation: "What are the students doing? What are you doing?" "What is the gap between what we see in this part of the video and the [exemplar]?"

	<ul><li>Present classroom evidence: "Half of the class wasn't unpacking the prompt. How does this impact student learning?" "What is the gap between [the exemplar] and class today?"</li><li>Present student work: "What is the gap between the [exemplar] and [student work] today</li></ul>
Name It 2 mins	**Action Step: What and How**
	Name the action step: <ul><li>"Based on what we discussed today, what do you think your action step should be?"</li><li>"What are the key steps to take to implement this action step?"</li></ul>**Punch it:** <ul><li>"So, your action step today is _____"—state clearly and concisely:<ul><li>*what* the teacher will work on (what-to-do directions, etc.)</li><li>*how* the teacher will execute (e.g., "1. Stand still, 2. Give a what-to-do direction, and 3. Scan")</li></ul></li><li>Have teacher restate the action step; then write it down</li></ul>
Do It Rest of meeting	**Plan, Practice, and Follow Up**
	Plan before practice: <ul><li>Plan the implementation into upcoming lesson plans<ul><li>"Where would be a good place to implement this in your upcoming lessons?"</li><li>"Take _____ minutes and write your script of what you will do and say as you implement your action step. I will also write a script so we can spar."</li></ul></li><li>Spar with the exemplar:<ul><li>"Let's compare our plans. What can we pull from each to make the strongest one?"</li></ul></li></ul>

- Perfect the plan before practice:
    - "Those three steps look great. Let's add _____ to your [script/lesson plan]."
    - "Now that you've made your initial plan, what will do you if [state student behavior/response that will be challenging]?"

Practice the gap:

- Round 1: "Let's Practice" or "Let's take it live."
    - [When applicable] Stand up/move around classroom to simulate the feeling of class
    - Pause the role play at the point of error to give immediate feedback
    - Repeat until the practice is successful.
- Additional Rounds: master it while adding complexity:
    - "Let's try that again, but this time, I will behave in a slightly more challenging way."
- (Once mastered) Lock it in:
    - "How did what we practice meet the action step we named?"
    - "Would you add anything to the action step based on the practice? Let's add it now."

Follow up:

- Plan for real-time feedback:
    - Agree on a predetermined cue for next observation: "When I come in, I will observe for ___. If I see you need support I will [give you a cue]."
- Set dates—teacher and leader write them down:
    - Completed Materials: when teacher will complete revised lesson plan/materials.
    - Observation: when you'll observe the teacher
        - "When would be best time to observe your implementation of this?"

- "When I review your plans, I'll look for
_____."
- (Newer teacher): "I'll come in tomorrow and look for this technique."
  - (When valuable) Teacher observes master teacher: when they'll observe master teacher in classroom or via video implementing the action step
  - (When valuable) Self-video: when you'll tape teacher to debrief in future meeting

A Growth Accelerator

Real-Time Feedback

If your experience is anything like most leaders, you likely feel like you don't have as much time as you would like to coach your teachers. Katie faced the same challenge: "Because of our union contract, I had limited time when I could meet with teachers each week, so I tried to figure out how to do it better. Real-time feedback was the game-changer."

Too often, we're hesitant to speak up at all, let alone to deliver feedback, while we're observing teachers in action. We fear that offering guidance while instruction is occurring will be interpreted as disrespect—as if we don't trust the teacher to get the lesson right without our aid.

But think of all the other professions in which real-time feedback is, if anything, the utmost sign of respect from a leader. When surgeons begin residency, they practice skills and procedures in the simulation lab with real-time feedback from more experienced surgeons. Then, they move into the surgical theater where they continue to receive real-time guidance. When soccer players take to the field, their coaches are as close to them as the rules of the game will allow, calling out the winning move at every instant. In these careers, real-time feedback from a coach says: "Your success is so crucial in every moment that I would never let you fight for it alone." Why wouldn't we take the same attitude with the professionals who educate our children? Why wouldn't we treat the minutes of a lesson as if they were as critical as the minutes that make up each quarter of a soccer match?

With the help of real-time feedback, we can. Delivering high-leverage feedback in the moments we observe creates immediate opportunities for students to learn more than they could have otherwise. When delivered effectively, real-time feedback does what any feedback does: it gives teachers what they need to grow, and by extension, it gives students what they learn. It just accelerates that process, so teachers and students get what they need faster.

Get Better Faster has much more information—including an extensive library of video clips—on how to conduct real-time feedback effectively. For now, however, here are two key criteria for determining whether an action step is right for real-time feedback:

- **Will the action step keep the lesson on track and improve student learning?** If giving the feedback right away will improve student learning right away, deliver it right away. If it would interrupt the flow of the lesson that is happening right now, table it because it would probably result in student learning lost rather than student learning gained.

- **Can the action step be implemented immediately without practice?** If the teacher would need to practice the action step outside the classroom to be able to implement it properly, work on it with the teacher outside the classroom. If you could show them how to do it right away, real-time feedback is the answer.

Here's a breakdown of the best strategies to use to deliver real-time feedback, ranked from least to most invasive.

Strategy	Degree of Invasiveness	When to Use It
Silent Signals	Least invasive	• When you and the teacher have already set up a silent signal to prompt the teacher to engage the action step
Whisper Prompt	Minimally invasive	• When you can deliver feedback quickly in a whisper while students are working independently
Model	Moderately invasive	• When the teacher needs to see a quick piece of feedback implemented to understand how to do it on their own
Extended Model	More invasive	• When the teacher needs to see a longer section of a lesson led differently in order to understand how to do it on their own

If you've modeled an action step for teachers during their class, make sure you continue observing when you turn the classroom back over to them. Then, debrief their progress either immediately or at your next check-in: "How did that feel? What are your takeaways?" Congratulations: once you've completed all these steps, you've sped up the feedback cycle exponentially!

SYSTEMS: MAINTAIN AND MONITOR YOUR FEEDBACK

Maintain—Spend Less Time Preparing and More Time Coaching

If you are like most leaders, another doubt could be creeping into your mind. If I am observing more frequently, that means I have more feedback meetings to prepare. How do I find the time?

It could be tempting to simply send emails with written feedback, yet leaders like Katie consistently prove that face-to-face feedback is the accelerator of growth.

Here is the good news. You no longer need to spend hours preparing. Utilize your Leverage Leadership App. You can prepare in minutes and give yourself the time to coach. All you need are your observation notes, a sense of the highest leverage action step, and your phone or laptop. Click here to see how:

Monitor: Follow Your Schedule

The easiest way follow up on your feedback is to keep observing and debrief your observations with your leadership team (more on this in Chapter 7). If you follow your observation schedule (from the opening of this book), you'll easily be able to see if your teacher is implementing the feedback and their next areas of growth. And if you use the Leverage Leadership App, you'll be able to see your previous meeting's action step and build upon them.

Some leaders also build their own observation tracker to make it visible. Here is a simple example built in Excel:

Observation Tracker—Individual Teacher Tab

Teacher	Current Instructional Goals	Previously-met Goals
Smith	1. **What to Do** 2. **See Your Students**	**Confident Presence**

Date	Action Step:	Strengths:
9/4	What to do: give crisp instructions with as few words as possible.	Opening procedures were very strong! The students got to work right away.
9/13	What to do: check for understanding with three students before beginning the activity	Maintained procedures.
9/21	See your students: choose 3-4 places where students often get off task to scan constantly	Oral review was crisp! Students were eager to participate. Your pace was excellent—it was great to see you moving toward kids.
9/23	See your students: circulate the room with purpose	Most students are following your directions. It was especially impressive to see all the students so thoroughly engaged in the independent practice!
9/30	See your students: circulate the room with purpose	The transition out of the room was quick and silent.
	Total Observations: 5	**Days Since Last Observation: 7**

Observation Tracker—Summary Page
All-Teacher Summary Tab

Name	Total Obs (last date observed)	Major PD Goal	Latest Key Action Step
Smith	5 (Sept 30)	1. What to Do 2. See Your Students	Circulate with your hot spots in mind.
Doe	3 (Sept 23)	1. Habits of Evidence	Ask 'Why?' and "How do you know?" after students generalize.
Raines	3 (Sept 10)	1. Narrate the Positive 2. Engage All Students	Narrate the positive after giving directions. Add brief (15–30-second) Turn and Talks after each part of your "I Do"
Antanov	4 (Sept 28)	1. Write the Exemplar 2. What to Do	Script exemplar response to the task into the lesson plan Deliver crisp 3–5 word directions for classroom routines like passing out papers.
Beck	5 (Sept 30)	1. Model the Thinking, not just a Procedure 2. Universal Prompts	Narrow the focus to the thinking students are struggling with.
Avg Obs per Teacher:	4.0		

From this simple tool, you can gain some powerful insights:

- **Patterns across classrooms:** What are the action steps that are occurring most frequently across the school? Are they limited to new teachers? Just the math department? This information can be invaluable to plan a PD session that meets the needs of a group of teachers or to train your instructional leadership team on a particular action step that is causing difficulties

- **Patterns across leaders:** Are all of your instructional leaders observing equally? Are all teachers receiving similar numbers of observations? Are there leaders who you need to push to do more observations or teachers who need more support?

Now imagine using this with your school leadership team. You can observe teachers not only to see where they need to grow but also to see if the feedback they've received matches what you see. You have a tool not only to strengthen your teachers' development, but also your leaders'.

TURNAROUND—WHAT TO DO FIRST

A legitimate question to ask is how do you implement a new observation/feedback cycle like this one with teachers who have never experienced anything like this before? Won't they resist such a change? And how do I find the time with everything on my plate?

We will talk more about overcoming resistance in Chapter 6 (Staff Culture) and how to roll out a culture of feedback. For the second question (how to find the time), make everything work together.

Katie shares, "I had so much going on I needed one consistent focus. So, I just linked all my PD and feedback to a single action step from *Get Better Faster* and worked on it with the whole staff." She would introduce it in a PD at the faculty meeting, observe for it, and give everyone feedback on that same action. "If teachers were nailing it, I just affirmed them and focused on those who weren't," shares Katie. PD. Observe. Feedback. Follow up. Repeat. All on one high-leverage action step. Start this way when you are facing a culture shift or turnaround!

When teachers see that a culture of practice is happening across the school—teachers are practicing reteaching in data meetings, role playing teacher actions in feedback meetings, and doing the same in professional development sessions (next chapter)—practice becomes the norm and not the exception.

When launched effectively, the real turnaround will not be teacher resistance, but your own resistance: resistance to stepping foot in people's classrooms far more often, getting out of your office, locking in consistent meetings, and asking people to practice. The driving force of turnaround is your persistence and constancy.

> **Core Idea**
>
> The real turnaround challenge will not be teacher resistance, but your own.
> Lock in your schedule for observation and feedback meetings,
> and you will make the turnaround a success.

CONCLUSION

Observation and feedback makes a difference at schools like Katie's because it doesn't operate in isolation: its impact makes the super-levers, data, and student culture stronger as well. Want to build a school that grows great and keeps growing greater? Then get in your classrooms like Katie does, and coach your teachers to greatness. "Our classrooms feel different now," asserts Katie. "Time will never be enough, but it's how you spend your time that matters. This work is super hard, but it is so worth it."

> **Core Idea—Keys To Observation And Feedback**
>
> - **Observe Frequently and Consistently:** lock in frequent and regular observations
> - **Identify the Key Action Step:** identify the 1–2 most important areas for growth
> - **Give Effective Feedback:** give direct face-to-face feedback that practices specific action steps for improvement
> - **Monitor and Follow Up:** develop systems to monitor teacher development and follow up accordingly

Action Steps for Principals

Observation and Feedback

	OBSERVATION AND FEEDBACK—KEY ACTIONS IN SEQUENCE
	Plan
Obs/ Feedback	1. **Build weekly observation schedule for yourself and other instructional leaders/coaches:** • Establish and maintain own observation schedule & observation tracker. • Set observation schedules for leadership team to effectively distribute observation of all teachers. • Adjust the schedule as needed to address trends and/or support struggling teachers 2. **Prepare:** Stick to an exemplar script (See It, Name It, Do It feedback protocol) to ensure that your prompts are clear, economical, and aimed at the highest leverage action step. 3. **Set mastery goals for the staff:** Utilize the Get Better Faster sequence of teacher action steps to determine individual and schoolwide goals to strengthen teacher execution or mastery
	Execute

	Action Steps
	4. **Identify highest leverage schoolwide and individual teacher action steps:**
	• Use your tools (Get Better Faster Scope & Sequence, student data) to create action steps that are:
	  ◦ Highest leverage (will student achievement improve tomorrow as a result of this action step?).
	  ◦ Measurable, bite-sized and sequenced (connected to previous action steps)

	Effective Feedback Meetings
	5. See It—see the success:
	• Prepare and deliver precise, authentic praise rooted in previous action step(s).
	• Ask teacher to describe the impact: "What has been the impact of this on your classroom?"
	6. See It—show a model & see the gap:
	• Show a model—video, live model, script, lesson plan—that highlights key actions for the teacher
	• Fully unpack the model: start with the end in mind and ask precise questions to identify all key actions (e.g., What is the purpose of. . .?" "What did she do next?")
	• Ask "What is the gap between what you just saw and what you did?"
	7. Name It—punch it:
Obs/ Feedback (cont'd)	• Punch the action step by naming the "what" (e.g., see your students) and the "how" (e.g., circulate among the desks) clearly and concisely.
	• Be bite-sized, not book-sized: limit the action steps to what the teacher can master in a week
	• Have teacher write it down and check for understanding to make sure she has it.
	8. Do It—perfect the plan before you practice:
	• Give teacher time to script out her actions before starting practice and between rounds of practice.
	• Spar: Use exemplar to perfect the plan "What can we pull from each plan to make the best one?"
	9. Do It—practice the gap:
	• Practice the gap: set up practice so that the teacher practices the actions that are most critical for the action step: anticipate what teachers or students could do/say incorrectly during the practice and plan for those mistakes.

Obs/ Feedback (cont'd)	**10. Do It—practice: go from simple to more complex:** • Practice with upcoming lessons/meetings to apply the skill to multiple scenarios. • Start with simple practice; when the teacher masters it, add complexity (e.g., student wrong answer). • Stop the practice, provide real-time feedback, and redo.
	Monitor and Follow Up

	11. Do It—follow up: articulate clear next steps:
	• Set dates for deliverables with clear timelines written into both the leader's and teacher's calendar
	• Establish follow up and (when applicable) real-time feedback cues to be used during the observation.
	
	12. Provide Real-time Feedback:
	• Choose highest leverage moments for real-time classroom feedback.
	• Use least-invasive method for real-time feedback that is appropriate for the teacher.
	   o Silent signal
	   o Whisper Prompt (name what to do, state rationale, say what you'll look for—all in 45 secs max)
	   o Model or Extended Model (model a whole class period)

Pulling the Lever

Action Planning Worksheet for OBSERVATION AND FEEDBACK

Self-Assessment

- How frequently are your teachers being observed? ___/year or ___/month

- What is the current ratio of leader-to-teacher? ___ teachers per full-time instructional leader

- Review the principal action steps for Observation and Feedback above. What are the biggest gaps in your implementation that you want to close first?

- (Note: The action steps are listed in priority order, so "think waterfall"; start at the top and stop at the first major growth area.)

_____

_____

_____

_____

_____

Planning for Action

- What tools from this book will you use to improve observation & feedback at your school? Check all that you will use (you can find all in the LL App):

  ___ **Effective Feedback One-Pager**

  ___ **Real-time Feedback One-Pager**

  ___ **Tool for Building Observation Schedule**

- What are your next steps for improving observation and feedback?

Action:	Date:

Chapter 4

Professional Development

Living the Learning: The Impact of PD

An elementary school teacher is in front of the classroom, with a reading passage on the whiteboard. She is in the midst of modeling for her students. "So, what is this prompt asking me to do? Hmm . . . I have to understand why Fred is different from Lena. Ok. So what evidence will I be looking for when reading?" As she speaks, she points to her head for a moment to indicate to her students that she is thinking.

What's remarkable about the practice above is that the teacher isn't actually addressing her students—she's speaking to fellow teachers. What's more, that teacher isn't alone: multiple teachers are rehearsing simultaneously around the room, asking themselves thinking questions while their peers observe and give feedback. They are all teachers are Montgomery Academy.

A few minutes in, principal Jasmine Woodward brings the room back together. "Now's our chance to give feedback," she says. "What would be the top piece of feedback you would give to your teacher to improve their model?"

After participants spend a minute reflecting, the room grows active again as they exchange high-leverage feedback. Practice begins again. By the end of this session, all participants will have had the opportunity to drill the steps that will make their think alouds more effective.

 WATCH Clip 24: Woodward—Do It (Practice)— Leading PD

Take a moment to remember the best professional development (PD) session you've ever attended. Maybe it was a session with a specialist on the science of reading that finally made sense of all the disparate advice you'd heard previously about teaching your students to read. Maybe it was a session on leadership—something you were grateful you got to experience in your career as a school leader because it made the immense task of leading a school more manageable for you.

Whatever it was, chances are the reason this PD still sticks in your mind is because it made a difference to who you became as a person, teacher, or leader. The PD that matters is the PD that marks us and changes us.

What if you could lead PDs that made that kind of difference to everyone: not just the hungry learners, but the entire staff? Think back again to the session that made such a difference to you and imagine the impact if everyone made the same improvements you did. If every PD gave every participant the right tools and motivation to become better at their work, the results would be transformative.

The question is: how can we craft PD that results in that kind of change? We can't do it by relying only on our most avid learners. We have to reach everyone—every time.

This was the story of Jasmine Woodward. When she arrived at Montgomery Elementary School in the UK, the school was struggling and in turnaround. "No one felt a sense of purpose, and it showed. We knew we needed to create a new vision, and we needed to do so quickly." What Jasmine soon realized was that setting a vision is very different than making it a reality. "Before, I believed that if we presented clear information to the staff, they would understand perfectly and would implement perfectly. How wrong we were!" Jasmine then learned a different way of delivering PD, and everything started to change. "See It. Name It. Do It. stripped away all the extraneous stuff and helped us focus on what actually works. We reduced our leader talk and increased our leader modeling."

Core Idea

Want to change your results?
Reduce your talk and increase your modeling.

Over the next three years, Montgomery went from turnaround to above the district average to one of the highest achieving schools in the entire UK, and they haven't stopped. Montgomery hasn't fallen below 80% proficient for seven consecutive years through 2025. Move from talking to modeling, and good things happen.

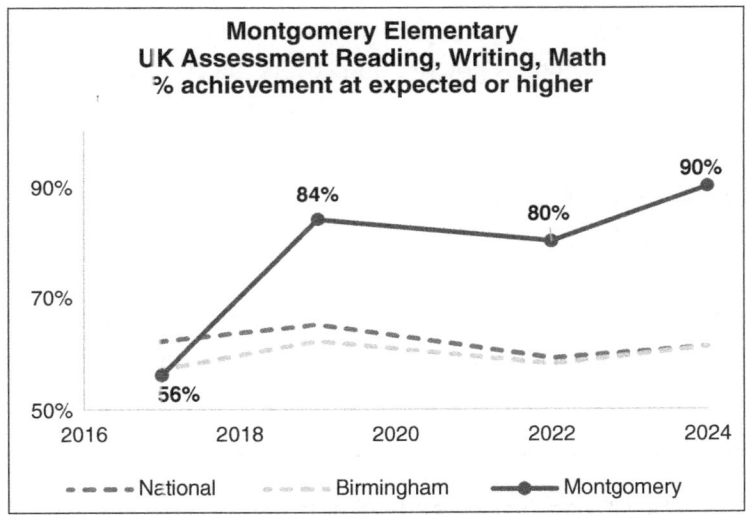

PD alone will not achieve these results. Nearly every school in the world has some sort of PD at some point, and that does not guarantee improvement. PD is the weakest of all the levers because it only works when in concert with the others. Yet PD can play a powerful role in a school once you link it.

Jasmine's experience speaks to a recurring theme that we've already seen play out in every lever thus far: great leadership is tied to what people practice. What teachers can do at the end of the PD determines the quality of the PD. It's not about our intent: it's the quality of what we practice.

> ## Core Idea
>
> Your PD is as powerful as the quality of what you practice.

How, then, can your professional development be an arena for purposeful practice? With the familiar structure of See It. Name It. Do It.

Give a large group of people a clear model and the opportunity to practice a high-leverage action step, and you will create a multiplier effect. You enhance feedback meetings, data meetings, and planning meetings by introducing a key action, and you raise development for a large group of teachers simultaneously.

The remaining sections of this chapter will show how to design a workshop that follows a structure that facilitates practice and covers material worth practicing. We'll start at the beginning: determining what you'll have participants practice in your PD.

WHAT TO TEACH: FOLLOW THE DATA

Every leader in this book has used PD to support their implementation of a key lever. Let's take a look at two of them more closely: Katie Harshman (whom you just met in Chapter 3) and Stephanie Amaya (you'll meet her in Chapter 6). As you read the scenarios below from each of them, what do you notice about how they determine where to focus?

Behind the Scenes: From Paper to Practice

Scene 1:

Katie sits down with her leadership team on Tuesday. "Pull up your observation tracker," she says as everyone opens their laptops. "We set a goal to master What to Do directions with our team this week. Let's look: how are we doing? What are our strengths and where are our biggest growth areas?"

Her third grade team leader comments: "Our staff is mastering the precision of their instructions, but they're not following up to make sure students follow them." She pauses as she pulls out her Get Better Faster Sequence. "I think we need to focus on seeing your students: making eye contact with students and circulating the room with purpose." Two other team leaders nod, commenting that they are seeing the same thing.

"Sounds right," agrees Katie. "So, what are the criteria for success for this action step that we want to see in classrooms next week?"

Scene 2:

Amaya walks quietly down the hallway on a Monday afternoon. She has just spent the past few hours observing weekly data meetings of each of her department chairs. She ponders to herself, "The Math department has been making the strongest gains in achievement on the interim assessments, and I noticed their data meetings were the only ones that got to multiple rounds of role playing the actual reteach lesson. The other teams just stayed planning the lesson and never stood up to practice it." The agenda of her upcoming leadership team meeting starts to materialize very clearly: she needs to show a model of how to lead effective planning and practice for the data meetings. She makes a quick note to follow up with the Math department chair to film her next data meeting.

●

Stop & Jot

What do Katie's and Amaya's processes have in common?

_____

_____

_____

_____

_____

_____

_____

Katie and Amaya have never met each other, but they've both landed on the same key principle: PD matters when it responds to a need, both for teachers and for your leaders. You cannot determine that by reading a textbook: you do that by monitoring your school.

The entire purpose of your PD is to close a gap that's undermining learning. Sounds simple, but too often we forget our primary focus and get distracted by everything we could be doing during PD.[1] Effective PD responds to real needs at a real school: yours.

Core Idea

Effective PD responds to real needs at a real school: yours.
To run PD that makes a difference, focus on practicing the gap.

Like many busy school leaders, Katie and Amaya have plenty of opportunities to outsource PD to presenters from outside their school. Ultimately, however, they keep most of their PD "in-house." Why? Because they choose application over theory. To drive a school's growth, PD must meet teachers' or leaders' needs *precisely* where they are. Having a company come in and provide a workshop for you may seem like a time saver, but in the long run, the only way to make time invested in PD time well-spent is to figure out what your teachers need. If the PD doesn't reflect where your teachers are on their way to meeting those initiatives, it's not a good use of their time. "I make sure our PD is tied directly to what I observed that week," shares Katie. As she mentioned in the last chapter, then she follows a simple cycle: Observe it. Coach it. Follow up.

Follow the Data . . .

The first step to identifying a worthwhile PD objective is to determine the highest leverage actions teachers are struggling to implement. Data from your school is the only way to accomplish this. Here are the three sources of information that leaders like Jasmine use to craft the PD their teachers need.

- **Assessment Data/Student Work:** Assessments are the first place to look for schoolwide areas for curricular or instructional improvement. By analyzing interim assessment data or even daily exit tickets, leaders like Jasmine are always on the lookout for larger patterns that cut across classes and grade levels. The simplest way to do that? Just track the key gaps that are being worked on in Weekly Data Meetings—both the standards and the key areas where teachers are struggling to reteach. From that analysis, Jasmine can choose a succinct focus for PD for her reading teachers.

- **Observation of Teachers & Lesson Planning:** As noted in Chapters 1–3, when you observe effectively, you can review the lesson plan and see the quality of execution at the same time. In doing so, you can more easily determine where the breakdowns are occurring.

- **Walkthroughs for Culture or Rigor:** Finally, as you will see in the upcoming chapters on student culture (Chapter 5) and managing school leadership teams (Chapter 7), leaders can use school rubrics to take a subjective area like student culture or rigor and quantify it—and then choose what dimensions of student culture that they'd like to improve.

Culture Walkthrough Data

Scores on Student Culture Rubric

CLASSROOM SYSTEMS	ADVANCED	PROFICIENT	WORKING TOWARD	NEEDS IMPROVEMENT
Transition between Activities	• Efficient, time-saving (30 sec) routine. • Teacher initiated using economy of language. • Immediately after the transition, students begin task. • Students know how to adjust the physical setting. • Evidence of a routine.	• Efficient, time-saving (up to 1 min) routine. • Teacher facilitated. • After the transition, students are waiting for directions. • Students know how to adjust the physical setting. • Evidence of a routine.	• Inefficient, more than one minute. • Off task talking, too noisy. • Teacher has to repeat directions. • After the transition, students are off task. • Physical setting is not adjusted. • Not a clearly established routine; teacher has to redo the transition.	• Inefficient, more than one minute. • Off task talking, too noisy. • Teacher has to repeat directions. • After the transition, students are off task. • Physical setting is not adjusted. • Not a clearly established routine; teacher has to redo the transition.
Student Joy and Engagement	• Students seem to be joyful and excited to be in school. • 90–100% of students are engaged in classroom activities.	• Most students seem to be joyful and excited to be in school. • 80–90% of students are engaged in classroom activities.	• While many students seem joyful, there are notable instances of student arguments and/or lack of joy. • 70–80% of students are engaged in classroom activities.	• Students generally seem disinterested in school. • Fewer than 70% of students are engaged in classroom activities.

(Continued)

CLASSROOM SYSTEMS	ADVANCED	PROFICIENT	WORKING TOWARD	NEEDS IMPROVEMENT
Exit	• Class ends on time with sufficient time to line up students. • Teacher uses a consistent system to have students line up that is organized, quick, and efficient. • Teacher leads students to the next class.	• Class ends on time. • Teacher uses a consistent system to have students depart that is organized, quick, and efficient. • Teacher leads students to the next class.	• Class ends in a rushed or hurried way or goes over time. • Teacher lines up students in a disorganized way or does not check to see that all students are ready to be lined up. • Teacher does not lead students all the way to the next class.	• Class ends late or in a rushed or hurried way. • No evidence of a systematic dismissal process is evident. • Teacher does not lead students to the next class. • Students are loud and disorganized during the transition.

With these resources at your fingertips, you have the right information to determine the highest leverage content and PD objective for your staff. Now the question becomes: how much can you accomplish in one PD session?

Then Narrow Your Focus

The natural tendency when designing a PD is trying to do too much, which leads to only one outcome: you end up talking too much. "We used to try to do too much," recalls Jasmine. "But as soon as we asked ourselves whether or not they would have time to practice, we had to narrow our focus."

So, what are some helpful tips to narrow the focus of our PD to what matters most? Start with the opening question of this chapter: what do you want them to practice?

Core Idea

The best way to narrow the focus of your PD is to ask a simple question:
What do you want them to practice?

In the end, what they practice is what they learn. We already learned the key criteria for effective practice in Chapter 3 on Observation and Feedback—make sure the practice is highest leverage, sequenced, measurable, and bite-sized.

Practice What Matters

Keys to PD Objectives

Great PD objectives are:

1. **Highest leverage.** The objective must be the most important skill teachers currently cannot do that will increase student learning and teacher proficiency.
2. **Sequenced.** Each action step builds on the preceding ones.
3. **Measurable.** Can anyone practice this objective? Can a leader easily measure if teachers have met the objective (via observation, rubric, data, etc.)?
4. **Bite-sized.** Can you accomplish this objective in the time allotted for this PD?

Note: Making your PD bite-sized depends on the time you have for PD—an hour, a half day, a full day, or even multiple days. What you can accomplish can grow with the amount of time that you have.

Generating a high-leverage, measurable, bite-sized objective can be daunting, especially if you're trying to do it on your own. No worries: we bring the team to you.

Over the past 20 years, we have crafted action steps that you can use in your PDs—for teachers and for instructional leaders. You've already been introduced to them: The Get Better Faster Sequence of Action Steps, and the Leverage Leadership Sequence of Principal Action Steps. The latter have been the action steps at the end of each chapter. Rather than start from scratch, start here. Then tailor it precisely to what your team needs. Try it!

Stop & Do

Open up the Leverage Leadership App. Pull up (or print out) either the Get Better Faster Sequence of Action Steps (for teacher PD) or the Leverage Leadership Sequence of Principal Action Steps (for leader PD).

LL App

Select a practice-worthy objective for your PD.

Takeaways:

_____

_____

_____

_____

_____

Once you know what you're going to practice, you're ready to think about how to facilitate.

HOW TO TEACH: LIVE THE LEARNING

Jasmine wasn't born a natural workshop deliverer: she built her skill little by little, workshop by workshop, until it became a staple of her leadership. The key to her transformation was meticulous preparation and using the See It. Name It. Do It. framework. Let's see how.

See It

Leading PD can be incredibly complex, especially when focusing on teaching content. The solution to this complexity is the same as in feedback and data meetings: let participants see it. Observe how Jasmine does this at the start of her workshop on how to monitor student's comprehension when they are reading independently:

 WATCH Clip 25: Woodward—See It (Model). Name It—Leading PD

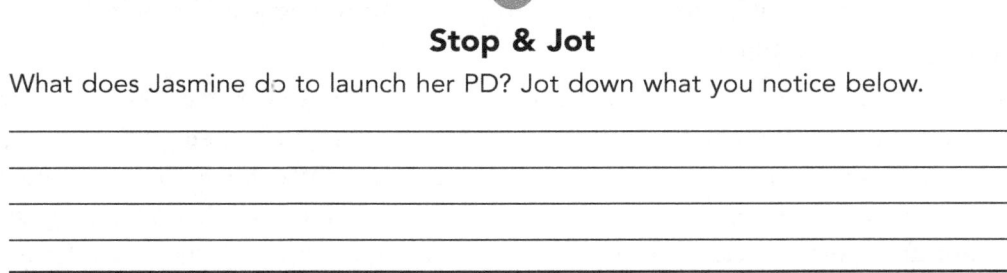

Stop & Jot

What does Jasmine do to launch her PD? Jot down what you notice below.

_____

_____

_____

_____

_____

Watching how Jasmine's teachers respond to the model makes it clear why this strategy works: seeing is believing. Jasmine's teachers see Jasmine modeling the thinking, and now they know exactly what it looks like. Just as was the case in feedback meetings, seeing the exemplar sets teachers up to be able to put it into action.

Core Idea

What's good for feedback is good for PD:
If you want a teacher to get it, get them to see it.

Of all the actions Jasmine took, these contributed most to making the See It effective:

- **Choose the best model for what teachers need:** In this case, what teachers most needed to see was how to build a model that modeling the thinking process for unpacking difficult tasks. Video clips of exemplary teacher are one of the most powerful ways for teachers to see the model. If you don't have one from your school, you can use one from another campus. Even more, there are many effective teaching clips that you can find in the books _Get Better Faster, Driven by Data 2.0, Teach Like a Champion, Love & Literacy,_ and _Make History._ If exemplary video of an action is not available, an equally strong option is to model it yourself, just like Jasmine did! You can immediately earn your staff's respect when you are willing to model what you'd like them to do as well: you show that you are "walking the walk." (We'll talk more about the importance of leading by example in Chapter 6 on Staff Culture.)

- **Keep it short.** Jasmine knows that a long See It won't hold participants' attention and will take valuable time away from practicing. Accordingly, she keeps it short: no longer than five minutes.

- **Target the focus.** The goal of the See It is to codify what makes the exemplar great, not to get caught up in its flaws. That's why Jasmine kicked off the activity with a targeted question *before* watching the model: "Watch what I do to model the thinking." Her questions drew participants' attention to what matters most, not unimportant details. Jasmine also kept these questions visible (on a Power-Point screen or handout) while the exemplar is being observed. This keeps your participants' thoughts on what you want them to notice, and it will ensure they remember the questions even as they devote their full attention to the exemplar.

Name It

Once teachers have had time to review the model, Jasmine leads them in a discussion as to why each part of the exemplar was important. After they mentioned the key concepts, Jasmine stamps their understanding—Name It—by showing a "Core Idea" slide and summarizing the key components that the group mentioned.

Those few minutes are highly valuable. By sharing a key idea with them, Jasmine gives the participants a common language with which to remember what they've just discovered. She also makes it memorable and pauses long enough to let it sink in. Put words to what they see, and they will see it more clearly.

Core Idea

Put words to what they see, and they will see it more clearly.

Here, again, you'll see a connection to observation and feedback: the steps that made Jasmine's Name It effective are similar to those that make a feedback meeting powerful:

- **Prompt the group to focus on the key actions.** Jasmine asked a series of prompts that pointed her teachers to the key takeaways from See It without giving those ideas away. She started with a Turn and Talk to allow every person in the room to share and crystallize their thoughts. When they then shared out in a large group, she used especially effective universal prompts like "What is the purpose?" or "Why is that important?" By using prompts that didn't reveal the answer she was looking for, Jasmine quickly got PD participants to do the thinking, so they learned on their own.

A Word on PD Facilitation
Prepare to Listen, Not Just Talk

As a part of my work with my Leverage Leadership Institute, I personally coach 25 leaders each year in their PD facilitation to certify them to lead trainings on the levers of leadership. As I've done that over the past 15 years, one thing has become clear: you need to practice listening just as much as talking.

One of the dangers of planning a PD is you think about everything you want to say, but you sometimes forget to practice how to listen. If you pick a great See It (a model of what you're teaching), the participants should be able to identify the key elements without you having to say much. Too often, a facilitator isn't really listening and just wants to talk themselves. That takes away all the learning from the participant.

Practice listening, and your staff will do the talking, not you.

- **Punch it.** Once the participants had generated the most essential cognitive work, Jasmine punches the core idea with formal language: "The quality of your pre-work dictates the quality of your classwork." Even at this point, she keeps her language succinct and precise—a two-sentence summary, not a lengthy explanation. By following these steps, Jasmine puts the famous advice of Bill Graham into action: she makes the complicated simple and the simple powerful.

Core Idea

"Make the complicated simple and the simple powerful."
—Bill Graham

Do It

All that See It. Name It. is intended to do is set you up for teachers to have effective practice. Let's see how that looks with Jasmine's PD. Watch what they do first:

WATCH Clip 26: Woodward—Do It (Plan)—Leading PD

Stop & Jot

What actions does Jasmine take to make her teachers better? Jot down what you notice below.

_____

_____

_____

_____

_____

_____

_____

Anyone who's ever stood up to rehearse a set of actions can testify that without thinking ahead, you freeze up on the spot. Jamsine anticipates this challenge by giving her participants the opportunity to plan before they practice. That sets everyone up to practice perfectly.

Core Idea

The precision of your plan determines the quality of your practice.
Perfect the plan before you practice.

Jasmine took three steps to lock in the success of this planning time:

- **Script it:** Have participants script what they will do and say before the actual practice. That way, Jasmine knows that when teachers stand up to practice, they'll already have their first moves down.

- **Use your tools:** Utilize resources to make the plan as specific as possible. Jasmine prompts teachers to use the resources they already have to optimize their plan's precision and effectiveness on the first go: guides on lesson planning, exemplar lesson plans, etc.

- **Tighten it:** Have participants give feedback on each other's plans before they transition to practice. Getting this feedback from their peers gives participants an additional layer of relevance and precision before they dive into practice.

When the plan is in place, it's time for participants to take that plan live! We saw the practice from Jasmine's PD in the opening clip. Let's see how fellow leaders from across the ocean do the same. Here we see examples of Yanela Cruz and Monique Cincore leading practice with their staff:

WATCH Clip 27: (Cruz and Cincore)—Do It (Practice)—Leading PD

Stop & Jot

What do all these leaders do before and during the practice to maximize its effectiveness? Jot down what you notice below.

_____

_____

_____

_____

_____

Jasmine and her peers have arrived at the heart of the PD. Let's unpack what they did to make their practice—and their entire PD—powerful.

- **Deliver clear, step-by-step instructions:** When the time came to begin practicing, Jasmine made sure to deliver clear step-by-step directions for the practice. Why is this so impactful? It makes it easy for participants to know what to do. Unclear directions make practice confusing and it's more likely that someone will opt out. Make it easy to say yes to practice.

> ## Core Idea
> Your PD is only as powerful as what you practice.

These principals' PD practice directions always include what materials you need, who is your partner, what the main participant who is practicing will be doing, and what the other participants in the group will be doing during that time.

- **Practice the gap:** They made sure the practice focused on the part of the skill participants were learning that would be most difficult for them to master. When you lead this part of a PD, initially keep the practice simple and straightforward, and then add layers of complexity (such as role playing student confusion) in subsequent rounds.

- **Target the feedback:** They prepared a "feedback cheat sheet" to point participants to the highest leverage areas she anticipated they'd need to receive feedback on. Other ways to optimize feedback include monitoring practice and responding to participants' struggles.

- **Do It Again:** The goal of the PD is not simply to experience practice: it is to practice perfectly! As such, they make sure each participant has a chance to do it again to incorporate the feedback and get even better.

Reflect

When we are learning something new, one factor is often overlooked: time. Learning a new skill is just like weightlifting. The real magic of long-term gains is not just in the practice but in the quiet that ensues after. A weightlifter needs sleep and nutrition for the body to consolidate gains and build strength. Without recovery, it does not matter how much the weightlifter trains because he or she will not make progress. For the learner, that translates to time to process and internalize.

For years, PD deliverers focused on squeezing as much content into one session as possible, assuming that the participants need more knowledge or skill to be effective. This was to the detriment of time to practice or even simply reflect. Yet research confirms the need for targeted time for reflection. Giada Di Stefano and Francesca Gino from HEC Paris and the Harvard Business School have looked at models for organizational learning in their recent working paper "Making Experience Count: The Role of Reflection in Individual Learning."[2] One of their core findings is that once an individual has practiced or built experience in doing something, reflecting on their experience adds far more value than additional practice without reflection. This helps not only in the cognitive mastery of a skill but also in increasing the participant's belief in their ability to master the skill.[3] And this takes remarkably little time to add to our PD!

To see how that plays out in PD, watch what happens in the final moments of the PD led by Jasmine:

 WATCH Clip 28: Woodward—Reflect—Leading PD

To lock in learning, Jasmine had participants reflect on what they'd learned about the skill they were working on before diving into practice. Here's how she made that reflection valuable.

- **Keep reflections brief.** Most individuals only require one to three minutes to reflect on a given topic. Jasmine allotted one minute for individual reflection, and then a final two minutes for a large group share.

- **Provide a single place for reflections to be written down.** Jasmine provided her participants with a colorful sheet of paper where they could record all reflections. They'll walk away after the workshop with a single, easy-to-find sheet of key takeaways.

- **Share out at key moments.** Finally, Jasmine had participants share their reflections aloud so the whole group could hear key takeaways.

Reflection only takes a few moments, but it dramatically improves the internalization of the PD. It gives time to memorialize the learning and to clear space in the brain to learn what's next.

Core Idea

Lock in learning by writing down your reflections.

See It. Name It. Do It. Reflect. When you have these steps in place, PD can produce powerful outcomes.

Ready to take it live? Get some help planning out your session plan, and then you can focus your time on listening to your teachers during the PD and coaching them.

Stop & Do

Open up the Leverage Leadership App. Name an area of focus for your teachers, and have the app write a precise PD-worthy objective for you. Then ask it to design a PD for the allotted time that you have. In just a few minutes, it will give you:

- Session plan
- Recommended model (where to find a video if available or how to live model)
- Plan for practice

LL App

Takeaways:

_____

_____

_____

_____

Here's a simple guide to remember for leading PD:

Leading PD—Living The Learning Cycle

Lead Effective Professional Development

	Your objective is determined by what they will practice
Objective	• **Highest leverage.** Practice the teacher gap: the most important skills to increase proficiency • **Clear and measurable.** You can easily evaluate if they have accomplished the objective • **Bite-sized/Doable.** You can accomplish the objective in the time you have allotted

Prepare	<table><tr><td colspan="2">Plan the PD aligned to your objective</td></tr></table> **Align the model to the practice to the gap:** • Select a model that targets the participants' gaps; align the practice to that model and gap • ID the purpose of each model and what key ideas you will listen for • Keep PPT slides concise: essential words/images and nothing more • Tell the story—connect one activity to the next: ◦ "We just looked at _____. Now we are going to add on to that by _____"
See It	**See It: a model of what the Do It will look like** **Frame it:** • "We are going to see [model]. As you observe, what does [model] do and say during ____?" **See the model** (keep it short! <5 min): • Video clip of teaching/leading • Written exemplar or case study • Live model
Name It	**Name It: formal language to describe the Do It** **Think-pair-share:** • Give time to reflect (individual), share with partner (Turn and Talk) and share large group • Always visible: keep questions visible during the discourse **Prompt—focus on the key elements of the Name It:** • "What happened in _____ [certain part of the model]?" • "Why is that important?" "What's the purpose of that action?" "What's the value?" • "What would have happened if we didn't do that?"

	Punch it: • Wait until the end: let participants do the cognitive work first; then name it with formal language: "So, we've come to a key idea. . ." • Say the key line, pause, then say, "Think about the significance of this." Then restate. • Limit the words: keep framework succinct and precise (3–5 bullets, one-pager)
Do It	**Do It: Put it into Practice** **Plan before practice:** • Give participants time to script prompts/actions/activities before diving into practice • Use tools: encourage them to use one-pagers/resources provided during the workshop **Clear What-to-Do:** • State what the audience will do: cue cards, pre-prepared student work samples, etc. • State what main participant will do: the protocol timing, where to practice, and with what tools, etc. • (If group is large) ID what group facilitators will do: feedback tips, what to look for, etc. **Practice:** • Practice the gap: practice what participants will struggle to master on their own • Monitor the room with exemplar in hand: ID common errors in implementation **Give feedback and do it again:** • Give large group feedback on common errors; model again if necessary • Peer-to-peer: use feedback cheat sheet to target feedback • Do it again: each person implements their feedback before moving on • Add complexity (e.g., student errors) in subsequent practice rounds

	Reflect: Lock in the learning by writing it down
Reflect	**Brief and written in one place:** • "Take 1 minute to write down: What are your key takeaways?"
	Repeat the Cycle as needed

A Word On . . . Preparing Presentations

In keeping with the theme of this book, transformative professional development is about making every minute count. To get the most out of each session you lead:

Rehearse, rehearse, rehearse: Scripting and practicing the entire presentation will make it far more polished and effective. Even if it feels awkward presenting in front of a mirror or to a colleague, it will make the final performance much better.

Anticipate tough responses: Because the See It. Name It. Do It. model is driven by audience participation, presenters need to be ready to deal with challenging audience responses, such as wrong answers during framing or confrontational reactions. Preparing questions to guide your audience back can be invaluable at dealing with these situations. Although these will vary depending on the situation, remember that scripting in advance will help you keep your cool and remain confident even if the questions or responses are challenging.

Build time for movement: Building in more kinetic activities is a great way to keep engagement high. Movement can be built into presentations by having participants "share out" on bulletin boards, switching groups in the middle of the presentation, or building in frequent breaks.

Pre-plan transitions: Taking the time to script and plan for transitions between activities can make a big difference. For example, pre-positioning binder supplies rather than handing them out can save several minutes and will make the presentation feel much more dynamic.

HOW TO MAKE IT STICK: FOLLOW UP

The Impact of Your Levers

How the Instructional Levers Hold Teachers Accountable

It is a Wednesday afternoon, and Jasmine is standing in the hallway with one of her instructional leaders. They have just finished observing a number of coaches' teachers and are pausing to debrief. "Consider the ideal actions we wanted to see coming out of our PD, what are we seeing?"

Her leader responds: "We saw good mastery of the discourse cycle from about half of the teachers. Those who were struggling either didn't use a Turn and Talk to increase the number of voices, or the Turn and Talk was too long and students got distracted."

"Agreed," responded Jasmine. "We can schedule a follow-up practice clinic with that group of teachers. What should be our focus to close the gap?"

"Let's work on making sure they note when to do Turn and Talks in their lesson plan, and then how to know when it's time to end a Turn and Talk and come back to the large group. They need to learn to see when students are wrapping up by watching their body language."

"Nice," comments Jasmine. "I hadn't thought of that detail. That will really help us with a clear model."

Jasmine knows that however excellent her PD is, it may not be remembered. How many times have you learned something only to forget it a few days later? What keeps that from happening is follow-up: someone who helps us make those actions a habit.

For school leaders like Jasmine, that means seeing it in action. A PD without practice won't lead to learning, but practice without follow-up won't make it stick.

Core Idea

A PD without practice won't lead to learning,
but practice without follow-up won't make it stick.

The good news is that the other levers in Leverage Leadership give you everything you need to make PD last. Let's take a look at how Jasmine does it.

Observe . . .

Jasmine maximizes the power of PD by looking for it. "We shared examples of what "good" looked like during the PD and then observed for it. That sends a message that the PD is not just an activity—it defines our classrooms."

Follow-up observations become easy if you have already created a weekly observation schedule for yourself (Chapter 3)—it integrates PD into your daily practice. You can also schedule a targeted walkthrough with your leadership team to observe the most recent objective in action (similar to what Katie described in Chapter 3).

And Coach

As we saw last chapter, observation is only valuable when it leads to coaching. Like every school leader, Jasmine has limited time. So, she leverages her existing schedule for the follow-up coaching:

- **Real-Time Feedback.** Chapter 3 on Observation and Feedback gave a brief overview of the power of real-time feedback (see page 179). This is especially true after you have led a PD. You can easily establish non-verbal signals to use to communicate with the teacher. For example, if you are working on the Habits of Discussion, you can simply post universal prompts on a poster in the back of the room, and you could point to them while observing to encourage the teacher to use them. Given that all teachers just took the PD, they will be attuned to you observing for those skills, which makes the feedback in the moment even more powerful.

- **Practice clinics: give them more time to practice.** Kauffman Schools are some of the highest achieving in Kansas City. When I observed leader Hannah Lofthus in action one day, I was blown away by what she could accomplish in 25 minutes before school started. While a few teachers were covering breakfast, she would gather the rest of the staff in a classroom for a quick huddle that she called a "practice clinic." They would pass out announcements on a piece of paper that the group would read silently for 1 minute, and then Hannah would immediately dive in. She would model something in 2-3 minutes, debrief it quickly, and for 15 minutes all the teachers would spread out to practice. It was like doing a See It. Name It. Do It. cycle on steroids—in 25 minutes everyone had learned a new bite-sized skill. Since then, I have seen leaders do this during lunch, after school, with small groups of teachers or whole staff. It has sped up improvement across the staff by leaps and bounds. "These take so little time and yield such impactful results," comments Katie. "It's a no-brainer for me to use them." To see what practice clinics look like in action, see this video of Matthey Rooney and Eddie Rangel leading a practice clinic at Adelante Schools in Indianapolis, IN.

WATCH Clips 29 and 30: Rooney/Rangel—
Do It (Plan & Practice)—Practice Clinic

- **Integrate the PD objective into upcoming feedback, data, or planning meetings:** In every type of coaching meeting you've learned about in this book, the Do It is about practicing the teaching. What better place to incorporate the teacher action step from the PD? You're still focused on the student work (data meeting) or lesson plan (planning meeting) or personalized action step (feedback meeting), but this can be integrated to create a coherent learning and coaching experience for the teacher. That allows the teacher to get more personalized one-on-one practice on areas of struggle, and it creates coherence between all aspects of coaching. That has a ripple effect on their response to all subsequent PD.

TURNAROUND—WHAT TO DO FIRST

When a school is in turnaround, the first priorities are clear: get data-driven instruction and culture up and running. Those are the engines that drive change. Professional development plays a supporting—but still critical—role. Its power lies in reaching the whole staff at once, allowing you to roll out new instructional or cultural priorities quickly and consistently.

The best way to leverage PD, then, is to make use of its time to reinforce culture and DDI, using that time for what matters most: practice. When PD is focused on rehearsal and skill-building rather than talk, it becomes a force multiplier for the systems that truly drive results. Here are two ideas to maximize it:

➤ **Add practice clinics** for targeted groups of teachers during the morning, lunch, right after school, or prep periods. When you have restrictions on how often you can gather with the staff, be creative. Turnaround principals have acquired a grant to offer PD stipends to be able to have teachers attend more PD sessions or practice clinics, offered voluntary PD sessions that are so impactful that many want to attend, or re-designed common planning blocks to include practice clinics.

➤ **Remove announcements** from faculty meetings and put them in a weekly memo. Make the 40 minutes of the meeting purely PD. Never sacrifice practice, no matter how little time you have.

CONCLUSION

Montgomery Academy, with Jasmine's leadership, is now one of the most successful schools in the UK. Looking back on the growth, Jasmine notes, "The See It. Name It. Do It. cycle stripped away the extraneous stuff and helped us focus on what actually worked. It was so clear and supportive, and teachers really started to grow. And once that happened, they thrived."

When integrated alongside the other levers, PD will shape who your teachers—and their students—become. Master the other instructional levers in this book, and you can get any individual teacher to succeed. Master PD, and multiply the impact to get whole schools—even whole districts—to the same level of excellence.

Action Steps for Principals

Leading PD

	LEADING PD—KEY ACTIONS IN SEQUENCE
	Plan
Lead PD	**1. Use Goals and Gaps to Plan August PD, Year long PD Calendar, and Weekly Sessions:** • Identify highest leverage topics for PD based on assessment, culture, or observation data and narrow focus to what matters most • Develop flexible year long PD calendar that identifies the highest leverage topics that teachers will need **Plan High Leverage, Individual PD Sessions** **2. Create the Do It:** • Start from the end: what do participants have to be able to <u>do</u> by the end of the session—break it down into the precise steps that they practice (this is your objective!) • Script out precise instructions and scenarios to make practice as authentic & effective as possible. • Build in sufficient time to "practice perfect:" plan, practice, and re-do each action that the participant needs to master. • Write exemplar script for practice to ID exactly what you are looking for when monitoring. • Develop/adapt monitoring tool to track proficiency during practice. **3. Create the See It:** • Design effective activities that allow teachers to "see" an effective model (video, written exemplars, models, etc.). • Observe high outliers to ID the strategies and practices that will close the gap. • Align each See It activity to the Do It components: they should reveal what teachers have to do.

Lead PD (cont'd)	4. **Create the Name It:** • Ask targeted questions before and after the activity that enable teachers to unpack and discover the best practices. • Give clear, concise language that describes the core actions teachers need to take. • Develop Core Ideas and Name It slides. • Design one-pagers of guidance for teachers to help them implement the PD. 5. **Design the Follow-up:** • Develop clear plans to ensure 90+% implementation of the PD. **Prepare to Deliver—Internalize the Session Plan:** 6. **Name your Exemplar:** • Identify what you want participants to say in each section of the agenda: identify when you are looking for the right answer (e.g., leading to a core idea) or the right thinking (e.g., thinking of the right action step for a feedback meeting) 7. **Anticipate the Gaps:** • Identify where participants might struggle, and plan your prompts/facilitation techniques to manage
	Execute
	8. **Tell a Story:** • Weave the story between the slides and activities: plan for entry and exit • Say "We're going to take a journey. . . ." or "You hit on many of the key points" • Connect each part of the content: "We just looked at ___. The question is how do we do ___? Let's take a look at someone who is doing just that. . . ."

Lead PD (cont'd)	9. **Bring it:**
	• Modulate the inflection in your voice to convey excitement; don't let your energy drop even if participants aren't excited
	• Keep an open face:
	◦ Watch your eyes: look at the audience
	◦ Keep your eyebrows up: don't let them furrow!
	◦ Smile and nod when participants are speaking
	• Use calm, slow hand movements
	10. **Engage—Switch it up**: vary engagement strategies to increase participation in the thinking
	• Utilize a combination of Turn and Talks (or online breakout groups), charting information, whole group share outs and reflection time
	11. **Connect:** make participants feel seen and heard
	• Use participant names—when calling on someone, thanking, shouting out
	• Honor their expertise (even when it's not apparent): "Just like Keith said. . . ."; use the collective "we"
	• Break the plane: circulate around the room
	• Cold call a group or individual: "It looks like there are five voices we haven't heard from yet. I'd love to know your thoughts."
	• Shout outs—make time in sessions for participants to shout out each other
	12. **Punch the Core Ideas**
	• Create "Core Idea" slides to drive home your most important points.
	• Gather the wisdom from the room—when they identify key points:
	◦ "Why is this important?"
	◦ "What's the purpose/value in doing that?"
	◦ "What would have happened if we didn't do that?"

- Deliver the Core Idea—"So, we've come to a key idea. . . ." Say the key line, pause, then say, "Think about the significance of this." Then re-state it. Narrate why this idea is important.

13. **Make it clear and concise:**
    - Reduce your words and cut all extra "throwaway" language
    - Give clear, concise directions, breaking them down to bite-sized steps, and delivering one at a time. Ideal order for practice:
        - Materials to have in hand
        - Group and location
        - Roles—designate, then describe with a lesser role
        - What to remember
        - Time. . .launch!

14. **Pacing—Create the illusion of speed**
    - Call on the next participant right after the previous one has shared (anticipate who you will call on while listening)
    - Give time reminders—Make bite-sized time stamps to make time fly faster (e.g., "You have 3 min")
    - Give "time remaining" reminders & poll the room to see if they need more time.
    - End Pair-share or small group sharing when 15% of the room has finished (to eliminate dead time)

15. **Facilitate discourse when the comments go off track:**
    - Roll back: repeat the participant's answer so that she can self-correct.
    - Call on someone who will give a strong answer in response to the off-track answer. Ask that person, "Why is that important?"
    - Wait until the right moment (If the question/comment will be addressed later in the PD): "Great question: we will address that directly in the next part of the PD."

	Monitor
Lead PD (cont'd)	16. **Actively monitor and follow up to achieve 90+% implementation** • Conduct school walkthroughs post-PD and provide RTF on PD objective. • ID individual teachers who have not mastered/are not implementing the PD objective. • Plan additional follow up (model, focused observation feedback, practice, recurring small group PD). • Utilize walkthroughs and observations to inform adjustments to PD calendars. 17. **Plan and lead effective practice clinics (short practice session) to strengthen individual and schoolwide teacher Action Steps—Hook-Frame-Model-Practice:** • Hook: deliver a hook (short and sweet) that gives them the "why." • Frame: name what you want them to observe: "As you watch the model of [routine/procedure], pay attention to how I. . . ." • Short Model (1–2 min max): exaggerate the model to reinforce every action you want to see. • Practice: implement the model with teacher's own lesson plan; give real-time feedback to close gaps.

Pulling the Lever

Action Planning Worksheet for PROFESSIONAL DEVELOPMENT

Self-Assessment

- Review the principal action steps for Leading PD listed above. What are the biggest gaps in your implementation that you want to close first?

  (Note: The action steps are listed in priority order, so "think waterfall": start at the top and stop at the first major growth area.)

  _____

  _____

  _____

  _____

Planning for Action

- What tools from this book will you use to improve professional development at your school? Check all that you will use (you can find all in the LL App):

  ___ **Leading Professional Development One-Pager**

  ___ **Practice Clinics One-Pager**

  ___ **Professional Development Rubric**

  ___ **Videos of Effective PD**

  ___ **PD Materials for Action Steps in the Get Better Faster Sequence.**

- For what key topics do you want to use the See It. Name It. Do It. framework to deliver upcoming professional development?

  _____

  _____

  _____

  _____

- What are your next steps for leading PD effectively?

Action:	Date:

Part **II**

Culture

Chapter 5

Student Culture

Student Culture

An Environment Where Learning Grows

It is a cold wintry morning in Washington, DC, but you can feel nothing but warmth emanating from Burroughs Elementary School. As students trickle in one by one in the morning, they are greeted with a smile and handshake. The hallways are quiet as they make their way to their classrooms, where breakfast is being served to soft music. You can see all the students put away their coat and backpack and head to their seat. A few who have finished breakfast have already moved on to a brain game that's right at their desk.

In every classroom, it is the same. The teacher warmly guides the students to their seats, makes sure they have breakfast, and encourages them with their brain game when they're done. The learning has begun even before the morning bell has rung.

As the morning bell rings, teachers throughout the building launch the first lesson of the day. All the children have been welcomed and nourished, and they are ready to learn.

When LeVar Jenkins first arrived at Burroughs Elementary School in his first year as a principal, he admits that he was all over the place: "I wanted to do everything—my mind was going in so many different directions with no targeted approach." Thankfully, two years later, he received the help of a great coach—his new instructional superintendent Elizabeth Namba. On the first day, they walked the school, along with instructional leaders Kristina Kellogg and Tarsha Warren, and she asked him, "What do you expect to see?" LeVar had a clear answer, but none of the teachers were implementing it. "Have you modeled what you expect?" she asked. LeVar paused. He realized he hadn't. "Why don't we start right now?" Elizabeth prompted.

That began a journey that changed the trajectory for LeVar and for Burroughs. "Once I got over the fear of modeling and implementing a lever, everything began to fall in place." Coming back from the pandemic, LeVar heard a lot of "We can't because. . . ." Many adults felt that the challenges were too steep to overcome. No one was showing what was possible, and in turn, the students didn't expect to learn. But when LeVar started coaching to establish a solid student culture, that shifted to "We can and we will. . . ." Developing the skills of success came first; the belief followed.

Core Idea

Build the skill to build the will.

LeVar got the staff practicing, taking the actions that can change a school's culture. Every moment our students and adults practice the right things is a moment that builds habits of excellence and belonging. By contrast, every moment we allow our students to "practice" less than their best is a moment that builds habits of lost opportunity and isolation.

Core Idea

Culture is not formed by motivational speeches or statements of values.
It is formed by repeated practice, using every minute of every day
to build good habits.

The evidence of the importance of student culture can be seen in LeVar's results. In just a few years, learning started to skyrocket:

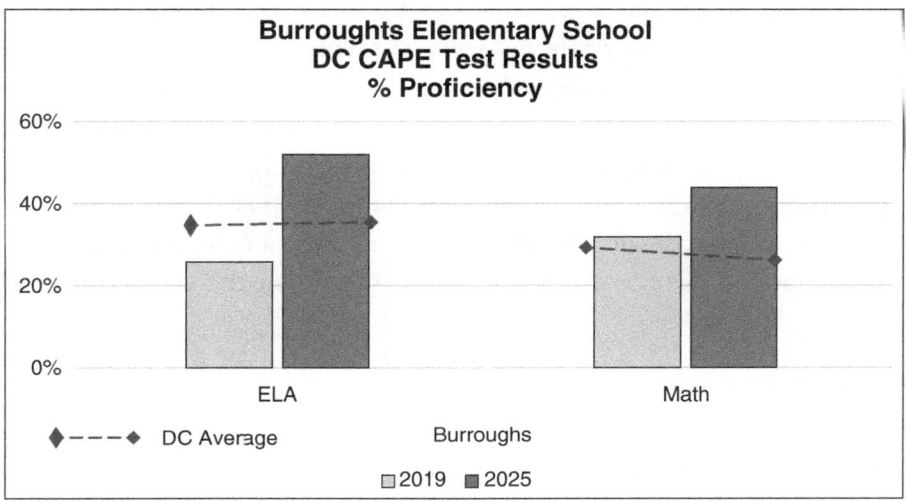

LeVar transformed Burroughs by recognizing something incredibly important: You can't blame your students for your school's culture—they simply follow the adults. LeVar had been told—as many of us have—that his students had "behavioral problems," and they were not teachable. But the more important problem at Burroughs was that adults weren't giving students consistent messages about what to do or how to do it. Children will rise to the level of our expectations; it's our job to set them—and teach them.

Core Idea

Children will rise to the level of our expectations.
It's our job to set them—and teach them.

LeVar's success is not an isolated case. His colleague Tiffany Johnson experienced the same, right down the road at Whittier School. So did Yanela Cruz at Libertas Academy Middle School in Springfield, Massachusetts. They replicated what Jarvis Sanford also pointed out in the first edition of *Leverage Leadership*[1], and every other leader highlighted in this book will affirm the same—student culture is a super-lever. But the truly good news they teach us is that we can fix it. You don't have to look as far away as Washington, DC, or Springfield to see the proof: you can see it in the instinctive ways children adjust their behavior when they enter your local library or place of worship. They know they are expected to speak in a respectful tone of voice, to walk rather than to run, and to treat property gently in these spaces. So, they do so—and whole worlds of opportunity to learn, discover, and grow open up. As adults, we can build those opportunities in our schools, too. The question is: how?

The answer lies in a single powerful idea: if you want a culture of excellence, you build it by repeated practice—performed by both children and adults. What follows is how LeVar did so:

- **Set the vision.**
- **Roll it out to your staff.**
- **Roll it out to your students.**
- **Monitor and maintain.**

Let's dive in.

SET THE VISION

You can tell a lot about student culture just by how a school feels. Imagine that you want to walk into a high school classroom and see students passionately engaged in a rigorous college-level seminar. Without a doubt, this ideal is worth working toward. But consider everything that needs to be in place for that seminar to happen. You could get to something that resembles what you imagined just by handpicking top students from your debate team who already thrive in these conditions. Yet in this scenario, only a select group experiences exciting intellectual engagement, rather than shaping an active learning culture for *all* students to experience every day. What needs to happen for that to change?

First of all, you need the seminar to be happening with a solid lesson plan that sets up a productive seminar and a unit that has provided the background material students need to participate in it. All students need to be invited, to have completed the prework, to be seated, and to listen intently to whomever is speaking.

Even with this foundation for an academic seminar in place, you'll also need ground rules for participation. The teacher needs to prompt without doing the work for the students; the students, in turn, need to ask good questions, express disagreement—and agreement!—constructively, and hear each other out without interrupting. And finally, the teacher needs to be ready to jump in when students go off track using intervention strategies designed to halt whatever's derailing the conversation and pull it back on course.

What do all these factors have in common? *Visibility*. We have high hopes for our students—intellectual rigor, a safe environment where they can learn—but our hopes alone don't create culture. What makes a student culture is what we can see.

Core Idea

Student culture is what you see, not what you hope for.

To build a strong student culture that everyone can see and belong to every day, you first need to articulate what you want it to look like in crystal-clear terms. The best way to see the culture you want is to answer a few simple questions about what should be happening at every moment in your school day (be it breakfast, classroom discussion, dismissal, etc.):

- What are students doing?
- What are teachers and leaders doing?
- What are teachers/leaders doing when students aren't doing what you expect?

These are the questions leaders like Anabel Ruiz and Cecilia Jackson ask themselves when they set out to lead student culture—not just for the first hour or the first day of school, but for every minute of every school day. Anabel Ruiz leads Bukhair Elementary in Richardson, TX, where she was named Principal of the Year. Cecilia Jackson leads Pioneer Academy in Queens. Look at these examples of their schools' arrival routines. What do these videos tell you about their schools' culture?

 WATCH Clip 31: Ruiz and Jackson—Do It— Student Culture

Based on this video of morning procedures, what are these school's values? How can you tell?

_____

_____

_____

_____

_____

At the heart of student culture is not only what students do but how they feel. When students feel accepted and respected, when they know they belong, they are far more ready to engage in rigorous learning. Belonging isn't just a nice-to-have—it is a pre-requisite for growth.[2] In a school that prioritizes belonging, routines and expectations do more than keep the room orderly: they create a signal that all students are valued, known, and capable, and that educators believe in their success. When you embed belonging into the daily design of your classroom and school, you amplify the power of strong routines and high expectations.

Anabel, Cecilia and LeVar lead schools where students are joyful and respectful, where their voice is elevated and they are dedicated to learning. They don't just hope for it—they make it happen every moment of every day, beginning with a warm welcome that sets them up to receive great instruction. Bukhair, Pioneer and Burroughs don't just preach a set a values; they live by them.

Core Idea

Strong schools don't just preach a set of values; they live by them.

When your school's values align with your behaviors—both for the adults in the building and the children—school culture becomes a living fabric that positively shapes everything you do.[3] When students don't do what they are supposed to do, we talk to them about what it looks like to live by those values. When a student helps a peer up the stairs, we praise the act as an example of values in action. Morning announcements and assemblies are geared toward teaching and presenting these values as essential. Time and time again, this commitment to moral values in student culture re-asserts itself.

In building from these core values, top leaders make an important insight. Ultimately, a culture of making every minute count and of constantly improving practice is not an end in itself; it matters insofar as it prepares students to be fully formed individuals. Without a school that builds culture meticulously and relentlessly, students will not have what they need to fulfill their potential. Values without visible expression are meaningless. And cultural systems without values are empty. Only together can they build the schools our kids deserve: a foundation upon which students develop virtuous action.

Core Idea

Cultural systems embody values upon which students develop virtuous action.

How can you do the same at your school? The keys are to see and name what you're striving for: seek out and define exemplary routines, identify the gap that separates those routines from the way your school looks now, and craft minute-by-minute action plans that will make your vision a reality throughout the school day. Let's address that step by step.

Identify and Define Your Model

When LeVar set out to reshape school culture at Burroughs, his first step was to identify and define model school routines to replicate schoolwide. Without selecting a model to follow, LeVar and his team wouldn't have known how to pass on their vision for Burroughs's culture to their teachers which was a sure way to prevent it from ever becoming a reality.

Here are the steps LeVar followed:

Find bright spots in-house. It is likely that your most successful teachers are using routines that drive strong student learning results effectively. By observing them and noting what they say and do, you can replicate their success throughout your school, rather than having to develop and teach a new routine from scratch. As an added benefit, you strengthen staff culture by acknowledging and reusing your teachers' work.

Find bright spots beyond your school. On the other hand, if your school doesn't have an exemplary routine you can roll out campus-wide, you can look elsewhere to find one. LeVar found two key strategies especially constructive: visiting high-performing schools to record what teachers, leaders, and students say and do; and seeking out videos of school culture run well, such as those included in *Leverage Leadership 3.0* and *Get Better Faster 2.0*. LeVar and his team choose the models they want to replicate and create a plan to enact them.

Define teacher, leader, and student actions. For each of the whole-school and in-class procedures that would uphold school culture every day, LeVar and his team start by naming the concrete behaviors and actions that they want to see during each part of the school day. Here's an example of what this might look like for the routine that sets the tone for the remainder of the school day: the students' arrival on campus.

A Sample Vision
Burroughs School Morning Arrival

- **What is the *leader* doing?**

  Before doors open, school leader (SL) is doing quick school walkthrough to ensure all teachers are in their classrooms and all leaders are at their positions. The custodian has brought the breakfast crates to each classroom, and teachers are setting up the brain games at student desks.

  SL opens door at student arrival time and stands outside of the front door. SL has a bright smile to greet students and shake their hands. If a student doesn't shake her hand or greet him in return, SL has students "do it again."

  Once breakfast finishes, the custodian posts the late sign, and SL enters the building.

- **What are the *teachers* doing?**

  Lead teachers set out breakfast, brain games (engaging mental math activities and challenges), and pencils. Assistant teachers transition to homework check-in station and set out homework bins and check-in binder.

  Once students arrive, the lead teacher greets each student with a bright face and circulates to ensure they are either eating their breakfast or working on bright work. The lead teacher ensures all breakfast is thrown out when students finish. The assistant teacher ensures all students place their belongings in their cubby, deposit any snacks or lunch, hand in their homework, and checks student homework. Performing arts teachers play CD of soft background music.

- **What are the *students* doing?**

  Students greet the SL upon arrival at the door. Students shake hands with a smile and wear compliant uniform. Students then walk to their classrooms where they greet the teacher. Then they walk straight to their cubby to greet assistant teacher and deposit their book bag and any snack and lunch from home. Students hand their homework to assistant teacher and then move to their desk where their breakfast is set out. Students eat breakfast or begin working on their bright work and signal hand on head when finished eating.

  If student is late, he/she goes to the main office with parent to sign in then report to class.

Define actions to take when a student doesn't follow directions. It is no surprise that schools (even those with excellent student cultures) are challenged by students who don't follow directions. LeVar's team anticipated the need and developed responses that are effective and immediate. Again, see how this looks for morning arrival.

Plan Your Vision: Morning Arrival

- **What will happen immediately when a student doesn't follow instructions?**

  Teacher will first try the least invasive redirect first (proximity, non-verbal, modeling what to do). If a student is still non-responsive, teacher repeats direction and has student do it again, provides a countdown. If the student is still non-responsive, teacher pulls him or her aside to talk to reset or sends student to another teacher. If the student still refuses to follow instructions, teacher will refer the student to the assistant principal and the assistant principal will follow up.

Create a tool to evaluate success. Finally, LeVar defines what each routine in his school will look like when it's implemented at a high level and when it's not. He then consolidates the success measures in a handy school culture rubric or checklist that makes it significantly easier to evaluate Burroughs's culture once the year is underway. Here's how the morning circle section of the rubric looks.

Plan Your Vision: Community Gathering

SCHOOL-WIDE SYSTEMS	ADVANCED	PROFICIENT	WORKING TOWARD	NEEDS IMPROVEMENT
Community Gathering	• Circle is organized such that all students can see and actively participate in circle activities. • All circle topics address school values, college, or community needs. • All students are attentive and listening. • Students are engaged and participate enthusiastically. • Leader encourages student participation through relevant questions and/or student presentation. • Leader provides opportunity for teachers to present or give input.	• Circle is organized such that almost all students can see and actively participate in circle activities. • Almost all circle topics address school values, college, or community needs. • 95% of students are attentive and listening. • Students are engaged and participate. • Leader encourages student participation through relevant questions and/or student presentation. • Leader provides opportunity for teachers to present or give input. • Transitions are mostly quiet, smooth, and efficient.	• Circle is somewhat disorganized such that some students are unable to see and participate in circle activities. • Circle topics may not be connected to values, college, or community needs. • There are some side conversations, and not all students are following the speaker. • Students participate begrudgingly. • Leader does not encourage student participation with questions or student presentation. • Leader infrequently opens the floor for other adult voices.	• Circle is poorly organized, limiting students' ability to see and participate in circle activities. • Circle topics are not connected to values, college, or community needs. • Side conversations disrupt the flow of Circle • Students do not participate. • Other adults do not participate. • Transitions within circle are almost always noisy and take too long. • Leader does not model teaching techniques (narrative the positive, cold call, CFU).

SCHOOL-WIDE SYSTEMS	ADVANCED	PROFICIENT	WORKING TOWARD	NEEDS IMPROVEMENT
	• All transitions to/from the gathering are quiet, smooth, and efficient. • Leader always models teaching techniques (narrative the positive, cold call, CFU).	• Leader consistently models teaching techniques (narrative the positive, cold call, CFU).	• Transitions to/from circle can be noisy or take too long. • Leader occasionally models teaching techniques (narrative the positive, cold call, CFU).	

A complete sample school culture rubric is available on the LL App, as well as templates you can use to complete each of the steps above.

Find the Gap

Once LeVar has set the bar for culture at Burroughs, his next step is to see the gap between the vision he's defined and the way each routine looks currently. Evaluating the gap looks slightly different depending on whether LeVar is introducing a new system or relaunching an existing one. If the routine has never been implemented at Burroughs before, LeVar has to anticipate what the gap might hypothetically look like when he rolls it out, asking himself these questions:

- **What would the students be doing that would indicate the system was being implemented poorly?**
- **What would ineffective leaders and/or teachers be doing?**

If, on the other hand, LeVar is revising or relaunching an existing system, his goal is to pin down the actions that are currently causing the system to break down:

- **What student actions or inactions are indicators of the problem?**
- **What teacher actions or inactions are causing the problem?**
- **What leader actions or inactions are causing the problem?**

Identifying the actions that would define ineffective implementation of school routines, as well as those that would show it had been implemented successfully, leaves LeVar prepared for the final phase of setting his vision for culture at Burroughs: crafting a minute-by-minute system for each of these routines.

Move Beyond Superman—Craft Minute-by-Minute Systems

Too often, when we think of transforming student culture we envision a superhero: a charismatic, show-stopping leader who gets all students to be invested. Yet everywhere I travel, the school leaders who drive strong culture are not superheroes (although they certainly should be admired!). Rather than lead culture by sheer force of nature, they build systems that make culture a habit among all staff. Your vision won't become a reality nor be durable without a system to lock it in.

Core Idea

Rather than lead culture by sheer force of nature,
build systems to build habits.

Findings from the Field
Lock in Culture with Systems, not Superheroes

"We used to manage student culture by trying to be magical, but there aren't that many magicians. We used to tell the superman story, but how many superheroes are there? Having minute-by-minute systems has given us the ability to systemize culture. This way, I don't need to be standing right there every moment to make sure it gets done."

—Candace Young, principal, Northeast Elementary School, Farmington, NM
(See Candace's more complete story in Chapter 1)

LeVar epitomizes this mantra. Quiet and unassuming, LeVar leads by example, and by building systems that empower everyone to do the same. (This approach dovetails seamlessly with communal Staff Culture—Chapter 6.) His work to establish Burroughs's culture isn't complete until he's named what leaders, students, and teachers will do during each school routine in a comprehensive, sequential, and minute-by-minute plan, including materials he'll need and actions that will be taken when students do not follow directions. If he's revising or relaunching a procedure, he makes sure to account for the breakdowns identified. To give you a sense of how detailed this plan needs to be, here is a sample. Many more examples for nearly every routine are available in the Leverage Leadership App.

Sample Minute-by-Minute Plan
Elementary School Morning Arrival

Prior to doors opening:

7:15 AM

- Custodian puts out breakfast crates and computers for breakfast sign in
- School leader (SL) does a walkthrough of the building making sure to stop by the teacher work room, copy room, and commons room (with notebook in hand to record anything that requires follow-up)

> **Materials:** Crates with breakfast already in them (pick up from walk in refrigerator), notebook

7:25 AM

- SL goes to front door for morning arrival
- All lead teachers report to their breakfast tables and set out bright work on stools and pencils on tabletops
- SL greets scholars as they arrive. All teachers make sure scholars pick up their breakfast
- All assistant teachers report to their morning homework check in station
  - Prepare to greet students as they arrive
  - Prepare to collect homework

> **Materials:** bright work bins with bright work folders and pencils, empty homework bins for collection of homework, check in binder, and notebook (each teacher)

Doors open and students enter:

7:30 AM

- SL opens the door begin to greet students and parents
- Performing Arts teacher puts on music (calming) and gets out materials for circle

  Materials: CD with calming music

- Scholars square up/stand still and greet SL by shaking his or her hand with a bright face and saying good morning
- SL does a quick scan of each student's uniform to ensure compliance and has any non-compliant students "do it again." SL gives a five-second pep talk for certain students to set them up for success.
- Scholars enter the building and walk quietly down the steps (holding on to the railing)
- When scholars reach the bottom landing they are greeted by a teacher
- Scholars stop by the computer station to scan their hand for breakfast or keep going if they are not eating breakfast
- Scholars enter the commons room and go to their cubby
- Scholars greet assistant teacher
- Scholars put their belongings in their cubby, submit homework binder, and put snacks in yellow bin and lunch in red bin (if they brought their snack or lunch)
- Scholars then walk to their table with hands by their side and greet the lead teacher
- Scholars sit down and begin to eat their breakfast (if they already ate they begin their morning bright work)
- Lead teachers are circulating, monitoring, and interacting with students (low tone of voice)
- After eating breakfast, the scholar gives the non-verbal signal (hand on top of head) to signal he/she is finished eating and ready for clean up
- Teachers will respond to the scholar by doing one of the following:
  - Go to the scholar and pick up the finished breakfast and throw it in the trash
  - Give the scholar a non-verbal signal (head nod) to throw breakfast away
  - Assign student helpers (2) who circulate during breakfast and respond when they see the non-verbal cue signaling a scholar has finished their breakfast

  Materials: Yellow snack bins, red lunch bins, morning bright work, and pencils

7:55 AM SL enters the building

- SL goes to the commons room in preparation for morning meeting
- Custodian puts out the late sign, closes the door, and reports to the commons room for morning

Materials: Late sign stand

8:00 AM Performing Arts teacher gives the signal (clean up song) for teachers and scholars to begin final clean up and prepare for morning meeting or dismissal

8:05 AM SL greets student body

- SL does the all-school clap and scholars respond (if SL does not get 100% they "do it again")
- SL verbally greets the student body and circulates
- SL gives signal for scholars and teachers to begin transition for morning circle

Late Arrivals:

- Any scholar who arrives after 7:55 must report to the main office with an adult to be signed in
- Office Manager gives the scholar a pass and the scholar reports to the commons room (if it is prior to 8:20 AM) and to the classroom (if it is after 8:20 AM)

All adults should use the least invasive form of redirects

- Non-verbal redirects
- Use of proximity—stand beside or behind a student
- Modeling what to do

Scholars who do not follow directions during arrival/breakfast:

Step 1:

- Teachers go through the set of non-responsiveness strategies (e.g., give the direction again using a strong but low voice, provide students with a count-down to do what is asked, give a consequence-pull to the side for a discussion, send to another teacher)

Step 2:

- The scholar is sent to the assistant principal and that person will do the follow up
- If assistant principal is out of the building, the scholar goes to the Instructional Leader for that grade level

Want to start building your own more quickly? Open the Leverage Leadership App and get started.

Stop & Do

Click on Student Culture. Pull up a sample minute-by-minute plan that you can adjust or build your own.

Measure It

Think back to Chapter 1 (DDI): assessments are the starting point for instruction, not the end. Similarly, LeVar's detailed planning is the foundation to measure and evaluate success (and take remediating action when called for). You cannot evaluate until you know where you are headed! He does so with the following:

- **What is the outcome?** LeVar always sets a concrete, measurable goal that he'll use to determine when the system has been successfully implemented, for example, "hallway transitions will reduce to one minute," or "one hundred percent of students will be celebrated in community meetings at some point during the year."

- **How will we measure it?** There are a number of different tools to measure student culture. Either you can create a student culture rubric (go to the LL App for an example), or you can create a checklist of actions you are looking for when observing. (*Get Better Faster 2.0* is a fruitful tool for observing in-class student culture.) Make this tool transparent so that everyone (staff and students) knows what success looks like and how it will be measured.

It's one thing to set your vision as a leader, and another thing to get everyone else in your school to follow it. Leaders like LeVar translate their cultural systems from paper to practice in two steps: roll it out to your staff, and then later to your students. Let's see what a staff-facing rollout looks like first.

ROLL IT OUT TO YOUR STAFF

For most marathon runners, race prep is simple: doing practice runs of a certain pre-scribed length each week, getting enough sleep, and eating right. Through these efforts, runners will get in shape, improve their form, and earn good times. For elite maratho-ners, however, training is much more rigorous and exacting. In the months before race day, elite marathoners plan *obsessively*: creating strategies for each hill, each turn, and each drink station. In the hours before the race, they don plastic bags to reflect sunlight, working to save single calories for competition. These runners aren't training to partici-pate; they're preparing to win. And when the goal is victory, it's the details that separate contenders from weekend warriors.

> ### Core Idea
> The details separate contenders from weekend warriors.

How can we apply this? Follow the leaders in this book.

When Katie Harshman (whom you met in Chapter 3) began at Minnequa Elemen-tary School, she needed to reset student culture. Let's consider how Katie's rollout of student culture differs from a traditional school leader, whom we will call Ms. Smith. Both Tera and Ms. Smith want to put strong school culture into place. To prepare, both lead a professional development session for their staff. Yet the similarities end there.

Case Study
A Tale of Two Leaders Launching Student Culture

Leader 1: Ms. Smith

Ms. Smith begins her staff professional development with a presentation on the general principles of the culture she wants. The slideshow is elaborate, containing instructions on a variety of classroom and school wide norms. In pairs, Smith has her teachers read a recent article on the "opportunity gap" in America before partner groups discuss how this work connects to the school's overall mission. After narrating what each procedure might look like, Smith leaves her teachers to determine how each procedure will be applied to their individual classrooms. During the days that lead up to the start of school, teachers create templates of their student rules and make them available to the school leader for feedback and suggestions.

Stop & Jot

What pitfalls might keep Ms. Smith's culture launch from succeeding?

_____

_____

_____

_____

_____

Leader 2: Katie

Here's what it looks like when Katie rolls out culture with her staff. How does her rollout differ from Ms. Smith's? What makes it effective?

▶ WATCH Clip 32: Harshman—Do It (Roll Out)
Student Culture

Stop & Jot

How does Katie's rollout differ from Ms. Smith's? What makes it more effective?

_____

_____

_____

_____

_____

Katie's talking was brief, but the change was real: they practiced the vision, and in doing so made it a reality. In the marathon that is building strong student culture, Ms. Smith is a weekend warrior. She has good ideas, works hard, and may make a positive impact. But she will not build an extraordinary school.

Katie, on the other hand, is a champion. She has built an exceptional school like LeVar Jenkins's, and this video makes it clear how. Like an elite marathon runner, she trains her staff down to the smallest details. They set a meticulous vision and work relentlessly to achieve it. In short, leaders like Katie and LeVar do not leave learning to chance. Let's break down how they do this.

See It and Name It

Watch how Katie introduces the new routine to her staff. As you watch, note as many as possible of the actions Katie takes to introduce the routine effectively.

 WATCH Clip 33: Harshman—See It. Name It (Roll Out) Student Culture

Stop & Jot

What did Katie say and do to lead an effective See It when she rolled out her cultural routine to her staff?

_____

_____

_____

_____

_____

_____

The actions of LeVar and Katie are strikingly similar, and they follow the principle we saw in previous chapters: if you want them to get it, get them to see it. Here's how:

Hook: Katie inspired and empowered her staff to learn this routine by letting them know up front why it mattered, and what it looked like. As you can see, there is a place for motivational speeches! She just keeps it short and sweet (less than two minutes) to allow her to focus most of her time on the model.

Frame: Before transitioning to a live model, Katie took an important step to ensure her staff was prepared to master the routine: she named what would happen sequentially during the model her teacher was about to perform. She told them what to look for, which allowed them to see it more clearly.

Model: For her part, Katie didn't model the routine halfway: she dove in completely. She fully performed all the actions as if students were in front of her, and she exaggerated the actions she wanted to see teachers replicate so they couldn't possibly be missed.

Debrief: Finally, Katie stamped her staff's understanding of the model by asking them to unpack what they had seen. (Verbal cues leaders can use to complete this step include "What did you notice? What actions did I take and what did I say?") Just as importantly, she pushed them to name why those actions had been part of the model.

Modeling doesn't just show the way, notes LeVar. "Whenever I model for the staff, we create collective efficacy—everyone carries the same culture together to create a welcoming, learning environment." In short, modeling is the method by which your vision comes alive.

Core Idea

Modeling is the method by which your vision comes alive.

Do It

Just as with leading PD, the value of a student culture rollout comes with the practice. The first step is to let your staff know exactly what actions they'll be practicing. Take a look at this video to see how Katie introduces practice.

RE-WATCH Clip 32: Harshman—Do It (Roll Out)
Student Culture

Stop & Jot

What does Katie say and do to lead an effective practice of the routine?

_____

_____

_____

_____

_____

_____

Plan: To set practice up for success, Katie delivered clear What-to-Do directions to her staff that let them know the following:

- **What the main participant will do.** Katie made sure to delineate the tasks of the key people in each group who were taking on the main practice role during the role play. She also gave them time to plan and script their actions, which would make them far more successful during the practice than if they went off the cuff.

- **What the audience will do.** Katie also set clear roles in place for the members of her staff who would be playing the role of students while someone else practiced the teacher role in the routine. This made the practice that much more relevant to what it would be like for teachers to roll out this routine on the ground.

Practice: All of the planning sets the teachers up for effective practice:

- **Round 1: Build muscle memory—start simple.** Katie started by having participants rehearse the routine at its simplest from start to finish. To ensure her staff spent this time building the muscle memories of what it felt like to rehearse the routine correctly, Katie delivered feedback in real time when staff members made an error and had them try again, starting at the point where they had stumbled. Remember, you need to know how to lift a bar before you add the weight.

Core Idea

Keep the first practice simple to build muscle memory:
you need to know how to lift a bar before you add the weight.

- **Round 2: Add complexity.** Once the basics are mastered, Katie can add complications like student misbehavior to the practice. This is the heart of the most effective practice: add the complexity once a participant is ready for it.

Practice is so simple in its concept; yet the first time we try it, it can feel so unnatural. "The first time I rolled out culture," shares LeVar, "when I asked my staff to practice I sensed so much fear—and I felt it, too! But as soon as I did it, it started to become natural. If you're able to get over your own reservations, you will fly."

A Word on . . . The Day One Dress Rehearsal

When you participate in a play, most of your practices leading up to it focus on one scene, one act, or even just an individual song. But as you get closer, it becomes essential to put it all together for a dress rehearsal. As any actor or actress would tell you, it's one thing to know each individual part, it's another to string them altogether in a full performance!

Many of the most successful school leaders imitate this by engaging in a full "dress rehearsal" a few days before school begins. The dress rehearsal is a minute-by-minute walkthrough of the school's entire day, from morning breakfast to detention dismissal. Teachers and leaders walk through what they will be doing in each part of the day, finishing the exercise by rehearsing their systems in pairs, offering critiques and suggestions as they refine their systems. For example, they stand in the hall outside their classrooms "watching" students enter, teaching students to sharpen pencils and how to put away books.

Don't underestimate the power of a rehearsal. Even if some will protest at the beginning, by the time the real students finally arrive two days later, every teacher knows exactly where he or she is supposed to be and exactly what he or she is supposed to be doing at all times. All the students see is a fully coordinated, united front: the first strong message of what to expect for the rest of the year.

Stop & Do

Open up the Leverage Leadership App (LL App).

If you don't have a minute-by-minute plan for a routine, ask for help in drafting it. Once you have one, plan out the rollout for staff, tightening your model and what you will practice.

_____

_____

_____

_____

ROLL IT OUT TO YOUR STUDENTS

After the staff is prepared to roll out culture as a team, it's the students' turn to learn the routines. Let's see what that looks like in the school of Trennis Harvey, principal of Heritage Academy in Atlanta:

WATCH Clips 34 & 35: Harvey—See It. Name It.
Do It. (Rollout to Students)—Student Culture

What works for adults works for children as well: hook, frame, model, debrief—and then get them to practice. The two structures for rolling out student culture, then, are nearly identical.

> ### Core Idea
>
> What works for adults works for children:
> hook, frame, model, debrief, practice.

While leaders like Trennis and LeVar follow the same structure for both rollouts, they tailor how they communicates to students so they are more likely to hear, respond, and adopt the desired behaviors:

- **Challenge and affirm:** The magic of Trennis's rollout to students is how he challenges them to do a task that could otherwise be menial (for example, lining up to exit class). He makes it an exciting opportunity for them to show leadership. To do so, he speaks with urgency and importance that makes it hard for the students not to follow suit.

- **Leaders and teachers together:** Trennis knows that if he asks the students to do something and the teachers don't make the same request, the culture will not work. As such, Trennis and his teachers work together to give feedback to students as they learn each part of a routine.

MONITOR AND MAINTAIN

Imagine you telling children to brush their teeth every night before bed and monitoring them only the very first evening after you give them these instructions. That first night, the children will go to bed with clean teeth. Tell any parent that the children now automatically brush their teeth every night, however, and you'll be met with justifiable laughter. The reality is that people of any age need to be monitored and supported in the process of making routines into habits.

By the same token, the benefits of student culture will only become durable if you monitor and maintain it. The steps in this section will show you how. They'll prevent you from having merely a "honeymoon period," to keeping the celebration of strong culture yearlong.

Lead Publicly

Whenever I visit a school that has a strong student culture, I immediately am left with the impression that the school leader seems to be everywhere. This is not by accident. School leaders like LeVar make sure they're visible at key times and places during the school day—like lunch, troubled classrooms, or hallways—after his staff- and student-facing rollouts. And they are more than just present: they leverage that time to craft culture.

Model by example. "As a school leader you have a lot of power," shares LeVar, "but the ultimate power you have is the signaling to staff—modeling with your daily actions what it should look like. The staff gravitates to your example, not your words."

Core Idea

Staff gravitate to your example, not your words.

Provide real-time feedback. When LeVar's supervisor Elizabeth first walked the school with him and prompted him to give in-the-moment feedback to a teacher, he was caught off guard. LeVar laughs when he remembers. "I think I responded by saying, 'You mean coach them right now?'" He was out of his comfort zone. "But as soon as I tried it, I saw the positive impact. When I debriefed with Elizabeth, that was an aha moment. We can move so much faster!" This was a change in mindset—moving away from email feedback or waiting for a meeting to fixing it in the moment. (You can find more on real-time feedback in Chapter 3. Feel free to turn back to that section for more ideas of how to use: non-verbal cues, whispering something to a teacher or student, or jumping in to model.) All of these actions communicate a singular message: I care about you and your learning, and I'm not going to let you fail.

How can LeVar do that and still stay on top of all of his work? He is relentlessly intentional about how he manages his time. He knows when he'll be walking around, when he'll be observing/leading meetings, and when he'll do other things. And he coordinates with his leadership team to make sure someone is present when he is not. (More about that in Chapter 8 on Finding the Time!).

A Word on . . . The 30-Day Playbook

Bill Walsh was one of the most successful professional football coaches of all time. One of his many legacies was the way he called plays for his offense.

At the time Walsh was coaching in 1980, every coach made a decision in the moment of which play their offense should run. This would happen roughly 65 times a game. Each team had hundreds of plays to choose from, and each coach needed to decide within a few seconds.

At one point, Walsh realized that he wasn't at his best when trying to make decisions this way. So, one night he decided to script the first seven plays of the game. No matter what the defense did, he told himself, he would stick with those plays.

His strategy worked. The team looked better, advanced the ball farther, and had more success in those first plays than later. Walsh kept expanding the number of scripted plays until he reached 25, or the equivalent of nearly the entire first half. And his teams were wildly successful on offense.[4]

In many ways, leading student culture is like coaching a football team. There are at least 60 moments in a day when leaders must decide rapidly what they are going to do: what to say during breakfast, how to talk to a student who's upset or angry in the hallway, whether to restart a routine or not, etc.

To help leaders who weren't instinctually good at leading culture, we have experimented with our own version of Walsh's success—we established a 30-day scripted Playbook for schools. Given that the first 30 days are essential to establishing culture, leaders made a minute-by-minute script of what they would do throughout those first 30 days to set in place the right habits.

- 7:00: Arrive at school and quickly check emails—anyone sick? Any emergencies?
- 7:15: Walk around to great the early-arriving teachers: How are they? Any concerns?
- 7:20: Go to stand outside to great students and parents. Look for the 15 students who need extra "love" to start the day strong—make sure to give them a particularly positive message.

And so on.

What was the impact? It was a game-changer for Yanela Cruz as a new principal (more on her in the turnaround section later in the chapter).

> "I needed total focus to address the challenges of culture and it's hard to keep distractions from getting in the way. I made a playbook for the first four weeks of exactly what I wanted the school to feel like, look like, and sound like, with clear roles for each staff member and myself. It was very liberating because I didn't have to overthink and could just do. It allowed me to set my leadership feet on firm ground while I was still learning to be a principal."

For any principal who is working on changing or improving their student culture and building new habits, a playbook frees your mind to look at the big picture while it moves your feet in the right direction. We have a sample of a 30-day playbook here and a complete version in the Leverage Leadership App. Adjust it to what works for you and your school.

The 30-Day Playbook: High School Version

Between 7:40 AM and 7:58 AM: Student Breakfast

- **Student Culture Observation—Breakfast:**
  - Observe student behavior at breakfast and note gaps in teacher presence or teacher actions

---

- If needed, pull aside a student who is not following the norms: model for teachers a quiet correction

> **What to Scan for and Fix:**
> - Staff not present in the lunchroom, not seen looking
> - Students too loud or shouting
> - Students blocking the entrance to the cafeteria, or going to different rooms without approval
> - Students standing, wandering
> - Students leaving without permission or pass

- **Real-Time Coaching:**
  - Note any teachers not coaching students for 100% behavior. Real-time coach using whisper prompts and/or modeling if necessary
  - Debrief quickly: "What did you notice me do? Why did I do that? What was the impact?"
- **Public Leadership Moment:**
  - With five minutes remaining in breakfast, model the hand raise procedure with all students: expect 100% of hands raised and silent within three seconds. Use Do It Again technique until success is achieved
  - Give public, precise praise to key students to build positive culture. Clearly state the expectations
- **Cue the Transition:**
  - Restate the expectations for hallway transitions and let students know that staff will be watching them to ensure success:
    - Moving with purpose, not lingering in the hallway
    - Talking quietly, no shouting
    - Entering classrooms quietly

Evaluate Progress

While on the ground, LeVar can keep track of what he is seeing and evaluate progress. The school culture rubric (like the one we introduced in the first section of this chapter) is a blueprint for a student culture-specific walkthrough. LeVar and his staff simply monitor each cultural system in action, give their school a score on the rubric, and make an action plan to close the gaps. As he walks the school, LeVar asks the following questions:

- What student actions or inactions are indicators of the problem?
- What teacher actions or inactions are causing the problem?
- What leader actions or inactions are causing those problems?

These questions embody a core principle: Adults create the school culture. Monitor students to see *where* the breakdown is; monitor teachers and leaders to see *why*.

Core Idea

Adults create the school culture.
Monitor students to see *where* the breakdown is.
Monitor teachers and leaders to see *why*.

Quite often, LeVar can close these gaps immediately with real-time feedback to adults and children. Occasionally, however, that is insufficient. When that happens, LeVar does the following.

Manage Individually

Sometimes an individual teacher or student is struggling to meet cultural expectations, and LeVar has an individual meeting with them. During these conversations, LeVar makes it clear not only what concrete actions the individual needs to begin performing, but also what the constructive impact is on the community when everyone works to perform these actions consistently. (We dive more deeply into these types of conversations in Chapter 6 on Staff Culture: accountability conversations.) He closes the loop on implementation by working with the individual to set a prompt timeline for them to begin performing those actions themselves.

Lead a Whole-School Reset

In other moments, monitoring student culture leads LeVar to discover that a school routine needs to be reset—the habits have slipped and the routine is no longer functioning effectively. A "reset" follows the same steps as a rollout with a few small adjustments—it is short and targeted to close a gap. If you look more closely at Trennis's clip from earlier, you'll see he does just that:

RE-WATCH Clips 34 & 35: Harvey—See It. Name It. Do It. (Rollout to Students) Student Culture

- **Hook:** State the gap you are trying to close (or have teachers identify the gaps themselves)
- **Frame:** Name what you want them to observe, particularly the area where you have been seeing gaps around the school
- **Short model:** If members of the school community are repeatedly not following a system, that indicates the community needs to revisit the exemplar that shows what the routine should look like. Start there, either by showing a video of the model or by performing it yourself! For a reset, having a live model is generally more effective because it reminds them what is possible.
- **Practice the gap:** Spend the rest of the time re-practicing the techniques needed to reset the routine. Students and teachers alike walk away not only with a sense of the gap but also actions to close it, and they know everyone else will be doing the same thing in their classrooms. That creates collegiality as well as results.
- **Celebrate progress until the goal is met:** As you monitor progress, keep your staff in the loop. Celebrate progress and stamp next steps each day until the routine looks in your school the way it does in the model!

Leading Student-Centered Culture

See It. Name It. Do It.

See It	See It: Set the Vision for Success
	See the Model: • Identify the models for your school to guide your vision: ◦ Internal models: What are your strongest examples of student culture in your school that you want to replicate? ◦ External models: Where are models of the culture you wish to create?

	• Visit high performing schools and observe what teachers, leaders, and students say and do
	
	• Look at video examples (Leverage Leadership, Get Better Faster, etc.)
	
	See the Gap:
	
	• Before school year—Anticipate the gap (What will it look like if executed poorly?):
	
	    ○ What would ineffective leaders/teachers be doing?
	
	    ○ What would the students be doing if it was implemented poorly?
	
	• During school year—See the gap via a school walkthrough
	
	    ○ What student actions or inactions are not meeting your vision/values?
	
	    ○ What teacher actions or inactions are not meeting your vision/values
	
	    ○ What leader actions or inactions are causing these actions?
	
	• Determine key habits or behaviors that need to be relaunched or introduced

Name It	**Name It: Start from Your Values to Create the Systems**

	Name the Behaviors to Define Your Values:
	
	• Identify the behaviors
	
	    ○ What behaviors would leaders, teachers, and students demonstrate that would create the ideal student culture?
	
	• Craft your vision for your own school's culture at every moment of the day:
	
	    ○ What will leaders, teachers, and students do and say?
	
	    ○ What will happen when students or staff are not doing what you envisioned?

Create the System:

- Craft specific, observable, written procedures for whole-school, classroom, and staff routines/moments:
  - Name what leaders, students, and teachers will do in a comprehensive, sequential plan.
    - What will staff say and do? What will be its tone and demeanor?
    - How will it build and leverage relationships?
    - What will happen when students and staff are not meeting expectations/maximizing inclusion?
  - Adaptive: name the resources/tools provided for students who need extra support (executive functioning, social-emotional, etc.)
  - Determine what materials and staff you will need and where they will be located.

Measure It:

- Create a school wide culture rubric that defines the following:
  - Evidence of habits/behaviors for all schoolwide and class-room gatherings, rituals, and routines
  - Common language that students, teachers and lead-ers will use
  - Management systems: in-class systems, how to work with students sent out of class, etc.
- Set goals and deadlines:
  - Set a concrete, measurable goal
    - E.g., hallway transitions will be 3 mins; 100% of students on task during independent practice
  - Identify when the system will be introduced and when the goal will be met.
  - Determine the tool for measurement (student culture rubric, etc.)

Do It	Do It: Plan, Rollout, and Monitor

Plan:

- Plan the rollout of all major routines, procedures and whole school moments (see details below)

Rollout for Staff—Hook-Frame-Model-Debrief-Plan-Practice:

- **Hook:** Deliver a short and sweet speech that shares the why—connect the routine back to your values
- **Frame:** Tell staff what to look for: "As you watch the model of [routine], pay attention to. . . ."
- **Model:** Exaggerate the model: fully dive into the model to reinforce the habits you want to see.
- **Debrief:** Name the what and stamp the why: "What did I say and do?" "Why is that [action] important?"
- **Plan:** Put a script of the routine in the hands of each teacher and give them time to prepare individually and/or adjust to their environment
- **Practice**
  - Rehearse:
    - Deliver clear what-to-do instructions
    - Make practice authentic: e.g., utilize the space where you will implement the routine
    - Give feedback during practice: narrate the positive and correct in the moment
  - Final Debrief: "How did that feel? Where could we improve the routine?"

Rollout for Students—Hook-Frame-Model-Debrief-Plan-Practice:

- **Hook:** Deliver a short and sweet speech that shares the why—connect routine to school values/mission
- **Frame:** Tell the students what they are going to do: "I'm going to model for you, look how I do/say. . . ."

- **Model:** Exaggerate the model: fully dive into the model to reinforce the habits you want to see.
- **Debrief:** Name the what and stamp the why: "What did I say and do?" "Why is that [action] important?"
- **Plan:** Develop clear directions and roles for both teachers/leaders and students.
- **Practice**
  - Give clear what to do directions
  - Give feedback: narrate the positive, correct in the moment and do it again
  - Final Debrief: "How did that feel? What do we want to remember to do every time?"

Monitor and Follow-Up:
- Lead publicly:
  - Be present and be seen in key areas (lunch, classrooms, hallways, etc.) during and after rollout
  - Celebrate: publicly and individually share success for students and staff
  - Confident presence: stand and speak with purpose
    - Warm-demander register: use a warm formal register, including tone and word choice
    - Utilize non-verbals to lead and redirect calmly
  - Provide feedback:
    - Narrate the positive; Do it Again until 100%; Challenge ("Can you do it, too?")
    - What-to-do: use concrete phrases and actions that teachers/students can use
    - Immediate: address challenges before they escalate: de-escalate the situation with the least invasive intervention

- Manage individually—have accountability conversations with struggling teachers and students:
  - Identify the challenge/gap and state the impact
  - Make bite-sized action plan with prompt implementation on a set timeline.
- Evaluate progress:
  - Do culture walkthrough, assessing strengths and weaknesses with your culture rubric
  - Identify whose needs are not being met
  - Make action plans to close gaps and/or redesign systems if they are not working
  - Work with teacher leaders to set and monitor team goals: target their support to teachers
- Plan and lead effective practice clinics (short practice session) to strengthen individual and school-wide teacher Action Steps—Hook-Frame-Model-Practice
- (When needed) Lead a Whole-School Reset of a specific, high-leverage routine:
  - Do a new rollout of the reset (Hook, Frame, Model, Debrief, Plan, Practice)
  - See the gap: have teachers/leaders identify the gaps
  - Execute a daily walkthrough to monitor the targeted action steps
  - Communicate to staff the progress and next steps on a daily basis until the goal is met

TURNAROUND—FIXING A BROKEN CULTURE

Sometimes, culture faces more serious problems. If normal "wear and tear" in culture can reduce performance, sometimes the culture frays so completely that it breaks down. And often, once that happens, it is incredibly difficult to fix: This is why under-achieving schools often stay that way for years. Yet that doesn't have to be the case.

Yanela Cruz is the principal of Libertas Academy Middle School in Springfield, Massachusetts. When she was first named principal in 2020, the school was in the 16th percentile of state performance, and the pandemic hit. "It really was a mess," Yanela recalled. "Students were completely unengaged, morale was low, and as a result we also had high teacher turnover." Yanela was undeterred. She followed all the steps that LeVar followed from earlier in the chapter: she created a minute-by-minute plan for every schoolwide and classroom routine, clearly named the role for leaders, teachers, and students, and created a playbook for the first four weeks of school.

Then she followed the cycle of modeling and practicing relentlessly. "To set all things culture, you need to have thoughtful PD that constantly brings it to life. We did a See It. Name It. Do It. cycle on every routine in the school." Time for announcements? That was left for a weekly memo. Other topics? Left until later.

Fast forward two years later and the school was transformed. With Yanela's focus on the two super-levers of culture and data-driven instruction, the results showed. In student growth percentile, Yanela's students were #3 in ELA and #5 in Mathematics of all 977 elementary schools in Massachusetts.[5] The growth in the percent of proficient students was equally impressive:

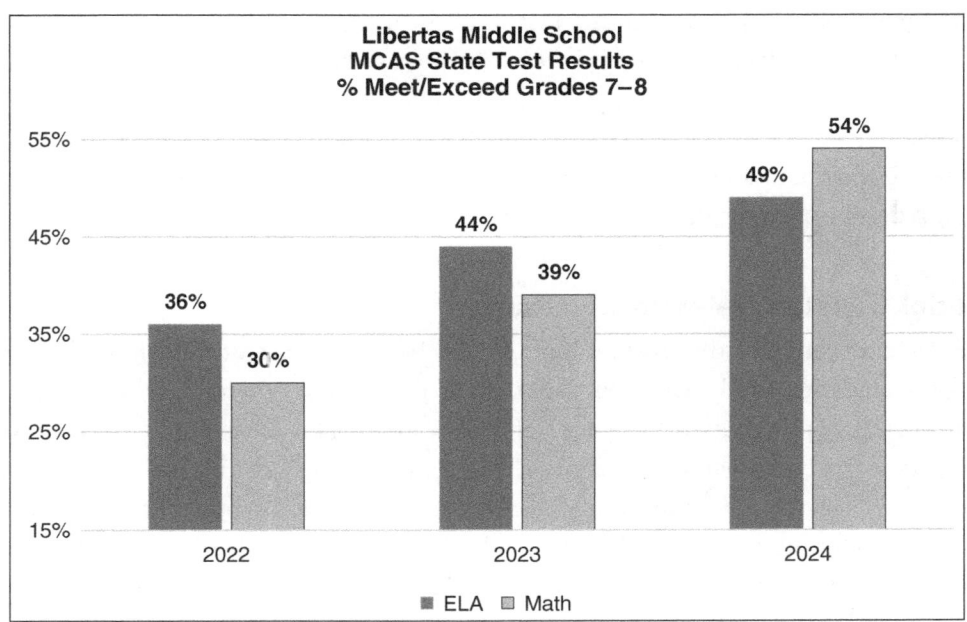

What is most striking about Yanela's results is that she followed the same actions of leaders who simply had to maintain a solid culture. The core actions don't change, but how you manage the pushback does (and when you reset a culture, pushback will surely come). Get most of your staff invested and manage the pushback from those who aren't.

> ## Core Idea
>
> In turnaround work, get most of your staff invested and manage the pushback from those who aren't.

Face the Brutal Facts—of Students and Staff

In *Good to Great*, management guru Jim Collins famously says that we must face the "brutal facts" of our situation before we can improve it. In a broken culture, the facts are two-fold: what this will look like for your students and staff.

In many schools, the brutal facts of broken student culture look like one of these:

➤ Mass student apathy and lack of engagement

➤ Students completely off task or sometimes even violent—lack of safety

These are easy to spot: they overwhelm the senses when you walk through the school.

The even more important "brutal facts" are the actions or inactions that adults are taking that are contributing to this culture. If students rise to the level of expectations placed in front of them, they can devolve to lower expectations just as easily.

Yanela described these actions when she first arrived at Libertas. "It was troubling to see the way that adults were talking about children—as if they were problems to be managed rather than brilliant young minds."

Model Constantly—with Constancy

The Rollout section of this chapter highlighted the importance of modeling: showing staff and students exactly what you want them to do. As LeVar mentioned earlier, modeling doesn't stop during the PD: your staff will be looking to you as a model at all times. Are you consistently following the model you set in the rollout? This is doubly important in turnaround, where too often teachers have been led by previous leaders who talked a good game but didn't follow through. Initiatives didn't work out, and they were often abandoned before taken to completion. Understandably, then, your staff could be jaded toward a new idea, and they will be reticent to your desire to fix the culture. That reluctance goes deeper.

At our core, we humans are often resistant to change. (As I like to quip at workshops, if you don't believe me, just ask your loved ones!) School leaders like Candace Young (see more of her in Chapter 1) recognize this, so instead of trying to deny it, they enter their reset with eyes wide open. "I knew that many staff members were not going to be open initially to the change—they needed to see first if it would work," recalls Candace. "So I didn't spend too much energy trying to convince all of them, but to remain constant: unwavering in the setting of a new vision. I didn't expect to be liked; but if I could remain consistent and fair, I hoped at least to earn their respect."

Candace, LeVar, and Yanela did so in the following five ways:

1. **Set the norm with your leadership team for "all hands on deck."** In successful turnaround, the leadership team of the school makes a commitment to lead culture equally. If an assistant principal walks down the hall and ignores the culture issues, it sends a message to the students that school culture is dependent on the individual. The leadership team needs to commit to all taking the same actions if they want the teachers to do the same. Note, too, that all hands on deck means that people are paying close attention to culture at critical times of the day, and have a common set of indicators to look for and either reinforce or correct in real time.

2. **Start with the staff who are most invested in change.** It is next to impossible to address the issues going on in every classroom at once. Yanela starts with the staff who are willing to make the change and that helps build momentum. (In Chapter 6 on Staff Culture, we'll talk more about how to manage those who aren't as invested.)

3. **Follow the rollout plan: hook, frame, model, debrief, plan, practice.** Once you've invested in those that you can, follow the process for rollout laid out earlier in the chapter.

4. **Put aside instruction for one or two days and reset.** Acknowledge that a reset takes time, and give teachers a few days to retrain all the routines and procedures established in the PD session without the need to cover material. Just like Yanela, follow the rollout plan for each routine: hook, frame, model, debrief, plan, practice. And on those critical days right after the reset rollout, spend all your time in their classrooms, observing and supporting wherever necessary.

5. **Remain emotionally constant.** Turning around a culture is not easy—but it is eminently doable. For your staff and students, you want to be the calm within the storm. No matter what students still push back at the beginning or no matter which teacher will have a resistant comment, your best action is calm, consistent, repetitive action. It's not charisma but constancy that creates culture. (More on this in the next chapter on Staff Culture.)

"Turnaround work takes consistency and clarity," shares Yanela. "Remember: the roots are bitter, but the fruits are sweet."

CONCLUSION

The importance of creating a student culture where students are welcomed, loved, and motivated to excel is more important than ever. In 2025, Common Sense Media reported that nearly 72% of US teens have used AI companions for friendship and emotional support.[6] These teens are turning to AI for a variety of reasons, including a sense of always-available companionship. Yet in the process, they are less engaged in community and relationship-building, and additional negative impacts that are not yet fully known. With fewer communities existing in the societal fabric, schools become even more important.

Student culture matters not only because it gives our students a solid foundation on which to learn, but it's a place for them to build community with their fellow students and find connection and purpose. And it's our opportunity as adults to communicate to our students how much we believe in them, and that we will support them in becoming their best self. Isn't that what we want from all our mentors?

When you stand before your staff and then your students to teach them your cultural routines, remember the "why" behind those actions: we build great school cultures so our students never forget they are capable of greatness.

> **Core Idea**
>
> Build great cultures so our students never forget
> they are capable of greatness.

Action Steps for Principals
Leading Student Culture

LEVER	STUDENT CULTURE—KEY ACTIONS IN SEQUENCE
	Plan

Student Culture

Set the Vision:

1. **See the model:**
   - Identify the models for your school to guide your vision
     - Observe high-performing schools/classrooms
     - Look at video examples (e.g., *Leverage Leadership, Get Better Faster, Teach like a Champion*)
     - Record what teachers, leaders, and students say and do.

2. **Anticipate the gap:**
   - Anticipate the gap:
     - Determine what it would look like if student culture was executed poorly.
     - What would ineffective leaders and teachers be doing?
     - What would the students be doing if it was implemented poorly?

3. **Name It—name the behaviors to define your values:**
   - Name the ideal behaviors:
     - Identify the behaviors leaders, teachers and students would demonstrate that would create the ideal student culture at every moment of the school day:
       - What will leaders/teachers/students do and say?
       - What will happen when students or staff are not doing what you envisioned?
   - Name the values that embody these behaviors
     - Name the 2–5 student-facing values the school will embody that encompass the ideal behaviors

Student Culture (cont'd)	4. **Name It—build a system for every routine, procedure and all-school culture moment:**
	
	• Craft specific, observable, written procedures for each whole-school and classroom routine/moment of the day: arrival/breakfast, hallway transitions, in-class routines (including first and last five minutes of class), community gatherings, celebrations, lunch, dismissal, etc.
	
	  ◦ Name what leaders, students, and teachers will do in a comprehensive, sequential, minute-by-minute plan.
	
	    ▪ Identify what will happen when students/staff are meeting expectations and when they are not
	
	    ▪ Adaptive: name the resources/tools provided for students who need extra support (executive functioning, social-emotional, etc.)
	
	5. **Name It—build systems to manage student discipline (asst. principal, dean of students, etc.):**
	
	• Set a weekly/daily schedule for the student culture leader to proactively reinforce student culture
	
	• Set up effective systems and routines for the leader who will drive student culture.
	
	  ◦ Create a clear protocol for responding to specific student discipline situations, including de-escalation strategies rooted in social-emotional learning
	
	• Build a standing agenda for principal culture leader check-ins that includes:
	
	  ◦ Data review of student discipline issues and most pressing student issues.
	
	  ◦ Feedback to the leader & to teachers who need support.
	
	  ◦ Review of send-out or suspension data to problem solve ways to prevent the behavior.

	6. **Measure it**
	• Create a school wide culture rubric that defines the following:
	◦ Common language that teachers and leaders will use
	◦ Vision for all schoolwide and classroom routines & systems
	• Set concrete, measurable goals and deadlines:
	◦ Measurable goal, e.g., hallway transitions will reduce to two minutes; 100% students on task during independent practice
	◦ Identify when the system will be introduced and when the goal will be met.
	• Plan your weekly observations and benchmarks to assess mastery
	7. **Tell the story for parents—Create training and guides around family communication**
Student Culture (cont'd)	• Storytelling: Create the story for your families on the vision of the school, proactively naming school and parents work together to support their child
	• Schedule and plan key moments in the year for all-parent communications (Report card conferences, Back to School Night, etc.)
	• Create routines for crisis/incident management to respond effectively to parent concerns

Roll Out

	8. **Roll out with staff—Hook-Frame-Model-Debrief-Plan-Practice:**
	• See It—model the routine/procedure:
	◦ Hook: deliver a hook (short and sweet) that gives them the "why"
	◦ Frame: name what you want them to observe: "As you watch the model of [routine/procedure], pay attention to how I. . . ."
	◦ Model: exaggerate the model to reinforce every action you want to see.

Student Culture (cont'd)	• Name It—debrief the model:
	    ◦ "What did you notice? What did I say and do and what did students do?"
	    ◦ Narrate for why: "Why is that [action] important?"
	    ◦ Stamp it: "Jot down your key takeaways before we jump into practice. . . ."
	• Do It—practice the routine/procedure:
	    ◦ Plan before practice:
	        ▪ A script of the routine in the hands of each teacher and time to prepare individually
	    ◦ Rehearse:
	        ▪ Deliver clear what-to-do instructions
	        ▪ Authentic practice: standing in the classroom
	        ▪ Give effective feedback during practice: narrate the positive and correct in the moment
	9. **Roll out with Students—Hook-Frame-Model-Plan-Practice:**
	• See It—model the routine/procedure:
	    ◦ Hook: deliver a short and sweet speech that shares the why in student-friendly terms—connect routine to the school values/mission.
	    ◦ Frame: tell the students what they are going to do: "I'm going to model for you [or show a model]: look how I do and say. . . ."
	    ◦ Model: exaggerate the model: fully dive into the model to reinforce the habits/expectations you want to see.
	• Do It—practice the routine/procedure:
	    ◦ Give clear what to do directions
	    ◦ Narrate the positive
	    ◦ Correct in the moment & do it again

Student Culture (cont'd)	10. **Roll out with student culture leaders (e.g., assistant principals, deans of students, etc.)**
	
	• Roll out and practice protocols and routines for leading publicly and privately (e.g., leading students publicly and interacting with them one-on-one)
	
	Execute
	
	11. **Lead publicly:**
	
	• Be present and be seen in key areas (lunch, hallways, struggling classrooms, etc.)
	
	• Celebrate: publicly and individually share success for students and staff
	
	• Confident presence: stand and speak with purpose
	
	   ◦ Warm-demander register: use a warm formal register, including tone and word choice
	
	   ◦ Utilize non-verbals to lead and redirect calmly
	
	• Provide real-time feedback:
	
	   ◦ Narrate the positive; Do it Again until 100%; Challenge ("Can you do it, too?")
	
	   ◦ What-to-do: use concrete phrases and actions that teachers/students can use
	
	   ◦ Choose least invasive method of real-time feedback (see Observation and Feedback): silent signals, whisper prompts, or models
	
	   ◦ Immediate: address challenges before they escalate: de-escalate the situation with the least invasive intervention
	
	12. **Manage individually:**
	
	• Teachers—have "course correction" conversations when they have important areas of growth:
	
	   ◦ Identify the challenge.
	
	   ◦ State the impact.
	
	   ◦ Make bite-sized action plan with prompt implementation on a set timeline.

Student Culture (cont'd)	<ul><li>Leaders—implement check-in with the leader in charge of student discipline issues (AP/dean)<ul><li>Model effective student de-escalation and reflection techniques for the AP/dean and have AP/dean execute.</li><li>Monitor & give AP/dean real-time feedback to ensure AP/dean meets current action step.</li></ul></li><li>Students—lead effective discipline conversations by following the model:<ul><li>Listen: ask them to explain their version of what happened.</li><li>Name the problem and then the consequence.</li><li>Share why this is important (back to shared mission and long-term dreams for the child).</li><li>End with shared commitment to work together.</li></ul></li><li>Families—lead effective discipline conversations with families:<ul><li>Name the problem and then the consequence.</li><li>Listen: acknowledge their feelings and their concerns ("open face," eye contact, emotional constancy).</li><li>Economy of language: keep language concise and precise and stick to the script.</li></ul></li></ul>13. **Master the waterfall: utilize Get Better Faster scope and sequence to prioritize feedback around culture**<ul><li>Align culture action steps and feedback to Get Better Faster Management scope and sequence</li></ul>

<table>
<tr><td align="center" style="background-color:gray">Monitor and Course Correct</td></tr>
</table>

COLLECT DATA AND COURSE CORRECT

14. **See the gaps**

- Via a school walkthrough, identify students and teachers not implementing routines effectively and identify the action steps:

Student Culture (cont'd)	o With student culture rubric in hand, identify where the breakdown occurs:
	
	  ■ What student actions or inactions are indicators of the problem?
	
	  ■ What teacher actions or inactions are causing the problem?
	
	  ■ What leader actions or inactions are causing the problem?
	
	o Bring people outside your leadership team to observe your school and identify the big rocks to move your school culture forward.
	
	• Targeted improvements: choose one row on the student culture rubric and set a specific goal for a score by a specific date. Develop clear action steps and implement. Re-score that row on a regular basis.
	
	15. **Plan and lead effective practice clinics (short practice session) to strengthen individual and school-wide teacher Action Steps—Hook-Frame-Model-Practice:**
	
	• Hook: deliver a hook (short and sweet) that gives them the "why"
	
	• Frame: name what you want them to observe: "As you watch the model of [routine/procedure], pay attention to how I. . . ."
	
	• Short Model (1–2 min max): Exaggerate the model to reinforce every action you want to see.
	
	• Practice: Implement the model immediately with teacher's one lesson plan; give real-time feedback to close the gaps
	
	16. **Monitor student culture leadership (e.g., Dean of Students)**
	
	• Observe the leader in action and provide real-time feedback on both public and private leadership
	
	• Conduct joint walkthroughs with the leader

	17. **Lead a whole-school reset of a specific, high leverage routine/procedure**
Student Culture (cont'd)	• Do a new rollout of the reset (Hook, Frame, Model, Debrief, Plan, Practice)
	• See the gap: have teachers/leaders identify the gaps
	• Execute a daily walkthrough to monitor the targeted action steps
	• Communicate to staff the progress and next steps on a daily basis until the goal is met
	• Plan and execute action steps

Pulling the Lever

Action Planning Worksheet for STUDENT CULTURE

Self-Assessment

- Evaluate the state of student culture in your school right now (you can use the sample Student Culture Rubric in the LL App as a starting point). Where does the reality of student actions not match what you hope for?

- What items on the Student Culture Rubric are your biggest areas for improvement?

_____

_____

_____

_____

- What actions on the above list of key action steps around culture for school leaders would you want to implement right away in your school? Choose your top two or three.

_____

_____

_____

_____

Planning for Action

- What tools from this book will you use to lead student culture at your school? Check all that you will use (you can find all on the LLI App):

  ___ **Leading Student Culture One-pager**

  ___ **Student Culture Rubric**

  ___ **Student Culture Minute-by-Minute Plans**

  ___ **30-day Playbook**

  ___ **Videos of Effective PD**

  ___ **PD Materials for leading student culture**

- What are your next steps for improving your student culture?

Action:	Date:

Chapter **6**

Staff Culture

Staff Culture: Building Teams

It's 4:45 PM on a Wednesday afternoon, the end of a long school day at WH Adamson High School in Dallas, Texas. But you wouldn't know it when you hear the buzz coming from the library where staff have gathered for the weekly faculty meeting.

Teachers have just finished writing appreciation notes to each other to celebrate their support and impact in the classroom, and they are excitedly sharing them with each other. Smiles and laughter abound. On the PPT screen, there appears a list of seniors who were recently accepted to college, and a thanks to each staff member who helped them with their application.

Principal Stephanie Amaya raises her hand to bring the faculty back together. "Before we begin our PD, let's remember our mission that we wrote at the beginning of the year. What do we want to focus on today?" The staff turn toward the chart on the wall where the school mission is always visible: Accountability and a Unified Force. They are clearly used to this question as they turn toward each other in pairs and name a commitment they will make during this meeting to live by these values.

"Ok. We've been working on academic monitoring this month, and today we are going to focus on some simple strategies to respond to the data we collected while monitoring. I'm going to model for you a Show-Call: how to post a piece of student work on the board and have the students evaluate it. Watch as I. . . . "

After a model and precise directions, the faculty break into department teams and start practicing. Amaya and her leadership team float around the room, leaning in when necessary to give a few words of feedback.

By the time Stephanie Amaya arrived at WH Adamson High School in Dallas, Texas with more than 1,600 students, she had seen a lot. She had already worked at an elementary school and turned it around from an F rating to a B, and she had been through the trials of COVID-19. But high school was a different animal. Adamson served students who were 98% free-reduced lunch and 98% Hispanic—they had not seen any success for years. "When I first arrived, there was a lot of resistance: they felt like I was bringing an 'elementary' approach to high school and it would never work." Everyone knew the bad messages that were communicated about the neighborhood, and that negative mindset had seeped into the fabric of the school. Department chairs and instructional leaders were skeptical, many of whom had been doing things the same way for years. Most of them were simply planning to "wait out" Amaya until she gave up.

Fast forward four years. WH Adamson High School achieved an A Rating—the only comprehensive high school to do so in all of Dallas. Amaya was named principal of the year and her accomplishments received national and international recognition.

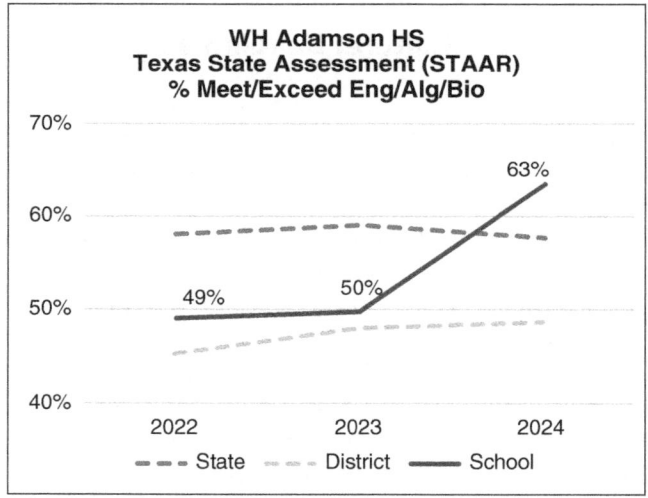

Where did it all start? With culture—culture for students and for staff. "We had to learn to become a community, in the real sense of the word," Stephanie shares. "A place where we can care for each other and push each other—where it's not okay to be less than our best."

Amaya reveals something powerful. In the end, your staff will come for the mission, but they stay for the people.

> ## Core Idea
>
> They come for the mission; they stay for the people.

No matter how noble our mission is in education, what keeps us going are relationships—people. They will come for the mission of serving children, but they will stay if there is a strong culture with their colleagues and with you.

Amaya is not alone in figuring this out. She is part of a community of leaders who have cracked the code on staff culture—and discovered that it makes all the difference in the world. Leaders like Kim Tymkowych, who led a successful turnaround at Winona Elementary School: "I asked my staff: what kind of environment do you want to work in and do students deserve?" Or leaders like Amanda McDonald, who dramatically transformed Lake Middle School (more about her in Chapter 7): "I had to build a staff culture to propel our student culture."

Without question, all of these leaders will tell you that student culture and data-driven instruction are the key levers to drive results, and that staff culture gets stronger as they achieve success in those levers. So, why address it separately? Because these leaders also all agree that staff culture amplifies the work of every other lever. "Students mirror what we do," notes Jasmine Woodward (Chapter 4). "If we are a community aligned to a common mission, they will also be drawn to it."

Instructional leadership gives your staff the ability to succeed; staff culture is about making sure they want to. It is to teaching what student culture is to learning.

> ## Core Idea
>
> Instructional leadership gives your staff the ability to succeed;
> staff culture is about making sure they want to.

Research confirms the many benefits of a robust staff culture. Authors from Judith Warren Little to Ron Edmonds to Michael Fullan have proven that strong adult culture creates more teacher expertise and higher achievement.[1] While the research is solid, schools have been slow to explicitly develop it. Why is that? Often, we make a number of assumptions:

- We assume we all agree on "unwritten rules" that guide how we treat one another and how we speak to each other.

- We assume that all of us take pride in a student-centered focus and know what that means.

- We are all adults. We know how to behave. That's common courtesy.

- If we get student culture working, staff culture will be taken care of.

These assumptions are understandable. We learn, from an early age, how to "fit in." Remember being a new hire, taking note of how your new colleagues dress, speak, and work together? You quickly sized up what gets rewarded and what doesn't. Culture is what we do to belong. So, how can we make the belonging serve a positive, affirming culture—more than just keeping us from being rejected?

When it comes to staff culture, leadership is indispensable.[2] It can make or break staff culture, mostly because leaders shape the conditions that let adults do their best work (or not).

Core Idea

Leaders shape the conditions that let adults do their best work (or not).

When you observe a strong family from afar, you are struck by the unity they display and the closeness of their relationships. You see the joy and the love. What you probably don't see, however, is the hard work that happens on a daily basis that creates that unity. The difficult conversations where you work through conflict. The moments where you have to push each other even when you're not feeling up for it. The same holds true for schools.

So, how do you get to that type of culture? Let's let Amaya show us the way.

SET THE VISION
Behaviors Define Your Values

When educators think about their dream staff community, they often begin with a list of key values. For good reason: if we want to succeed, we need to have a vision. For example, Jon Saphier has spent more than 40 years detailing what makes great teaching in his seminal text *The Skillful Teacher*.[3] He notes that great schools and teachers communicate ". . . the belief that all students are capable of working on rigorous material and meeting high standards, even if they currently are behind grade level."[4] This value of high expectations for students is at the bedrock of every excellent school.

Values abound in schools: high expectations, community, student-centered. They are far-reaching, hopeful, and ambitious but also unclear.

Values seem simple to name, but they can actually become emotionally triggering. Two different people interpret the same value differently, which can cause discomfort and frustration when others aren't living by the same understanding. For example, the value of honesty might be "in-your-face" truth-telling to some, and gentle nudging to others. Without clarity, your staff will be headed for unproductive conflict!

I stumbled upon this truth when I was a superintendent. I would lead coaching meetings or PD with instructional leaders, and I would notice some of them undermining the work: checking their phones when we were in PD together, stopping practice early (or just pretending to practice), not doing pre-work, or arriving late after a break. I was frustrated because I felt they weren't honoring our value of being "all in." Then my peer asked me, "Have you ever told them that?" I realized I hadn't. What's more, I assumed "my values" meant "our values." I thought they would understand my vision of being "all in" to align with what I expected of them.

Amaya did it better.

Prior to her arrival, her high school had a mission statement: "accountability and a unified force." She didn't spend weeks re-writing it; she leveraged it. She asked her staff to name all the negative behaviors that had undermined the school in previous years. Kim Tymkowych did the same thing when turning around Winona Elementary School in Loveland. She led an all-staff retreat before the year started and confronted the brutal facts. "I mirrored back what they had been saying about the children and the school. I asked them, 'Is that what you want us to be saying about the children and the school?' It opened up a conversation, with honesty, that started the transformation."

Then Amaya's staff named the alternative positive behaviors—resulting in clear, specific actions such as these:

- On-time arrival, ready for the day to begin, calm and focused
- Greet each other by name, with a smile, and make eye contact
- Ask for help and give help when asked
- If you have an issue with people, talk to them first—not about them
- Welcome feedback and act on it

The assignment was powerful because it showed clearly what the staff expected of each other. Behaviors define your values by making the invisible visible. "It's a pipe-dream until you name it out loud," shares Amaya.

Core Idea

Behaviors define your values by making the invisible visible.

Brené Brown is a trusted and oft-quoted researcher about courage, vulnerability, and clarity in relationships and leadership. She asserts that we get in trouble when we expect mind-reading, meaning when we hint instead of saying exactly what we mean and what "good" looks like. The research lines up with this: leaders who spell out expectations with brevity and clarity inspire better performance and motivation. Why? Because the direction they give is actionable without interpretation. Brown says it best: "Clear is kind."[5] And, I would add, empowering.

To make your values clear and concise, think of the behaviors you wish to see; then name the values. To help see the connection, here are some examples. In 2025, we interviewed some of the most successful leaders in the Leverage Leadership Institute and asked them what values they used with their staff. We also asked for some examples of the behaviors that defined those values. Here is a list of the most frequent values and sample behaviors.

Top Values of Leverage Leadership Schools and Behaviors Attached to Values

VALUE (ALTERNATE NAMES)	MEMORABLE HEADLINE	EXAMPLE BEHAVIORS
Belief in students (unapologetic focus on learning outcomes)	We believe. (We can and we will.)	• We keep the end-goal assessment as the starting point for our instruction. We don't lower the rigor of plans when students struggle, we just provide more access for students to get there.

VALUE (ALTERNATE NAMES)	MEMORABLE HEADLINE	EXAMPLE BEHAVIORS
		• Every choice starts with the question: will this improve student learning?
		• We use asset-based language, not deficit-based, when talking about our students.
Unity (shared purpose, teamwork)	We move as one. (We are better together.)	• We all follow the same procedures for students to give them a consistent, predictable experience.
		• No triangles: if you have an issue with someone, talk to them first—not about them.
Growth Mindset (open to feedback, continuous learning)	Hunger to learn. (We are all learners.)	• We engage actively in meetings: listen, question, and respond.
		• We embrace feedback and implement it.
Belonging (respect, joy)	Everyone belongs here.	• We greet every student, and each other, by name when they enter our school and our classrooms.
		• We immediately correct any student who makes fun of another in any space in the school.
Accountability with care (consistent follow-up)	Hold each other to high standards— with kindness. (Clear is kind.)	• We show up on time, prepared, and we are present for the duration without distraction (no cell phones, laptops, etc.), and we support each other in staying engaged.
		• We deliver clear, kind feedback to each other to hold each other accountable.
		• We own the outcomes of our students' learning, and we implement a plan when there is a gap.

I was struck by a few things after gathering this information. For one, high-achieving schools cannot exist with unity alone—that has to be combined with high expectations for student learning. (If not, your staff could be united but still reaching mediocre results for kids.) Another takeaway is that it is not the name of the value that matters—but the actual behaviors. In the end, naming the behaviors takes the mystery out of culture. It gives a clear path that engenders shared commitment.

> ## Core Idea
>
> Naming the behaviors takes the mystery out of culture.

Pause. Take time to reimagine the behaviors and values of the staff in your own school. Imagine observing them in the halls, before, during, and after meetings, in the lounge—wherever they interact. Take a moment and think deeply: what are the negative behaviors you wish didn't occur? And what are the behaviors you wish to see? Remember: you don't build staff culture by stepping away from the work—you build it by seeing the culture that has already emerged (both the good and the unproductive). Get as granular as possible: the more specific you are, the clearer you will be. Then you can distill those behaviors down to 2–5 core values (more than that is difficult to hang onto!).

Stop & Jot

What are the behaviors you do *not* wish to see among your staff? Be as specific as possible.

To help you get started, here are some of mine. Use whichever ones resonate with you:

- Being late to coverages, duties, or faculty PD
- Opting out of practice during PD, or ending it early
- Being on phones/laptops during meetings
- Gossip or negative talk about a student or fellow staff member at the school

_____

_____

_____

_____

_____

_____

What are the behaviors you wish to see among your staff? Be as specific as possible.

_____

_____

_____

_____

_____

_____

_____

_____

_____

_____

_____

Now distill all these behaviors down to 2–5 core values. That will make them easier to name and remember (you can use the prior box as a starting point):

Core Value 1: _____

Core Value 2: _____

Core Value 3: _____

Core Value 4: _____

Set Clear Roles and Schedules

Once Amaya and her staff named the behaviors that define her values, she didn't stop there. She made sure her staff were set up to succeed to make the behaviors habitual.

In TNTP's national survey of teachers, it discovered three statements that separate high-achieving schools from the rest. "The responses to three questions on our survey had the strongest connection with greater retention of successful teachers and higher student achievement in reading and math."[6] The three statements were:

1. "My school is committed to improving my instructional practice."

2. "Teachers at my school share a common vision of what effective teaching looks like."

3. "The expectations for effective teaching are clearly defined at my school."[7]

The first two are directly addressed in Chapters 1–4; the last one merits additional attention.

Clear and consistent roles are essential to build a team that executes its work harmoniously.[8] Put another way, confidence and performance grow from clearly defined expectations.[9]

> ## Core Idea
>
> Confidence and performance grow from clearly defined expectations.

Mike Mann has led Washington Park High School in Newark, NJ, for 20 years, and it has remained one of the highest achieving urban high schools in the nation. One thing does not fail about his leadership: he consistently creates a detailed list of all roles and responsibilities at the start of each year. It includes everything: your teaching load, your coaching load (if you are coaching a peer), your duties, your standing weekly meeting with your instructional leader, and even what prep periods you will be occasionally asked to give up to cover for an absent teacher. Here's an example of what Mike's document looks like:

Setting Clear Roles

Creating Equitable and Transparent Schedules

| TEACHER | TEACHING HOURS | DUTIES | | | | | OTHER RESPONSIBILITIES: | | TOTAL HOURS |
		MON	TUES	WED	THURS	FRI	HOURS	DESCRIPTION	
John	20	0.5	1.5	1.5		0.5	2	Journalism—newspaper	26.0
Mary	20	0.5	0.75	1.5		0.75	2	Yearbook	25.5
Derek	16	0.5	1.5	0.5	0.5	1.5	5	Curriculum & Asst Development	25.5

TEACHER	TEACHING HOURS	DUTIES					OTHER RESPONSIBILITIES:		TOTAL HOURS
		MON	TUES	WED	THURS	FRI	HOURS	DESCRIPTION	
Katrina	20	0.5	0.5	0.5		0.5	4	Dept. Chair	26.0
Tom	26			0.5					26.5
Meghan	22	0.5		0.5	0.5	1.5			25.0
Amy	19						8	Writing Ctr/Support teacher	27.0
Thomas	17	2	1.5	1.5	0.75	1	2	Curriculum & Asst Development	24.8
Ashley	24		0.5		0.5	0.5			25.5
Sam	18						8	Dept. Chair	26.0
Brittany	26	0.5			0.5				27.0
Tiara	26	0.75	0.5						27.3
Michael	21	0.5	0.5	0.5	0.5		3	Senior Research Project	26.0

This seems simple, but it adds so much value to staff morale. For one, when teachers know all of this in advance, they can schedule their time and plan accordingly. But they also benefit from knowing that everyone in the school is carrying their weight: we are in this together.

Clear weekly schedules are just as crucial. Beyond the standard school schedule are all the changes that occur each week in school life: a field trip one week, a fire drill the next, etc. The second key component is a simple weekly email to all staff that has all the changes to the standard schedule. Here is Mike's example. He starts with a bit of inspiration, and then brings clarity to the upcoming week and month:

Sample Weekly Email

Above and Beyond . . .

All of us who know Jared's story are proud of the young man he has become. Amir, who has known him and taught him since middle school, went out of his way this weekend to help Jared with a college visit: "Jared asked if I could help him with a college visit, because his mother wasn't going to be able to take him. So, I volunteered. Today, we went to Franklin & Marshall, and Jared was so impressive. His interactions with folks in Admissions were the epitome of professionalism. When he talked with Dr. Penn, professor of Neurophysiology, he made our community proud!" Thanks, Amir, for going above and beyond!

On the Calendar this Week . . .

☐ Monday: Advisory Spirit Competition (attached)

☐ Wednesday: Advisory video #1 on the International Day of the Girl

☐ Friday: Whole-faculty PD, 1:30–4:30 pm

Of note . . .

☐ Advisory Spirit Competition: Please see the attached flyer and be prepared to share this with your advisory on Monday. Each advisory is asked to create a video this week showing their spirit. Students will have a chance to work on this on both Monday and Tuesday. Thank you for your help with this!

☐ International Day of the Girl: Last Wednesday, October 11th, was the Sixth Annual International Day of the Girl, as declared by the United Nations. All advisories are expected to view the videos linked in the handout and to discuss the questions listed. Advisories that are still not finished with their spirit video by Tuesday will still have a chance to work on the video next week.

☐ Fire Drill, October 17th: We will be having a fire drill on Tuesday, October 17th; please review the Emergency Reference Guide located in the operations manual or on your classroom wall in advance of this drill. If you have any questions, please reach out to Connor before the drill takes place.

Kudos!

☐ **Boys Soccer:** Good luck in the County Tournament Friday!

☐ **Girls Varsity Volleyball:** It was "pretty in pink" this week as both teams rocked pink socks for a great cause for breast cancer research. Great cause and well done girls!!!

Month at a Glance. . .

WEEK	MONDAY	TUESDAY	WEDNESDAY	THURSDAY	FRIDAY
Oct 16–20	Advisory: Spirit Competition	Advisory: Connections Fire Drill	Advisory: Video & discussion	Advisory: Video & discussion	Faculty PD: Predicting IA performance
Oct 23–27	School Forum: Fastest Improvement	Advisory: Connections Tag Day	Quarter 1 Exams	Quarter 1 Exams	Quarter 1 Exams Faculty PD: Complete IA grading & begin analysis
Oct 30–Nov 3	School Forum: Personal Improvement Plans 9th grade Hike (group 1)	Advisory: Connections 9th grade Hike (group 1) Instructional Ldr PD: Leading Data Meetings	Advisory: reading & discussion	Advisory: reading & discussion 9th grade Hike (group 2)	Faculty PD: IA Data meetings 9th grade Hike (group 2) Quarter 1 grades due
Nov 6–10	Forum: Latinx Cultural Celebration	Advisory: Connections	Advisory: reading & discussion Quarter 1 Report Card Night	Advisory: reading & discussion Senior Class Tag Day	Half-day: No faculty PD

Notice the power of Mike's memo. First, it is pretty short because no one wants to read a long essay! Second, it gives a clear calendar of what is coming up in the next two weeks to plan accordingly. Finally, it includes a few accolades from that week.

Everyone gets excited to hear about the athletic teams' success, and it also makes it easier for them to feel better about the student who missed their class that Friday traveling to the tournament.

Clear roles and clear schedules mean a clear mind: you drive out the clutter and allow a teacher to focus on teaching. When they can do that, teachers will fly.

Core Idea

Clear roles and clear schedules mean a clear mind: you drive out the clutter and allow a teacher to focus on teaching.

Just as with student culture, once you have established your vision (behaviors that define values and clear roles), you roll it out.

ROLL IT OUT

See The Exemplar—Make Your Values Visible

I founded the Leverage Leadership Institute (LLI) in 2014, and a hallmark of the experience is an opening dinner where we launch the yearlong fellowship. After a chance to spend a little time with each other, I often share the story of Ross Lunceford, principal of the year in Ogden, Utah, and Shawn Mangar, a high-performing principal from New York City. They didn't know each other before joining LLI, but they formed an instant bond. One morning, I was walking back from working out around 6:00 AM, and I heard voices coming from our conference room. When I peeked inside, there was Ross rehearsing the PD he was to deliver later that morning—and there was Shawn, wide awake at dawn, giving him feedback. Shawn had no obligation to be there. But he was because his colleague needed him. That small moment made visible the values they lived: unity, collaboration, and commitment to each other's growth and practice.

In your schools, stories like these are far more powerful than written values or a mission statement. Stories give staff something they can see—a real moment, tied to real actions—that illustrates what great culture looks like. Vision statements are forgettable; stories aren't. Culture doesn't begin in a meeting. It begins in the stories of a school. Make your values visible via story.

> ## Core Idea
>
> Make your values visible via story.

That observation points to a more effective—and far more sustainable—approach to building staff culture. Instead of launching a stand-alone values initiative or spending days writing vision statements, great leaders simply tell stories. This helps teachers see and name the values already embedded in their best work.

Think about the most memorable stories you could tell about your staff. Stories where staff lived by and embodied the values you seek. Then follow the advice we give students when they write: Show, not tell. Paint a picture with the details (like I did with describing coming back from working out and hearing the sounds from the conference room). Pick the moment, not the entire project (I picked 6:00 AM, not the moment when Ross actually delivered the PD). And make the stories replicable, meaning actions anyone could take. When you do that, the vision for your culture comes alive.

Stop & Jot

Write a memorable story about your staff that illustrates one or two of the behaviors aligned to your values that your school has adopted—the more specific and aligned, the better:

- Pick the moment
- Show, not tell: paint a picture
- Keep it short

_____
_____
_____
_____
_____
_____

You don't have to be the only storyteller. Stories from the staff can be just as powerful or even more so. What great stories of ideal behaviors could your staff tell? Engage them and as the stories unfold the essential question will emerge: "What behaviors made these moments possible?" This is how culture becomes concrete. You are not declaring what the culture should be; you are helping them name what already works.

See the Gap—Flag the Unproductive Behaviors

In my LLI launch, I follow these inspiring stories with stories of what it *doesn't* look like to live by our values—the behaviors that don't embody them. It is less uplifting but equally powerful. By telling them what the values aren't, you make the values even clearer. You paint a picture of unproductive behaviors that eliminate the guesswork on how to act in your culture. Make it easy to say yes by making the implicit explicit.

Core Idea

Make it easy to say yes by making the implicit explicit.

Do It—Create a Culture of Practice

You will not find a single professional athlete or musician who didn't have a deep commitment to practice. An ethos of practice is also central to successful schools. Judith Warren Little and Jon Saphier—and a host of authors in between—have defined this as one of the key characteristics of a high-achieving school.[10] Every previous leadership lever has driven home the importance of practice, yet that culture isn't always apparent in schools. What do you do when your staff doesn't have a culture of practice? You show them.

For example, in the first weeks of her leadership, Amaya stated that they would be practicing—a lot. She used lots of sports analogies on the power of practice, she modeled what it looked like and had them practice giving feedback in the very first meetings. "I needed to create a staff culture of improvement, and that wasn't possible without a culture of practice." She followed the same formula you've seen throughout the book: See it (show examples of the power of practice). Name it (make it a behavior attached to your values). Do it (constantly ask them to practice).

In the end, staff culture isn't built in a meeting—it is revealed in their work. Name the values and practice until it's who you are every day.

The first time you ask a teacher to practice who has never practiced before, they might balk or have an attitude. The second time you do it, they'll react a little less. By the time you've done it for the fourth time in a row, they will understand that this is the way you do things, and your culture has been established. Be consistent even if it's awkward at the beginning. If they benefit (and they will), they will embrace it.

Launch With Your Staff Values

BEHAVIORS DEFINE YOUR VALUES	
See It and Name It	

Identify the Behaviors to Define the Values	• **Individually or as a Team—Name the Ideal Behaviors:**
	○ Identify the ideal behaviors you wish to see from staff at all parts of the day in casual encounters and established routines
	• **Categorize with Values:**
	○ Sort the behaviors into categories based on common characteristics
	○ Name 2–5 Core Values that are foundational to the behavioral categories or themes
	  ■ (Examples: top five values from surveyed highest-achieving Leverage Leadership schools):
	  ■ Belief in student learning
	  ■ Unity/teamwork
	  ■ Growth mindset
	  ■ Belonging
	  ■ Accountability

(Continued)

	- Validate: ensure that all ideal behaviors are assigned to one of your values
	- Option: Re-state each value with a headline that is memorable, simple, an unambiguous
	■ (Examples from Leverage Leadership Schools):
	■ Belief in Student Learning: "Kids come first"
	■ Unity/Teamwork: "All in," "Better together," "Commit as one"
	■ Growth Mindset: "Iron sharpens iron," "We are all learners"
	■ Belonging: "See each other"
	■ Accountability: "Warm demanders," "Clear is kind"
	**Make your values visible via story**
Roll It Out: See the Exemplar	**Share the Values that Carry your School's Culture:** - **Name It:** Share the core values and ideal behaviors associated with them **See the Exemplar—Tell replicable stories from school's history that embody the behaviors for each value:** - (Examples) - "When a new teacher in her grade team could not figure out how to address a particularly tricky student example, Maria spent time with her in her classroom practicing scenarios, helping her plan a call home to the family, and prepare a seating chart. That's what Growth Mindset looks like." - "Sean was really nervous about leading a PD for the English department. When I arrived to school at 6:30 AM before students arrived, I spotted him with his colleague Nikki, practicing together. She had volunteered to get up super early to practice with him the morning of the delivery. This is what commitment to Teamwork looks like." - **(For LT)** Share specific examples of how leaders in the room both embody the behavioral norm and hold others accountable to the norm

	Selective vulnerability—share examples of your own growth: • "I remember when I was a new teacher and my principal Eric gave me feedback during practice that I needed to improve my word economy with what to do directions. I asked him if he would help me with scripting after the PD and he stayed an extra 20 minutes just helping me rep language and cut words until I felt confident." **(Optional): Ask returning staff for examples:** • "Jermaine asked if he could share what it looks like to 'See each other' at school." • "Christopher, can you share. . . ." • "Can I ask any of our returners to share what _____ looks like?"
Reflect (and Refine)	**Reflect:** • "Which resonates the most with me about how to live these norms at our school?" • "How do these values help us be successful and feel supported?" **Share:** • Turn and talk; large group share out **Optional—Refine together:** • Revisit the behaviors and values you developed to clarify the language and get buy in on what you will "publish." Add or revise based on input and the stories your staff told. • Develop "headlines" together.
Name the unproductive behaviors via story	
Roll It Out: See the Gap	**Give counterexamples and what they communicate:** • Pushback on feedback: "When people push back on feedback in PD ("I get it. I know how to do that. It's just that it was a role play and not real."), they communicate the message: I don't have weakness, and your feedback is not valuable to me."

(Continued)

<table>
<tr><td></td><td>

- Opt out of practice: "When people don't take full advantage of the opportunity to practice ("I just finished early; that's why I'm not still practicing."), they communicate the message: I'm too good for practice—if I finish early there isn't more for me to learn or 'I just need to talk about it'"
- Lack of responsiveness to emails: "When people don't respond to an email, they communicate the message: Your emails don't matter to me because you don't matter to me, and I don't care about letting you down."
- **(For LT)** Share specific examples of how leaders in the room do <u>not</u> live by the norms, particularly when they don't hold staff accountable to them

(Optional): Ask returning staff for examples:

- Plan for who you are calling on and when
</td></tr>
</table>

Commit

Reflect and Commit	**Reflect:** Write your personal commitment: - "Which resonates the most with me about how to live these norms at our school?" - "What norms do I want to work on the most to be a strong team member?" **Share:** - Turn and talk; large group share out - Post publicly **Revoice and Reframe (if needed):** - Leader rounds up when necessary: "What I am hearing. . . ."

Practice

Practice	**Plan:** - Share scenarios where the norms can be practiced - Plan your response - (For LT) Anticipate the red flags that will occur during each part of the year. Plan the follow up conversations with staff members who are not living by the values.

> **Practice:**
> - Pair up new and returning staff strategically
> - Practice:
>   - Give directions:
>   - Name Partners
>   - Tell Recipient What to Do (the person not living by the norms)
>   - Give the Time Stamp & launch practice
>   - Practice: Float and give feedback
> - Time to reflect and share out

If you follow the guidance of this chapter, think about what you will have accomplished: you've rolled out your values, you've set clear roles, and you've created a culture of practice. So, how do you maintain that momentum throughout the school year?

MAKE IT DURABLE

Jon Saphier cautions that "healthy cultures are fragile things."[11] Amaya and leaders like her make their culture durable through a few key actions:

- Lead by example
- Maximize strengths
- Leverage accountability to maintain community

Lead by Example

On Amaya's first week on the job at Adamson, the Athletic Director was unexpectedly hospitalized. Without thinking twice, Amaya did what she would always do. She reached out, visited, and supported him. "I was just doing the right thing," she comments. "But looking back, I see that the care I showed him built a lot of trust with the rest of the staff. Those actions carried more weight than anything I had said."

This type of leadership-by-example makes your message congruent with your actions. If you want your staff to be kind to each other, be kind to them. If you want them to be receptive to feedback, receive feedback constructively. If you want them to act as one school with one mission, model that you are part of that one school and hold yourself to the same high standards. Corliss James is the principal of Leadership Prep in Memphis, Tennessee and her school earned Reward School distinction from the state.[12] She shares, "Some leaders just want to tell teachers what to do without rolling up their sleeves and doing the work side by side. Your example matters most."

Amanda McDonald (more on her in Chapter 7) had the same experience at Lake Middle School in Denver. She wanted staff to listen to each other—but it started with her: "How can I make sure staff feel valued? When I listen to them. If you pour into your people, they'll come with you." Cultural leaders don't inspire from the balcony; they model the work on the floor.[13]

Core Idea

Cultural leaders don't inspire from the balcony;
they model the work on the floor.

In every moment of the school day, people are watching you to see how you act and interact. Marc Brackett is a professor of Psychology at Yale University and the Director of the Center for Emotional Intelligence. Part of his research focuses on what makes great leadership. He makes a simple point: when people experience emotionally intelligent leadership, they report higher job satisfaction and lower burnout even when the workload is heavy.[14]

If you go a step deeper, most people sense your support as a leader based on how you act in your weakest moments, not your best. All of us can stay strong when we're doing well. The key is how you treat others when you are under duress.

Core Idea

They remember how you act at your worst more than at your best.

Amaya was well aware of this. She recalls her first years as a principal: "Being a principal is a stressful job, and there is a lot of pushback, especially in a turnaround context. That stress I was carrying initially spilled out in my interactions my staff. I tried both extremes—work harder to get it all done with little sleep and incredibly poor habits—and have a complete focus on self-care with little focus on my job. Neither worked."

By the time she came to WH Adamson, she found a middle ground. She still attended a multitude of high school athletic events, but "I found a way to fill my bucket" while doing so (like playing the drums with the drum corps!). She still had some long workdays, but she organized her weekends to maximize rejuvenation. And when she was in school, she still experienced stress, but she picked a partner to help her. "I called my assistant principal Oscar Rodriguez, Jr., to be my accountability partner. If I do these things that aren't ideal, that means I'm stressed out. Tell me so I can monitor myself."

What Amaya did is a master class in emotional resilience and her approach is consistent with research on emotional resilience that has exploded in recent years, from Mark Brackett to Brené Brown to Lauri Santos to Elena Aguilar.[15]

It has two key components:

- Build up your internal strength to minimize your moments of negative behavior
- Regulate your emotions when you feel your internal "heat" going up.

Be Centered

Leadership demands more than stamina; it requires recovery. You can't pour from an empty cup, and you can't project calm you don't feel. Just like Amaya did, the best leaders build simple, renewable habits—exercise, sleep, journaling, spirituality/meditation, connection, gratitude—that keep them grounded and present.[16] Emotional constancy, then, isn't about never feeling stress. It's about creating enough inner stability to convert stress into strength for yourself and those you lead. Centeredness isn't an act; it's a habit.

> ### Core Idea
> Centeredness isn't an act; it's a habit.

Regulate Yourself

No matter how hard we try, we will still have moments when we do not perform at our best. As Marc Brackett of Yale's Center for Emotional Intelligence notes, strong leaders don't avoid pressure—they regulate it.[17] They identify what they're feeling, pause to regulate, and then refocus on what matters most.

For those of us who struggle with this (myself included!), self-regulation doesn't come naturally, but we can practice. And just like Amaya, we can name a partner to keep us honest and help us. "I don't always succeed at this," reflects Amaya. "But when I don't, I name that I was wrong and start again." It's not charisma that builds culture—it's constancy.

Core Idea

It's not charisma that builds culture—it's constancy.

MAXIMIZE STRENGTHS

Just like we preach with students, if you want an energetic staff culture, reward the right stuff: praise the behavior, not the personality. Send clear messages about what you value by giving shout outs about the behaviors that embody your values. Celebrate a teacher who embraced feedback. Acknowledge the behavior when staff members go above and beyond to help their colleague.

When people can see "what good looks like," they hit it more often. Amaya targets her praise because a precise move spreads; vague applause doesn't.

Core Idea

Precise praise spreads; vague applause doesn't.

If praise and celebration isn't natural for you, you can get better with practice (we'll talk more about getting someone to hold you to that in Chapter 8 on finding the time). Here are some simple prompts to tell yourself when generating precise praise. Have your list of values and behaviors close by and answer the following:

- Where did someone exhibit one of these behaviors?
- What was the impact on the team or students?

You can also track it. Here is a sample communication tracker that a principal can keep for each staff member

COMMUNICATION TRACKER

Communication Tracker			Communication 1		Communication 2		Communication 3		Communication 4		Communication 5	
Recipient	Target	Total Communications	Type	Date	Type	Date	Type	Date	Type	Date	Type	Date
Taylor	4	3	Card	8/14	Card	11/22	Gift with Note	12/14				
David	4	2	Card	8/14	Gift with Note	12/14						
Julia	3	3	Email	10/2	Card	11/22	Gift with Note	12/14				
Asia	4	3	Card	8/7	Email	8/11	Gift with Note	12/14				
Marc	3	2	Card	8/30	Gift with Note	12/14						
Natalie	3	3	Card	8/30	Email	10/7	Gift with Note	12/14				
Olu	4	3	Card	8/7	Card	11/22	Gift with Note	12/14				
Christine	4	4	Card	9/13	Card	11/22	Gift with Note	12/14	Gift with Note	12/16		
Nick	3	5	Card	10/12	Email	8/30	Email	10/24	Card	11/22	Gift with Note	12/14
Monique	3	4	Gift with Note	6/21	Email	10/24	Card	11/22	Gift with Note	12/14		
Aisha	3	4	Email	7/16	Email	10/24	Card	11/22	Gift with Note	12/14		
Tom	3	1	Email	8/10								
Kevin	3	1	Gift with Note	12/14								
Brandon	4	3	Gift with Note	7/28	Card	10/4	Card	11/22				
Angelica	2	2	Email	7/28	Gift with Note	8/30						

You can use any template like the one above to help you leverage even brief interactions with your staff to build strong relationships with them.

For Amaya, precise praise was just the beginning. She also worked to maximize the strengths of the staff. With such a large, comprehensive high school, Amaya couldn't sustain culture on her own. We build culture collectively, not through individual heroics.[18] She needed "culture carriers": the people that others gravitate toward. Their example and relationships act like glue to keep the team intact and growing. She cultivated them, and together, they built the culture, one member at a time. Amanda did the same: she created cultural ambassadors to carry the staff culture. Slowly but surely, the staff who were resistant to the changes felt like they were going against the current rather than with it. That is the power of community.

What is important to note about Amaya's and Amanda's actions is that they didn't just name culture leaders: they empowered them along with the whole staff. When staff lead alongside you, your impact multiplies, and culture becomes the force that sustains success. When leaders grow partners, they build ownership that endures.

Core Idea

When leaders grow partners, they build ownership that endures.

COMMUNITY DEPENDS ON ACCOUNTABILITY

When you look at surveys of children of their favorite teachers and teachers of the leaders they respect the most, a common pattern emerges: consistency and high expectations. It matters less the type of personality the teacher or leader has but that each are consistent.[19] A durable staff culture relies on consistent follow-through. How do leaders do this? With vigilance and courage.

Saphier reminds us that healthy cultures are fragile and the most likely cause of their unwinding is "slow death by neglect."[20] No matter how well we work to establish a strong staff culture, it will weaken every time a staff member strays from the agreed-upon behaviors: not submitting a lesson plan by the stipulated time, not arriving on time to cover a lunch duty, speaking poorly about colleagues in the faculty room. Left unanswered, the unwanted behaviors become new, undermining behaviors—and they become your actual values. Too often leaders think corrective action is negative and even destructive to positive staff culture. Yet it is actually the strong, reassuring guardrail that engenders trust and unity. Accountability is the partner to community.

Core Idea

Accountability is the partner to community.

When you follow Amaya's lead and clearly establish your values from the beginning—including explicitly describing what it looks like *not* to follow them—accountability is so much easier. But you still have to look for it.

When Amaya walks into a room with staff, she is immediately listening to the "pulse": Are staff happily interacting? Is there tension? Does the room go quiet when she walks in? "If you look for it," shares Amaya, "you'll see it and feel it." Pay attention to the smoke, or unattended sparks will turn into a fire.

Core Idea

Pay attention to the smoke.
Unattended sparks can turn into a fire.

When Amaya follows up, she can determine what is happening and whether staff aren't following the behaviors for each value. Most often staff members will quickly recognize their error and work to correct it without you having to say much more than mention the values. If you consistently follow up quickly, "They will be expecting it," shares Amaya.

If you don't follow up quickly—or turn a blind eye to what they're doing—two critically negative things occur. Those people will feel like they can continue those actions, and others who were watching to see what would happen now feel the freedom to do the same. Then the culture starts to deteriorate even more quickly than you built it. At times, the negative action taken by a staff member will be such that a simple heads up won't suffice—you'll need to initiate a sit-down conversation; in other words, an "accountability conversation."

Lead Accountability Conversations

Either staff members don't realize they've broken a core value, or they are struggling to admit it. In moments like these, Amaya keeps a simple mantra in mind: In the stormy seas, anchor yourself in your values.

Core Idea

In the stormy seas, anchor yourself in your values.

Leaders like Amaya address these issues directly but also warmly. And they do so by following a simple framework.

State the issue and ask what happened. Directly state the issue that has warranted the conversation—state only the facts, not your opinion or speculation. Then ask them what happened. This allows you to let them explain, and it communicates to them that you want to assume the best.

Kim Tymkowych concurs: "When I was working with a teacher who was demonstrating reluctance to engage in the process, I always went back to the data and allowed for self-reflection. I tried to keep it as objective as possible."

State the impact. Share with teachers the impact of what they did. This is less about what teachers intended and more about the impact on their colleagues and the work. "I know you probably didn't mean this, but by arriving late you communicated to your peers that their time is not as valuable as yours and that the PD was not important. And, we didn't have time to complete all of the work on the agenda." This sort of language assumes the best of teachers: you are not making assumptions about their motivation, but you are explaining how that action could be perceived and how it could adversely impact the work. It makes the conversation easier and grounds it in what matters most: running an effective school.

Identify next steps and remove roadblocks. Finally, simply set a plan to ensure teachers know how to address the issue, and provide everything they need to do so. Asking a question like "What's getting in the way of you being able to do this?" allows a leader to show that they want to remove any roadblocks.

Go back to normal. After a challenging conversation, staff members will be monitoring how you treat them moving forward. Building relationships after accountability conversations maintains a virtuous cycle: build relationships, maintain them through accountability, keep building relationships, repeat. That's how holding your staff accountable can strengthen bonds and make your culture stronger.

Core Idea

Keep assuming the best
and they will try much harder to improve on the rest.

A Word on . . . Avoiding Email for Accountability Conversations

Email—the lifeblood of so much of our communication in the workplace—has major drawbacks for accountability conversations: your words can be misinterpreted, and you have no control over when or where the emails you send are read. Additionally, by its very nature, email conveys stress and hostility in a particularly clear way because you cannot see the tone/person behind the text. As a result, strong leaders of staff culture recommend, whenever possible, avoiding sending emails and seeking out the people you need to speak with in person. This way, they gain the opportunity to learn more about their staff, themselves, and the effectiveness of their communication because they are there to see how the information is received.

On the rare occasion that you need to use email, follow Julie Kennedy's simple advice: always wait a few minutes, or even hours, before sending an email. Sometimes, after 24 hours have passed, she may not send it at all.

TURNAROUND—COMING TOGETHER

Even the most successful schools can face serious challenges when it comes to building a rich and supportive staff culture. At schools where negativity has prevailed and where teachers have become factionalized, politicized, repeatedly chastised, or otherwise disengaged, the challenge of fixing adult culture is very daunting.

So, how do leaders overcome that resistance? A consistent implementation of the other levers gets you a long way: When they experience more success in their teaching, their investment grows. They also adapted the ideas of this chapter intently. Then they got creative to address the unique challenges in their school.

For example, Amaya led many team-building activities to start the year. "We needed to start to trust each other," she recalls. She also set term limits: "The staff had been there a long time without much turnover, so I instituted term limits on leadership roles and used the turnover to transition to a growth mindset."

As teachers and staff see and experience the impact of a well-defined culture, they begin to trust the process and the value of the named behaviors. They develop an appetite for more. Now you have momentum.

A Word on . . . Resistant Staff in Turnaround

In the vast majority of situations, naming your values, rolling them out, and openly addressing challenges early will resolve staff culture problems. Teachers genuinely want to do what is best for students, and most will respond. Sometimes, however, teachers will behave in ways that are entirely out of bounds or will repeatedly resist meeting basic expectations in ways that stem not from misunderstandings but from deeper disrespect or a lack of commitment to the mission. This is particularly likely to happen in "turnaround" situations where teachers may have developed a very different set of habits, attitudes, and expectations for approaching school and the principal's role. In many situations, it is very difficult to dismiss such a teacher.

In the long term, the best way to deal with this sort of challenge is often to change the culture *around* the resistant teacher rather than confront them head on. "Unify the majority around your values," shares Amaya, "and the remaining few will become isolated, and eventually they will either change or they will leave." Indeed, the more consistent a culture is, the more isolated such negativity becomes, ultimately leading the negative to move on.

CONCLUSION

Stephanie Amaya's leadership at W.H. Adamson High School reminds us of what's possible. She showed her team what it looked like to care, to practice, and to believe in one another until the staff didn't just follow her—they became her mission. In the truest sense, her success was shared.

Building a strong staff culture is not a mystery—and it's not reserved for the few. Any leader can do it. When you name the values and behaviors you want to see, when you help your team see what great looks like, and when you practice those habits together until they live in the daily fabric of the school—you build culture that lasts.

This is the compelling work that creates unstoppable momentum—where everyone moves together because everyone belongs.

Core Idea

Staff culture creates unstoppable momentum:
where everyone moves together because everyone belongs.

It's not magic. It's leadership done with intention and heart.

Keys for Successful Staff Culture

➤ **Set the Vision:**
- Behaviors define your values
- Set clear roles and schedules

➤ **Roll it Out:**
- See the exemplar—make your values visible
- See the gap—flag the unproductive behavior
- Do it—create a culture of practice

➤ **Make it Durable:**
- Lead by example
- Maximize strengths
- Community depends on accountability

Action Steps for Principals

Leading Staff Culture

LEVER	STAFF CULTURE—KEY ACTIONS IN SEQUENCE
Staff Culture	**Plan**
	1. **Set the vision for staff culture:** • Name the explicit behaviors you wish to see and what you do <u>not</u> wish to see: how staff will interact with students, with each other, and with coaches/leaders • Synthesize those behaviors into 2–5 values that are memorable, simple and mission-oriented • Set clear roles for staff and weekly schedules.
	Roll-Out
	2. **Lead PD to launch staff culture** • See the exemplar: tell powerful stories of the staff that make the values visible • See the gap: give examples of unproductive behaviors and how they are not aligned to the values • Do It: practice implementing those values collectively 3. **Create a culture of practice:** • Establish expectations for regular practice and give staff multiple opportunities to do so.
	Execute
	4. **Lead by example:** • Faithfully implement all the values of the staff culture in your own behaviors first and always. • Be present—conduct periodic check-ins with staff you do not coach and have "small talk" in staff workspaces, at social events, and at other less-structured times.

Staff Culture (cont'd)	- Implement simple, renewable habits that keep you centered (exercise, sleep, journaling, spirituality, social connection, gratitude)
	
	- Practice regulating your emotions: learn to identify when you are not your best self and implement strategies to regulate those emotions (breathing, physical movement, attention-shifting, self-talk)
	
	- Respond to harsh feedback/poor staff culture moments with emotional constancy.
	
	5. **Maximize the strengths of the staff:**
	
	- Create and use a staff tracker to track regular affirmation and positive interactions (small notes, acts of kindness, etc.): celebrate and affirm culture wins and student achievement data
	
	- Identify and cultivate "culture carriers": staff who act like glue to keep the team intact and growing and who are unafraid to push each other.
	  ◦ Establish regular touchpoints with them focused on staff culture
	  ◦ Through surveys and conversations, identify trends in staff culture and ID key areas to improve
	
	- Acknowledge your staff as experts: "That sounds great—I like your language there!" OR "So you've named the keys. . . ."

	Monitor
	6. **Identify and close the gap—create a plan to realign the school to your staff culture vision:** - Identify gap between current staff culture and ideal staff culture. - Develop 3–4 high-leverage, specific action steps to respond to poor culture. - Communicate your actions to staff with reference to their feedback.

Staff Culture (cont'd)	7. **Strengthen community with face-to-face accountability when staff are not living by the values:**
	• State what happened: ask if this assessment is accurate or what they would add/change
	• State the impact: what was communicated by these actions (e.g., "When you arrived late to PD, you sent a message, even if you didn't intend to do so, that PD doesn't matter or that you don't need it.")
	• Let the staff member react and state what she was intending/feeling
	• Identify next steps and remove roadblocks
	• Go back to normal: communicate positively and proactively in subsequent interactions

Pulling the Lever

Action Planning Worksheet for STAFF CULTURE

Self-Assessment

• Review the key action steps for successful staff culture. What are three steps you'd like to take right away?

_____

_____

_____

_____

Planning for Action

- What are your next steps for improving your staff culture?

Action:	Date:

Chapter 7

Managing School Leadership Teams

A picture can tell a thousand words. So, too, can observing a school leadership team meeting. It's not what they say, but what they do. Let's take a journey across the country from DC to Dallas to Denver to North Carolina. At each stop, we'll look at the actions of successful leadership team meetings to understand their power.

Leadership Team Meetings

A Painting, Part 1

It is a Friday morning at Whittier Elementary School, and the instructional leadership team is gathered around the conference table with their observation notes from this week in front of them.

Principal Tiffany Johnson dives right in. "Ok. So we had a goal this past week for every teacher to do the first steps in academic monitoring—a pathway and pen-in-hand feedback. Where are we? What patterns do you see? Turn and talk."

The team starts comparing notes and looking at each other's writing prompts—the energy is palpable. After a few minutes, Tiffany calls them back together. "Let's share out. What are the highest leverage gaps that you see?"

AP John Wiley starts it off. "We are excited to see that teachers are getting around the room to give feedback. But their feedback to students isn't very specific, and it's taking too long."

Coach Jannl Henry nods her head: "We saw the same pattern: only reaching a few students in each round of independent practice rather than most of the room."

Tiffany nods. "That's what I saw as well. Pull out your Get Better Faster (GBF) Scope & Sequence: what are the highest leverage action steps we should take to address this?"

A silence settles over the room as everyone pulls out their GBF tool and debates the action step. Finally, Math coach Monai Chavers jumps in: "I think we could do more efficient one-on-one feedback to students."

Jannl agrees and adds on: "For the second one, I think we can use the language from the tool: Cue students by a) affirm the effort; b) name the error; c) tell them to fix it; d) tell them you'll come back to check it."

"Excellent," affirms Tiffany. "Now that we know our focus, let's make a plan to address it . . .."

When Tiffany Johnson steps into the room, people listen. Not because she expects it, but because she's earned it. "I was originally the assistant principal at my school," recalls Tiffany. "It was hard for people to accept me when they named me principal: you have to reinvent yourself and how people see you." And she certainly did that.

Over the past three years, Whittier Elementary School, located in Washington DC, made dramatic gains in student achievement[1] and received EmpowerK12's "Boldest School Award" for multi-year, faster-than-average improvement since the pandemic.

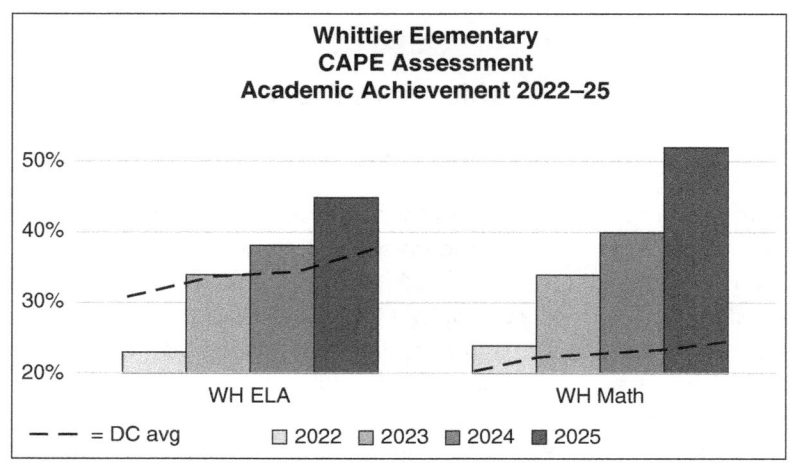

Tiffany used the levers of leadership extraordinarily. But she didn't do it alone. Look no further than her school leadership team meeting.

If you examine Tiffany's entire meeting, a few things jump out at you. This isn't a meeting with a bunch of announcements. And it's not focused on administrative tasks and compliance. Tiffany's meetings are spent on what matters most: student learning and teacher development. How did she get there? She was relentless about the way she used her time and the way her team used theirs.

Core Idea

Exceptional school leaders succeed because of how they use their time. And they get their leadership teams to do the same.

"In my first year as a principal," remembers Tiffany, "I was trying to fix everything myself—it was completely unsustainable. I had to learn to train others, and then our school began to take off."[2]

The previous chapters in this book have been about the key leadership levers for your own work. This one is about tripling your impact by getting your team to do the same. Let's find out how.

CHOOSE YOUR TEAM

We all know the power of a "dream team": the joy of working with colleagues toward a common goal, and the heights we scale together when we build on each other's strengths. Tiffany's leadership team is one of those dream teams, but it didn't get there by chance.

The first thing Tiffany had to do to set up an effective leadership team was to identify who her instructional leaders would be. The composition and organization of your leadership team will vary depending on the resources available to you at your school. Principals like Tiffany draw on assistant principals and instructional coaches that are built into their staffing model. Others get more creative and choose instructional leaders from their teaching staff. Regardless of the precise role each instructional leader holds, following these core guidelines as you choose your leaders will go a long way toward making your leadership team strong.

Look for Reliability and Receptiveness

Just as there is no one "principal personality," there is no one "instructional leader personality." More than anything, these leaders need to be reliable: their dependability will help to facilitate that of everyone else in the school, yourself included.

"The top advice I can give a fellow principal" shares Tiffany, "is to build a leadership team that is committed: consistently doing the work and always data focused. Do you believe all children can learn? Then you can be on my team." Tiffany needed to be able to trust that her leaders would implement the actions they decide upon, so reliability is a must.

Just as essential is openness to feedback. If instructional leaders are going to develop teachers with lots of coaching, they need to be models of being open to being coached themselves. And they need to be receptive to the leadership practices mentioned throughout *Leverage Leadership 3.0*. "They don't need to know how to do it," shares Principal Amanda McDonald (more about her a bit later in this chapter). "They just need to be willing to learn." Teachers or administrators who are not enthusiastic learners would not be good choices.

Remember 12:1—The Golden Ratio

As noted in Chapter 3 on Observation and Feedback, even the most diligent school principal usually cannot serve as a weekly instructional leader for more than 12 teachers. Fortunately, principals need not (and, indeed, should not) be the sole instructional leaders. Assistant principals, deans of instruction, coaches, and your strongest teachers (coaching 1–2 teachers each) are also excellent candidates for the role. Through the creative use of such personnel, nearly any school can meet this 12:1 threshold to ensure that every teacher is observed and receives key feedback. (If you can only get to 24:1, don't worry: that just means you'll have bi-weekly rather than weekly feedback for teachers).

To plan how much time it will take, use a 2-hour rule. For a new instructional leader who will also be teaching, assume a two-hour weekly time commitment for each teacher they will lead. Though the 15-minute weekly observation and 30-minute check-in take less than an hour, we build in an additional hour for the preparation work and lesson plan support that occur. With your Leverage Leadership App in hand, this is more than enough time! Based on these calculations, as a lead teacher takes on a teacher for instructional leadership, the principal reduces the lead teacher's other responsibilities (for example, by cutting back that teacher's lunch duties) or provides a stipend that is similar to what others would receive for a two-hour weekly commitment. When that teacher takes on more than two teachers, course load may need to be reduced or modified.

TRAIN YOUR TEAM—ROLL OUT THE VISION

Leadership Team Meetings
A Painting, Part 2

Across the country, in Dallas, Texas, Principal Alicia Iwasko has gathered her leadership team for their weekly meeting. They analyzed trends from their observations, and they identified five teachers who were struggling the most to produce lesson plans that met the standard.

"Let's review your schedules for the upcoming week," says Alicia. Each leader pulls out their observation schedule. "Given the patterns we just identified, what changes would you make to your schedule?"

All the leaders quietly look over the weekly schedule of observations that they had from the previous week. Instructional Coach Ms. Rodriguez starts: "I'm coaching three of our struggling teachers, so I'm going to change my coaching cycle to double down on their observations and feedback."

Assistant Principal Francis chimes in: "You know, I have capacity to support. Would you like me to observe your other teachers so you can focus on those three?" Miller nods in gratitude. "That would be great."

"Ok," shares Francis. "I will change my observation block from Tuesday afternoon to Tuesday morning so I can observe an extra third grade Reading block and second grade as well."

"Sounds good," replies Alicia. "And I can observe the other third grade teacher at 9:30 on Tuesday so that we can compare notes."

When you talk about what teamwork looks like, look no further than Alicia's meeting at Annie Webb Blanton Elementary School in Dallas. Notice they start with the evaluation (data), agree on how to use their time to address the need, commit to the where and when, and set a time to compare notes. Everything is working in synch.

So, how do leaders like Tiffany and Alicia create a productive, efficient team? Like a professional sports team, they organize, schedule, and train before the season starts.

Core Idea

Treat your leadership team like a sports team:
organize, schedule, and train before the season starts.

Here's how.

Build the Team's Schedule

A vision is meaningless unless we spend our time pursuing it.

Core Idea

A vision is meaningless unless we spend our time pursuing it.

The success of Tiffany's and Alicia's leadership team is the way they manage their time. First, each team member has a locked-in weekly observation and feedback cycle. As we discussed in the Observation and Feedback chapter (Chapter 3), developing a teacher is about consistent coaching, not one-off meetings. They had a consistent leadership team meeting time, so leaders can plan their coaching around that.

What might such a coach's calendar look like? For a full-time instructional leader, it can look very similar to the principal's schedule—which we'll show in more detail in the next chapter (Chapter 8: Finding the Time: Build Your Weekly Schedule). For someone who also teaches, it will look slightly different. Consider the schedule of a high school leader who splits time as an Algebra I teacher and Math coach:

Managing Leadership Teams
An Instructional Leader's Schedule

	MONDAY	TUESDAY	WEDNESDAY	THURSDAY	FRIDAY
6:00 AM					
		Morning greeter duty			
7:00 AM					
8:00 AM	Teach Algebra I (2 classes)	Teach Algebra I (2 classes)	Teach Algebra I (2 classes)	Teach Algebra I (2 classes)	Teach Algebra I
9:00 AM					
10:00 AM					
	Algebra II Planning Mtg				
11:00 AM		Obs. James	Feedback: James		
				Monitor lunch	Teach Algebra I
12:00 PM	Math Dept Weekly Data Mtc	Obs. Tiara			
1:00 PM	Obs. Jorge	Feedback: Jorge			
2:00 PM	Lesson planning/ grading time		Lesson planning/ grading time	Feedback: Tiara	
3:00 PM					

(Continued)

	MONDAY	TUESDAY	WEDNESDAY	THURSDAY	FRIDAY
4:00 PM		Tutoring			
5:00 PM					

As you can see from this sample, the instructional leader's role is, in important ways, a microcosm of the school leader's. By delegating these responsibilities, leaders of large schools can ensure that every teacher in the building is observed, receives feedback, and conducts data or planning meetings with an instructional leader.

In the next chapter (Chapter 8), we'll give you even more strategies for how to finalize the schedule. Once locked in, you can focus on how to use that time effectively.

Train Your Team

When Amanda McDonald enters a room, you sense her presence. There is no ego—just high energy and unwavering focus. When she arrived in 2020 to Lake Middle School in Denver, Colorado, it was the lowest performing school in the city. Four years later, they had not only erased the COVID-19 gap but had achieved the highest results in the school's history.

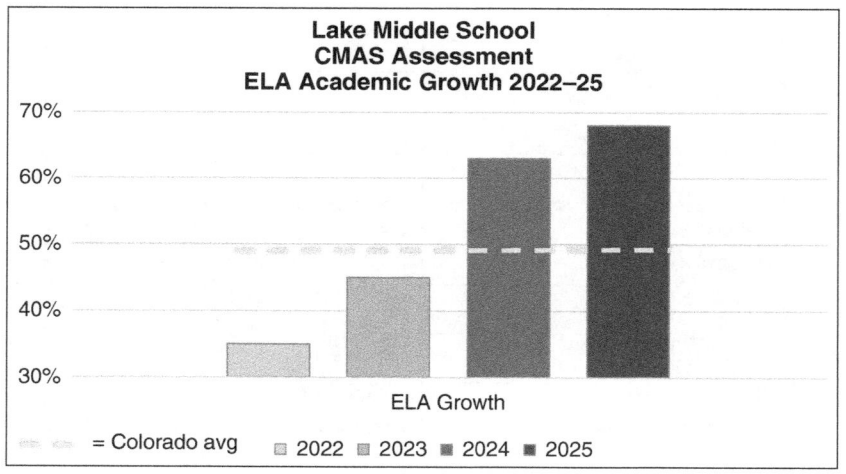

What is one of the keys to her success? The training of her leadership team. "You can trust once you train," she comments. "Train and trust." That's why she prioritizes the team every week with an initial Monday team meeting and a closing Friday team meeting. Let's see what those look like.

Leadership Team Meetings
A Painting, Part 3

"Let's pull out the videos you each took of the 'See It' of last week's Weekly Data Meeting," prompts Amanda. "To calibrate our feedback, let's start by watching Emily's video."

AP Emily Felsenthal smiles—she knew it was her turn this meeting! They project her video on screen up on the wall in Amanda's office.

"As you watch," instructs Amanda, "pull out your rubric for Weekly Data Meetings. Identify the areas where Emily was most effective and the top two highest leverage actions she could take to improve."

For the next few minutes, all you can hear is the sound of Emily's Weekly Data Meeting coming through the projector; and each leader takes notes and tries to generate an action step. A few moments after the video ends, Amanda opens the discussion. "What is your feedback for Emily?"

"I thought her launch was highly effective," commented AP Victor Aguilar. "She had all the student work ready, as well as their old Know-Show Chart from the previous meeting, and they were immediately able to name what students should know or be able to do." Heads nodded in agreement. "My highest leverage actions step for Emily would be to use a timer to make sure you get to practice. The team spent so long in the See It part of the meeting that they ran out of time to role play the re-teach."

"Agreed," shares Victor. "I think you could also remind the team to use the language of the Know-Show Chart to ID the gap sooner. That would get them there faster."

A few others add on praise and recommendations and Emily takes notes.

"Ok," shares Amanda. "Nice work. Let's all pull out our plans for this week's Weekly Data Meeting. Spend a few minutes revising your plans. In four minutes, we'll let Emily role play first, incorporating the feedback she just received." Team members pull out their laptop and begin revising.

Amanda realized early on: leaders need the same opportunity to plan and practice that teachers do. Leadership training is as important as teacher training.

> ### Core Idea
> Teachers don't get better faster without good coaching—neither do instructional leaders.

Delivering this training could be daunting. The purpose of this book, however, is to reduce that burden. Parts I and II of this text are devoted to making each of the levers of leadership clear to you. The Leverage Leadership App (LL App) takes it one step further: it has all the materials, scripts, and links to videos to train your instructional leaders in the same principles. It follows the same model you've learned throughout *Leverage Leadership 3.0*: See It. Name It. Do It.

If you're not sure where to start, remember that data-driven instruction and student culture are the super-levers. However, if you have instructional leaders who don't have to lead student culture, then you can choose data-driven instruction planning or observation and feedback as a starting place. Try it: plan your next leadership team meeting now.

Stop & Do

Click on the option for planning your training of instructional leaders. The App will guide you through selecting an objective and then providing you the resources to lead the PD.

Resources you can generate
Direct identification of videos of leaders in action (right from this book)
Agenda and script for your training of the leadership team
Clear guidelines of how to lead practice

MONITOR THE SCHOOL

Leadership team meetings don't only work at the elementary and middle school level as in the case with Tiffany, Alicia, and Amanda. They are also highly effective—and even more necessary—for high schools. Let's look at a sample of the leadership team meeting of Taro Shigenobu (whom you met in Chapter 2) at Henderson Collegiate High School. His leadership team meetings continue even after they've left the office:

Leadership Team Meetings
A Painting, Part 4

Taro and his instructional leader Jessica Evans are standing quietly at the back of the room, observing the teacher. They just finished walking around the classroom and looking over students' shoulders to see their work.

"What are you seeing?" whispers Taro to Jessica. "Well," she replies. "Nearly all the students answered #1 and #2 correctly, but most struggled with #3. Yet the teacher is reviewing the first two questions right now, which doesn't seem to add much value."

"Agreed," murmurs Taro. "So, what are you going to do?"

"I'm going to jump in and cue the teacher to skip ahead to #3."

"Ok," says Taro. "Let's get the action precise before you jump in. How can you give the feedback to the teacher in a way that least disrupts the class?"

They spend a few seconds rehearsing what to say. "Ready?" asks Taro. "Yes!" nods Jessica. And she starts moving toward the front of the room to get the teacher's attention.

The interaction narrated above is commonplace in Taro's school: leaders walk the school, observe, and coach together. "What's good for a teacher is good for a leader: monitor the learning side-by-side."

You saw the power of monitoring the learning in Chapter 1 on Data-Driven Instruction. Think about the impact here. Taro is not the only one monitoring the learning, and he's not just telling his school leaders what to do—they have a partner helping them get better while leading. That is the ultimate definition of a culture of practice: getting better is the norm.

Core Idea

Build a culture of practice for your leaders where getting better is the norm, not the exception.

Think back to each of the leadership team meeting vignettes in this chapter. They all follow the same steps: monitor the school, identify the highest leverage response, and commit to the actions that will make it happen.

No matter how often Taro, Tiffany, Alicia, or Amanda observe classrooms and walk around their schools on their own, they cannot see everything. The power of uniting a leadership team in this way is that you've exponentially increased what you can see and what you can do. These leaders and others like them set a process for the leadership team to identify gaps and address them quickly. If you think about it, they simply follow the same framework that you use with teachers: See It. Name It. Do It.

- **See It—Start from the Exemplar:** Before rushing to observe the "hotspots" of your school, make sure you know what the bar is. Taro starts by looking at his top teachers (or top examples from other schools): their culture routines, their student work, and everything in between. Then you can ask "What do you want to see?" You cannot find a gap until you know that answer.

- **See the Gap—Name the Pattern:** As a larger leadership team, you can look for patterns across the school depending on the needs of the school or the time of year:

  ○ **Data-driven instruction:** quality of student work and weekly data meetings

  ○ **Planning:** quality of lesson plans and execution of the plans

  ○ **Feedback:** quality of instructional leader coaching sessions

  ○ **Culture:** quality of student culture in each classroom or whole school routines

  ○ **PD:** quality of grade-level meetings or schoolwide PD

- **Name the Response:** Agree on the highest leverage action steps to close the gaps.

- **Do It:** Practice the gaps you see right away—while walking the school or during the next leadership team meeting.

LEAD EFFECTIVE LEADERSHIP MEETINGS

Leadership Team Meetings
Completing the Painting

"Ok," affirms Tiffany, "let's review. We know our focus area, and we've changed our observation schedule to monitor more closely. Let's plan out the week. What should we do at our next faculty PD to help close this gap? And what should we do at the Wednesday Practice Clinic for those teachers who need some extra at-bats?"

One leader starts by recommending "Let's give them a model of what effective feedback looks like during Academic Monitoring. I'll pull up a video to use and plan the meeting."

"Great," responds Tiffany. "Miller, can you plan the practice clinic?"

"Sure."

"Ok" says Tiffany. "Will you lead the clinic and I'll take the PD?"

"Sounds good," she replies. They proceed to finish the plans in the remaining time.

When I first asked Tiffany the keys to her success, her answer was immediate. "We were heavily focused on observation and feedback, making sure we observe what we expect. But the key was that it wasn't 'I' but 'we'—every member of the team was doing the same." When I asked her about the consistency and frequency, she was clear. "We design the time to make it happen. It's a non-negotiable shared commitment."

What is so striking is how infrequently I get that sort of answer. It is hard to maintain consistency of observation, feedback, and coaching. That's where Tiffany leans on her leadership team meeting. "It's all right there. If we plan it together, we can hold each other to it." The weekly leadership team meeting is the glue that keeps everything in place: your observations, your coaching, your data, and your culture.

> **Core Idea**
>
> Weekly leadership team meetings can be the glue that keeps everything in place.

Common Errors of Leadership Team Meetings

Of course, not every leadership team meeting is as successful as Tiffany's, Alicia's, Amanda's, and Taro's. The following actions do *not* meet the goal of enhancing the quality of instruction. Ask yourself if any of these errors are present in your own leadership team meetings:

➤ **More announcements than instruction:** Peruse the agenda for your leadership team meeting. How many items on the list are directly connected to student learning and teacher development? More importantly, how much time do those announcements and logistics take up of the actual meeting? Honing instructional leadership takes time, and it requires prioritizing.

➤ **More reading about leadership than doing:** Another trend in leadership team meetings is a book club or reading articles about leadership. If all you do is read this book, I can pretty much guarantee it will have little impact. What changes outcomes is persistent practice: putting the agreed upon responses into action to close gaps. This is beyond leaders sharing their big takeaways from reading: it means role playing or acting on the spot.

> **Core Idea**
>
> What changes outcomes is consistent, targeted practice.

➤ **More opinion than evidence:** Now look more closely at the agenda items that are centered around teachers. How often are leaders sharing opinions about teachers' development without evidence? There is a real danger to a principal simply listening to an instructional leader talk about a teacher's development. First, you are assuming that the leader has been observing regularly (if not, they could hold an opinion based on one observation of the teacher from more than a month ago).

Second, you assume they are correct in what the teacher is struggling with (but we know how hard it is to select the right action step, as seen in Chapter 3!). Third, you are assuming that their feedback to the teacher is fine, and the issue is simply the teacher's lack of following the leader's advice. You cannot have a real conversation without an observation tracker that lists the frequency of observations and nature of action steps and without having evidence of the nature of their feedback meetings. None of those are addressed by simply listening to leaders share interpretations and opinions.

➤ **Walkthroughs/observations without feedback:** Consistent walkthroughs or observations are a step better than simply sharing opinions about teachers: at least you can observe together and discuss what would be the best action step to focus on for the teacher's immediate development. But if we use these as our only tools for developing leadership we are still missing two of the four key components of observation and feedback: giving effective feedback and holding teachers accountable to that feedback. Walkthroughs can have their place in leadership team development but only when explicitly connected to feedback and follow through.

Core Idea

Talking about teaching is not enough.
You need consistent feedback and follow through.

Stop & Jot

What are the most common errors we make in our own leadership team meetings that we want to eliminate to become more effective?

_____

_____

_____

_____

_____

_____

Redefine the Agenda

What makes a leadership team the glue to a school is the content and the protocol. "The agenda drives the day," Tiffany underscores. "If the agenda is focused on effective instructional leadership, effective instructional leadership will be the outcome." What's critical during your leadership meeting isn't just *what* you spend time focusing on, but *how* you cover it. You've already learned the protocol in every chapter:

➤ **See the exemplar/model:** Start by establishing the exemplar: What do you want to see?

➤ **See the gap:** Look at the patterns across teachers/student works: Where are the biggest gaps to close?

➤ **Name It:** Select the actions to close the gaps

➤ **Do It:** Plan the schedule and plan/practice the actions that will close those gaps

---

Core Idea

What makes your meeting powerful isn't just *what* you cover;
it's *how* you cover it.
See It. Name It. Do It.

Depending on the lever, this protocol can take different forms. Here are examples of how to implement the protocol with each leadership lever.

See It—Do It For Every Lever
Agenda Frameworks for Leadership Team Meetings

Lever	See It—Model and Gap	Do It
Data-Driven Instruction	• Look at student work from weekly data meetings or reteach lessons • Analyze data from the last round of interim assessments • Observe weekly data meeting (in person or watch video of it)	• Plan and practice the weekly data meeting the leader will have with each grade-level team • Set the schedule to observe re-teach lessons and upcoming weekly data meetings

Lever	See It—Model and Gap	Do It
Planning	• Stack Audit: review a stack of teacher lesson plans from that day: what are the patterns of strengths and areas of growth? • Observe with lesson plans in hand: what are the patterns in execution of the lesson plans? • Review a leader's feedback to a teacher's curriculum or lesson plan. Is it the right feedback? Do teachers seem to be implementing the feedback?	• Plan and practice leading a weekly planning meeting • Monitor the learning with lesson plans in hand
Observation and Feedback	• Review the observation tracker: What are the patterns across the staff? Which teachers need extra support? Where are leader observations falling short? • Observe teachers: do the action steps in the tracker match the teaching? • Observe the feedback (in meetings or real time): How well is the leader implementing feedback?	• Plan and practice feedback meeting • Plan and practice real-time feedback • Practice observing and identifying the highest leverage action steps for teachers
Leading PD	• Identify the gaps via any other lever above • Observe a leader's PD session (in person or watch video of it): where can they improve in their planning and delivery?	• Plan and practice delivering PD that closes a gap

Lever	See It—Model and Gap	Do It
Student Culture	• Observe student culture in action (in classrooms or whole-class moments): what are the patterns or gaps in teacher actions?	• Plan and practice a whole-school roll-out or reset • Plan and practice a rehearsal/practice clinic with teachers • Plan and practice real-time feedback for culture

Here is an example of what a leadership team meeting agenda could look like. This is adapted from Jeannine Zitta (you can read more about her leadership in *The Principal Manager's Guide to Leverage Leadership*[3]):

Weekly Instructional Leadership Team Meeting:
Sample Agenda—60 minutes

Agenda

- **Review of Action Steps from Prior Week (3–4 minutes)**

- **Celebrations (2–3 minutes)**
  - Each leader will share out one thing they are most proud of from the week.
    - *Exemplary action:* link the celebration to the school's mission, vision, and values

- **Action Step Audit and Coaching Cycle Review (~30 minutes)**
  - Pull up Get Better Faster Tracker: review quality of action steps and teacher implementation
    - *Exemplary action:* instructional leader will review there data in advance of the meeting to focus the conversation on the gaps in action steps, quality of teaching and learning, frequency, and timing of walkthroughs, etc.
  - Each team member will name the patterns they see and the highest leverage gaps to close
  - Name the key lever(s) to use: feedback meetings, real-time feedback, practice clinic, faculty PD, and/or intervention plan

- **Plan and Practice (~20 minutes)**
  - ○ Plan the action that each leader will take (from above list)
  - ○ Practice either hot seat (one person practices and all others give feedback) or in pairs
- **Follow-up (~5 minutes)**
  - ○ Determine a focus "look for," as applicable
  - ○ Team members will adjust individual schedules to focus on these action steps
  - ○ Determine owners, deliverables, and deadlines for all group tasks (PD planning, practice clinic leadership, etc.)

Take a look back on each leader we highlighted in this book. Nearly all of them utilized their leadership team to accelerate the implementation of the levers of leadership. You can, too. And it's quite simple—leverage your tools. Haven't tried it in the LL App yet? Try it now.

Stop & Do

LL App

Click on the option for planning your training of instructional leaders. The App will guide you through selecting an objective and then providing you the resources to lead the PD.

Resources you can generate
Direct identification of videos of leaders in action (right from this book)
Agenda and script for your training of the leadership team
Clear guidelines of how to lead practice

Instructional Leadership Team Meetings (ILT)

Monitoring and Coaching Implementation of the Leadership Levers

Goal	Meeting Purpose
	• Identify schoolwide trends in culture or learning and practice the action steps that will address them.
Prepare	**Prepare**
	Tools in hand: • Leader: leadership calendar, exemplars for sparring • Team: current action plan/playbook, monitoring tools, follow up from recent coaching (sent in advance) **Prepare:** • Identify key data to review and analyze: ○ culture tracker, teacher coaching tracker, student mastery report, meeting debriefs, etc. • Create/acquire needed models or exemplars
See It. Name It. (15–25 minutes, or 50 minutes with walkthrough)	**Analyze and name shared trends in culture or rigor**
	See the success: • Build continuity: celebrate growth based on ILT goals set last week: ○ "What are specific teacher/student bright spots connected to our school wide goals?" ○ "What made us successful here? What leader actions led to those bright spots?" **See the model and the gap:** • Narrow the focus: ○ "Let's return our focus to our priority/action step from last meeting. . . ." <u>or</u> ○ "Let's focus on the upcoming priority from our playbook/calendar. . . ."

- Observe the exemplars:
  - Model <u>or</u> walkthrough the school <u>or</u> review teacher artifacts/student work <u>or</u> assign as pre-work
  - "What is happening with our exemplars that are making them successful?"
- Identify the gaps:
  - "What are the gaps in what we planned for and what we are seeing in teacher/student work?"
  - "What are the top trends: what are the highest priority gaps?"
  - "What is causing these gaps? ID the student and teacher actions leading to the gap. Be ready to spar and strengthen our analysis."

Name the action step:

- "Here is the student/teacher action step. What resonates? What would you add?"
- Follow up: "What are the most important actions we should take next week to close these gaps?"

  (Utilize examples of potential actions to spur thinking):
  - Practice clinics for Get Better Faster culture or rigor action steps
  - Real-time feedback on Get Better Faster culture or rigor action steps
  - Weekly data meetings or weekly planning meetings: adjust to focus on these teacher action steps
  - Culture action steps: whole class or whole school resets
  - Learning action steps: student work audits

Stamp it (3 minutes)

- "Write down your final action steps into your playbook/calendar and when you will do them."

(Continued)

Do It. (20 minutes)	Practice the Meeting: Weekly Data Meetings, Planning Meetings, Feedback, Practice Clinics, etc.

	Frame:
	• Name key things to remember before practice (e.g., "Remember to model the thinking, not just actions")
	
	Option 1: Practice upcoming coaching meetings with partner (WDM, WPM, Feedback, PD) (20 minutes)
	• Individual: pull up and rehearse/finalize script (3 minutes)
	  ○ Revise meeting to target whole school trends mentioned in first part of meeting
	• Practice most important part of the meeting (3 minutes)
	  ○ Option 1: Hot Seat (everyone watches one practice to learn from it)
	  ○ Option 2: Pair up so everyone practices
	• Feedback with cheat sheet (2 minutes)
	  ○ Review cheat sheet independently (30 seconds)
	  ○ Give feedback (1:30 minutes)
	• Re-do & final feedback (2 minutes)
	• Round 2: Hot Seat #2 or partner 2 goes (10 minutes)
	
	Option 2: Plan: Revise coaching meeting plans based on named action steps (20 minutes)
	• Revise scripts based on schoolwide action steps (8 minutes)
	  ○ Revise the See It. Name It. Do It. of their WDM, WPM, feedback, or PD to target school action step
	• Trade with partner, review, and give feedback (9 minutes)
	• Stamp final takeaways as a group (3 minutes)
	
	Option 3: Problem solve: Small group problem solving protocol (20 minutes)
	• Small group or whole group: IL shares what was tried/shares their action step/their follow up (3 minutes)
	• Q&A (2 minutes)
	• Brainstorm new solutions (5 minutes)
	  ○ IL revises plan with the whole team
	• Repeat with second leader

Everything Else (If needed: 10–20 minutes)	Plan and Practice for Key School Initiatives and Events

	Present a Model:
	
	 • Present minute-by-minute plan, session plan, or live model
	     ◦ Key events: report card conferences, parent orientation, gradebooks, DEI session, etc.
	     ◦ Additional leadership skills (trust generators, accountability conversations etc.)
	     ◦ Key rollouts (state testing, small group tutoring, etc.)
	     ◦ Whole school culture adjustments
	 • Ask clarifying question
	 • Stamp key elements to highlight
	 • Plan or practice (as needed)

Follow-up: Lock It In (5–15 minutes)	Confirm the follow-up plan and plan for monitoring

	Name key deliverables and dates: (5 minutes)
	
	 • 100% of leadership team members calendar action items, or establish a timeline to complete calendars
	     ◦ Co-observe classrooms and debrief
	     ◦ Observe or co-lead meetings and debrief
	     ◦ Real-time coach
	     ◦ Co-plan meetings
	     ◦ Provide additional resources
	
	 Revise IL schedule/playbook (5 minutes):
	
	 • "Pull out your playbook. Given what we discussed today, how will you adjust how you spend your time?"
	     ◦ When/how you will monitor instruction and student work
	     ◦ Real-time feedback needed in key classrooms
	     ◦ Additional meetings or practice clinics with teachers
	 • (If time) Peer feedback: "Read your partner's follow-up plan. What would you add/edit/change?"

TURNAROUND

In turnaround, with so many fires to fight, it can be tempting to focus on the rest of the school and wait on the leadership team. Yet you won't get very far without them. Kim Tymkowych notes: "For the leadership team, peer-to-peer doing and feedback is what matters. That's where the change happens." She also found she had to get them to believe what was possible, so they would start every observation by visiting bright spot classrooms. She noted what they saw, adding on when needed, and was immediately able to pivot to "how do we get our other classrooms to look like this one?" Then they would observe each other, and that raised accountability and commitment to common expectations.

We noted in Chapter 6 that Amaya creatively put term limits on leadership team participants to be able to fill it with people who were hungry to grow. The school leaped forward.

CONCLUSION

As we've shown throughout this text, a single leader can accomplish a lot. But schools like Whittier fly even higher when the whole leadership team is in formation. Get everyone in the right place at the right time, and together you can scale incredible distances in even the most challenging conditions. It's a lot easier to fly with a team than on your own.

Four Keys to Leadership Team Development:

➤ **Choose Your Team:** Identify instructional leaders.

➤ **Train Your Team—Roll Out the Vision:** Build your team's schedule, train them in Leverage Leadership, and equip them with the right tools

➤ **Monitor the School:** Start from the exemplar, see the gap, and take action

➤ **Lead Effective Leadership Team Meetings:** Find the patterns and take the actions to address them

---

Sample Instructional Leadership Rubric—Advanced Column

Category	Evidence of Advanced Implementation
Data-Driven Instruction	• **Assessment:** create, improve, or maintain high-quality, in-class assessments that are aligned to end-goal assessment, curriculum, college readiness, and cumulative (keep spiraling previous content) • **Analysis:** establish timely and robust systems to collect student work and analyze it • **Action:** ensure that analysis translates to long-term (6+ week) action plans and daily reteaching to improve student achievement via academic monitoring, activating knowledge, modeling, and discourse • **Data Meetings:** teachers receive active support in DDI via consistent data meetings
Planning	• **Units/Lessons:** ensure lessons are aligned to the rigor of end-goal assessments • **Anticipate. Activate. Adjust:** ensure teachers effectively adjust lesson plans to meet the learning needs of the students while also maintaining alignment to the end-goal assessments • **Content Knowledge:** PD and coaching meetings (planning meetings, etc.) build sufficient content knowledge for the teacher to teach the lessons at the rigor of the end-goal assessment
Observation & Feedback	• **Consistency:** ensure consistent coaching of teachers: both observation and coaching meetings (either observation/feedback meetings, practice clinics, week y data meetings, and/or weekly planning meetings) • **Time Management and Follow-through:** implement effective time and task management tools that guarantee follow through on each action
Results: Effectiveness of Coaching	• Teachers see gains in student achievement over the course of the year

Note: The complete Leverage Leadership Implementation Rubric can be found on the Leverage Leadership App.

Action Steps for Principals

Managing Leadership Teams

LEVER	MANAGING LEADERSHIP TEAMS—KEY ACTIONS IN SEQUENCE
Managing Leadership Teams	**Plan**
	1. **Create a distribution of leadership and individual leader schedules** • ID the responsibilities for each team member: instruction, culture, and (when needed) operations • Assign teachers, subjects, or grade levels to specific instructional leaders that have expertise • Build weekly schedules for each instructional lead that lock in observations, coaching meetings, preparation time, and leadership team meetings • Adjust schedule to provide time for collaborative planning time to prepare for all meetings 2. **Name the key behaviors and values for the leadership team:** • Develop leadership team values [See Staff Culture for details] with explicit exemplary behaviors and counter-example behaviors to make the values explicit for strong teamwork (on time and fully present, prepared and engaged, united ownership of every decision, etc.) 3. **Create protocols for effective Instructional Leadership Team (ILT) meetings** • Develop agendas to enable leaders to share data, share initiatives, and get feedback. 4. **Create a yearly calendar of ILT and PD** • Set clear priorities for each quarter of the school year (e.g., Academic Monitoring in Quarter 2) • Create scope and sequence for ILT meetings and PD (for staff and for instructional leaders) aligned to key actions each quarter

	5. **Develop tools and systems to ensure accountability**
Managing Leadership Teams (cont'd)	• Develop methods to track all action steps and follow up from meetings
	Roll Out
	6. **Roll out your values to the ILT**
	• See the exemplar: tell powerful stories of the leaders that make the values visible
	• See the gap: give examples of unproductive behaviors and how they are not aligned to the values
	• Do It: practice implementing those values collectively
	7. **Train instructional leaders on the levers of leadership:**
	• Lead PD for the ILT: coaching meetings (observation and feedback, planning, data), observations (identifying the action step, real-time feedback and monitoring the learning), PD (leading practice clinics and PD), and leadership (accountability conversations, utilizing leadership tools/trackers)
	Execute
	Lead Effective Instructional Leadership Team (ILT) Meetings:
	8. **See It:**
	• See the success: celebrations are named, attached to leader actions, and quantified and data-based
	• Be the model: Provide live models of effective leadership to push your leaders' development
	• See the gap: identify student, teacher, and leader gaps where implementation goals are falling short
	9. **Name It—name the key actions to take**
	• Name a key action from this Leverage Leadership sequence of action steps

Managing Leadership Teams (cont'd)	10. **Do It—plan/practice upcoming actions**
	   • Plan and practice upcoming coaching meetings, PD sessions, or practice clinics
	   • Determine weekly goals, additional coaching actions, and observation/feedback responsibilities
	   • Calendarize and track every action item
	
	11. **Pacing—lead efficient meetings**
	   • Utilize economy of language and precise what-to-do instructions
	   • Effectively manage time so that each leader leaves with a completed, practiced coaching meeting plan

	Monitor

	12. **Observe and give feedback to ILs on their implementation**
	   • Observe and give feedback on observations, real-time feedback, weekly data/planning meetings, etc.
	   • Co-lead a meeting with an IL that needs more support
	
	13. **Identify and invest in rising leaders**
	   • Find rising leaders and create a trajectory of short-term and long-term development

Pulling the Lever

Action Planning Worksheet for MANAGING LEADERSHIP TEAMS

Self-Assessment

- Evaluate each of the members of your leadership team on the instructional leader rubric: What is the average percent proficient for your team? ___ %

- What are the biggest gaps for your leadership team based on the rubric? Of those gaps, which is the highest leverage to address first? (Remember: start with the super-levers of data-driven instruction and student culture, then move to observation/feedback, then all the rest.)

_____

_____

_____

Planning for Action

- What tools from this book will you use to improve leadership teams at your school? Check all that you will use (you can find all in the LL App):

  ___ **Instructional Leadership Team (ILT) Meeting One-Pager**

  ___ **Leverage Leadership Implementation Rubric**

  ___ **Observation and Feedback One-Pager**

  ___ **Leading Weekly Planning Meetings One-Pager**

  ___ **Leading Weekly Data Meetings One-Pager**

- What are your next steps for developing your leadership team?

Action:	Date:

Part **III**

Making It Happen

Chapter 8

Finding the Time

One-On-One

Getting Ready for the School Day

It's 7:15 AM on a Friday morning, and students are about to start arriving at the Albany School of the Humanities. Principal Marie Culihan sits in her office in front of her laptop, finalizing the preparation for her fourth-grade Weekly Data Meeting that will happen later that morning. On her walls you see Know-Show Charts from previous planning and data meetings, as well as a data report from the latest assessment. You also see appreciation notes and warm photos of the students and staff.

What is striking is what Marie is *not* doing. She is not checking to make sure breakfasts have been put out for students upon their arrival and confirming coverage for a sick teacher—the home school coordinator is doing that. She is not walking the halls to make sure every teacher is at their post ready to start the day, and she is not yet at the front door to greet the earliest arriver—her assistant principal is doing that.

Instead, Marie is putting the final touches on what the teachers will practice in the reteach lesson. At that point, she hears a gentle knock on her open door. It is her secretary. "Students are starting to arrive," the secretary says gently. "Do you need a few more minutes, or are you ready?"

Marie smiles. "I'm ready." She grabs her observation schedule rainbow guide (her spiral bound copy of all the *Leverage Leadership* one-pagers and the Get Better Faster sequence and heads out the door—she won't be back in her office for quite some time.

Marie's story at the Albany School of the Humanities is nothing short of remarkable. Before and right after the pandemic, less than a third of students were proficient in Math and ELA. Since then, the school made 30+ point gains in ELA and 40+ point gains in Math, far outpacing their peers in New York state and earning the National ESEA Distinguished School Award.

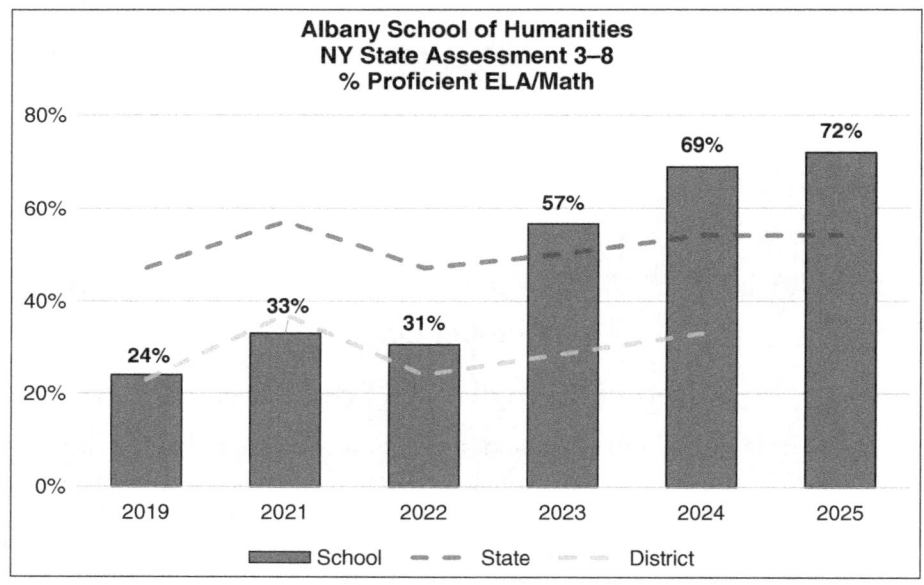

How did she do it all? "Preparation," she replies readily. "Consistency matters most, and preparation is 90% of the pathway to consistency. Once I've done that, I just stick to my playbook—and the waterfall," she says smiling, referring to the nickname for the Get Better Faster Sequence of Action Steps for teachers. Katie Harshman (from Chapter 3) agrees: "The more prepared you are, the more quickly everything goes." Follow the levers, she shares, and results will come.

In 1996, Kim Marshall wrote a powerfully accurate critique of the lives of most principals in which he diagnosed the overwhelming majority of school leaders—including, formerly, himself—with "Hyperactive Superficial Principal Syndrome."[1] Unfortunately, not much has changed since Kim coined the term. Principals are continually bombarded by students, parents, staff, and the mini crises that occur every day. Because of this, a principal can invest a tremendous number of hours—and heart and soul—into the work of the school without even stepping foot into a classroom. Is the intensity and nature of the job too difficult to overcome?

Marie offers an emphatic "No" to that question, and so does every other leader you've met in this book. And they have the systems to back it up. Many principals believe they don't have control over their time, but in reality, your time—not parents, not staff, not regulations—is the one thing you and every principal *can* control. School leadership is not easy—it is very, very hard. But the leaders in the book show us one thing: they were relentless about how they used their time—and that made all the difference.

Core Idea

So many principals believe they don't have control over their time.
In reality, your time is the one thing you *can* control.

Controlling your time doesn't mean you can stop your district from adding meetings you must attend or you can avoid the fight that will occasionally break out in the cafeteria (even though your good work on Student Culture will certainly limit the frequency of these occurrences!). You won't pretend these things won't happen; rather, you build a schedule that *anticipates* them and is flexible enough to adjust to what comes.

Although many have written about school leadership, few have offered a concrete path of how to put all the pieces together on a daily, weekly, and monthly basis. This is a serious mistake. Ultimately, even the best solutions are meaningless if you cannot feasibly put them into place.

So, how does this apply to you? Your school, like any other, is unique: you have your own strengths and challenges, be it the size of your staff, the number of additional instructional leaders, or the particular needs of your students. Yet over and over again, the number one factor that highly successful leaders have that others don't is consistency. Simply put, excellence cannot exist without consistency.

> ## Core Idea
> Excellence cannot exist without consistency.

In the pages that follow, you'll see that consistency (and time management) isn't about being so rigid you can't meet the ever-shifting needs of your teachers, your students, their families, or any of the other dynamic elements of your school's community. On the contrary, it's about putting systems in place and consistently using them to meet the most important of those needs first.

To make this feasible, this chapter offers a pathway for putting the vision we've outlined into practice:

➤ Identify and stop your "leaks" (Where does my time go? And how can I change that?)

➤ Protect Your Time

➤ Build Your Weekly Schedule

➤ Plan Backward—A Yearly Calendar

➤ Manage Your Tasks

IDENTIFY YOUR "LEAKS"

If time is a leader's most precious resource, then it is not enough to know how it should be spent; leaders also need to know how to prevent the pitfalls: how might a principal lose control of his or her calendar? Look at the following case study of a well-intentioned principal.

———————————————●———————————————

Defending Time Case Study
The Well-Intentioned Firefighter

Mr. Reynolds wants to transform his school, to conduct weekly observations, analyze data, and forge a strong student culture. Today, he hopes to conduct a schoolwide culture walkthrough, observe three teachers, and finish analyzing the first math interim assessment. After getting to school early to prepare for the day, he already has six text messages about sick teachers, an angry parent, and a bathroom not functioning. He abandons preparation work and responds to these until 7:30 AM, when he walks downstairs to the cafeteria to monitor breakfast and deliver morning announcements.

When he returns to his office, he sees 25 emails in his inbox and immediately starts to respond. As he works, a secretary shares the four phone calls he's received: two vendor requests and a call from a central office staff member. She also mentions the need to update a social media post about the field trip that has the wrong time. After calling each party back and correcting social media, Reynolds returns to his inbox, continuing to write. After two hours, he still has not watched a single teacher, analyzed a single data point, or observed classroom culture.

By the day's end, things are only marginally better. Reynolds's inbox is empty, he was able to monitor lunch and dismissal, and all phone requests have been dealt with. Yet Reynolds never stepped into the classrooms to observe or support his teachers.

If a school leader's main role is to drive student learning, then Reynolds did not do his job today. Despite his best intentions, he is playing whack-a-mole.

> ### Core Idea
> A well-intentioned firefighter is still not an instructional leader.

Have you felt like Mr. Reynolds? Have you felt time slip by and you don't know where it went? Welcome to the world of a school leader. You have countless colleagues who share this challenge with you—including Marie! The problem is not the challenge; it is what we do with it. But you cannot tackle the challenge until you identify it.

> ### Core Idea
> You cannot tackle the challenge until you identify it.

In working with thousands of leaders over the past few decades, we have created a Leverage Leadership Consistency Scorecard to help leaders identify their strengths and weaknesses. I have attached it here. Before you keep reading, stop and do the scorecard—it will make everything come more alive. Be honest: don't fill it out only thinking of your best week—think of a typical week.

Stop & Do

Leverage Leadership
Consistency Scorecard

4 = Exemplary implementation (90% of the time)
3 = Proficient implementation (75% of the time)
2 = Beginning implementation (half the time)
1 = Little/No implementation (less that half time)

Consistency	Team	Self
1. **Consistency of Coaching Teachers:** ensure consistent coaching of teachers: both observation and coaching meetings (either obs/feedback, practice clinics, weekly data meetings, and/or weekly planning meetings)	__4	__4
2. **Consistency of Coaching Leaders:** ensure consistent coaching of leaders to meet their own goals for their leadership development		__4
3. **Time Management and Follow-through:** implement effective time and task management tools that allow me and my team to follow through on our own tasks and those we coach	__4	__4
4. **Effective Whole-School Coaching & Resources:** consistently lead professional development and practice clinics that effectively close schoolwide gaps and ensure that teachers and leaders feel that they have the resources they need to be effective	__4	__4

What are my strengths in consistency?

_____

_____

_____

What are my top growth areas in consistency?

_____

_____

_____

_____

Now let's go a little deeper—where does it break down? We surveyed numerous leaders in our Leverage Leadership family and asked them the top things that break down during the school day and outside the school day that keep them from being consistent instructional leaders. We have shared these things below. Take the following survey and evaluate yourself—where are your breakdowns?

Stop & Jot
Consistency—Root Cause Analysis

During the School Day—Where Does it Break Down?
(Rating Scale: 1 (Rarely) to 5 (Frequently))

Star or circle your key areas of growth—as many as you'd like!:

- **Getting things done:**
  - Frequent interruptions and unexpected tasks disrupting the schedule.
  - Time wastage and inefficiencies in meetings and task execution.
  - Conflicts in managing and scheduling direct reports.
  - Over-scheduling and unrealistic time allocations for tasks.
  - Ineffective classroom observation scheduling and follow-up.
  - Lack of uninterrupted work time for strategic planning and tasks.
  - Poor use of energy peaks and troughs for scheduling high-energy tasks.
- **Follow-up:**
  - Timelines of follow-ups after meetings or assignments.
  - Thoroughness and clarity of follow-up communications.
  - Impact of follow-ups on achieving desired outcomes.
  - Accountability and tracking of follow-up actions.

Outside the School Day—Where Does it Break Down?
(Rating Scale: 1 (Rarely) to 5 (Frequently))

- **Physical/Mental Health:**
  - Lack of physical activity or exercise or hobbies/activities that energize you
  - Irregular mealtimes or healthy food

- Lack of sufficient sleep (signs: fatigued throughout the day; unable to maintain energy)
- Excessive time spent on social media and other non-productive activities.
- Lack of time for the spiritual/reflective/meditation/reading/quiet time
- **Social/Family:**
  - Frequency of conflicts between personal and professional responsibilities.
  - Lack of support systems in place (e.g., childcare, home responsibilities, etc.)

Reflections—where does it break down?

_____

_____

_____

_____

STOP YOUR "LEAKS"—BUILD NEW HABITS

Lofty goals and desires don't change our habits (this is why New Year's resolutions fail far more often than they succeed). Rather, you need to build new habits strategically. Here's what it looks like when Marie solved a problem by developing a new habit.

During the summer before school opened, Marie's office staff shared a concern. They often felt out of the loop because of how frequently she was in classrooms or circulating in the building. They wanted to be able to serve staff and families well, but they didn't always know what was happening across the school each day.

Instead of trying to "be more available" in vague ways, Marie built a habit. Together, they created a simple five-minute daily meeting from 7:25 to 7:30 every morning. In that brief window, they reviewed her schedule, the building schedule, and any key events or needs for the day. What happened next was striking: radio calls dropped, interruptions decreased, and the entire front office began to operate as a more cohesive, confident team.

For those who have read James Clear's work, you'll see parallels to Marie's new habit. Clear crystallized a lot of the thinking about what it takes to let go of unhelpful habits in his groundbreaking book *Atomic Habits*.[2] One of the most important points of the book is that you don't rise to the level of your goals. Rather, you fall to the level of your systems.

> ## Core Idea
>
> You do not rise to the level of your goals.
> You fall to the level of your systems.
> —James Clear

Marie needed a new system to develop a new habit with her staff. That started with understanding what it takes to build one. Clear points out four keys (which I have simplified slightly for ease of understanding for those who haven't read his full book):

- **Make it easy and obvious:**
  - Write a plan: "I will [BEHAVIOR] at [TIME] in [LOCATION]
  - Create the right environment: link habit to a place, make it visible, reduce negative cues
  - Stack habits: "After [CURRENT HABIT], I will [NEW HABIT]." Reduce friction for good habits
- **Build incentives and accountability:**
  - Bundle it: Pair an action you want to do with an action you need to do
  - Track it visually as motivation—habit trackers
  - Accountability partner: who will hold you to it?

If you look back at Marie's experience, you can see each of these principles at work. She made the new habit easy and obvious: every day at 7:25, in the main office, she and her team gather for a five-minute rundown. By tying the behavior to a specific time and place, she created an environment that cued the habit automatically. She stacked it onto an existing routine—the moment before the school day formally begins—reducing friction and ensuring it would happen without fail.

And because her entire office staff participates, the team itself became her accountability partner—everyone expects and prepares for the meeting they requested. Over time, that simple structure hardened into a reliable habit that keeps the whole front office aligned and informed.

Marie didn't just schedule a meeting; she built a system that made the right habit the easy habit. And that's the heart of habit formation for leaders: when you design the routine well, the routine does the heavy lifting.

So, how can you apply it to your own context? Let's walk you through the actions that Marie takes to solidify her habits. It starts by protecting your time. And you do that by empowering your team.

PROTECT YOUR TIME

Schools, as principals know all too well, are about far more than learning: communications, technology, compliance, food service, transportation, safety inspections—the list goes on and on. The first step is to recognize that your role is just as critical as the quarterback in football. So, build up the team around you to be the offensive line (for non-football junkies, that just means people to protect you!). Your team can be larger than you realize:

Add a New Special Assistant—Your Leverage Leadership App

Go back to the chapter on the AI Primer: the Leverage Leadership App can be your new special assistant—it's like having a new hire in your front line of defense. Once you get used to it, you can follow the path of countless leaders who have reduced their administrative burden by 50%, 70% or more. You can use it to:

- Build your task list and calendar (when to get things done)
- Plan all your coaching meetings and faculty PD
- Prepare communications
- Generate reports
- Unpack data more quickly

And for burdensome administrative tasks, you can prompt it or any AI the same way. Remember your framework:

- **Me:** Tell AI who you are and your context
- **You:** Tell AI who you want them to be (their role)
- **What:** What to do
- **How:** How to do it
- **Personal Touch:** Revise the final product to match your needs.

Stop: don't discard this recommendation. This is like adding a staff member without any impact on your budget. Not using it is like not using a staff member you have hired. Save multiple hours very quickly.

Appoint an Operations Leader

Managing your facility and the systems that keep it running bleeds time. An ideal solution is the designation of an operations leadership position as a single point of contact to address these tasks. Whether the person is an assistant principal, a dean, or even a secretary, this leader is in charge of managing each of the operation systems. Marie did this herself. "My home school coordinator was very talented and under-utilized, so I started giving her different operations tasks around the building, and she did it better than anyone! It freed me up and gave her a valuable role." Beyond saving time, there is a more subtle advantage to creating an operations leader: specialization. The skills of operations are far different than instructional leadership. Splitting the roles allows a principal to specialize in what matters most—culture and instruction—and someone else can get good at the rest.

If a single operations leader cannot be assigned, an alternative solution is an operations team made up of teachers, office managers, assistant principals, or others. Each member of the operations team would be assigned a set area of operations; for example, a veteran teacher might be responsible for all field trip logistics, while a head custodian might be responsible for building logistics. To facilitate this process, school leaders must meet with the operations team at the start of the year to record every major operations event (for example, closing down the school for winter break) and then assigning an "owner" to it. To streamline even further, make sure the team has a leader and it isn't you!

Shutting the School Down for the Holidays
Sample Operations Plan

Task	Who Owns It	Complete By
Turn off boiler	Jane	12/15
Monitor dismissal	Cassandra	12/15
Call lunch delivery to cancel	Jake	12/16
"Deep Clean" of all desks and hallways	Amari	12/17
Create flyer to send home with students	Carla	12/17

Designate Who to Go to For What

One of the best ways to protect your time is to stop the need for staff to come to you with everything. Marie created a simple guide: "Whom to Go to for What." And her name was never first on the list. The mantra is clearly stated at the top, "Three before Marie."

Whom to Go to for What
Three Before Marie. . .

 **Albany School of Humanities**
Got a question?? Here is who to go to...
Three Before Marie

Curriculum/Instruction	Kelly - Instructional Coach
Social-Emotional Behavior (RULER)	Erin, Amber
Maintenance Concerns	Shaliem
Attendance Concerns	Tara, Susannah
Med Concerns/Needs	Sally, Debbie
Buses	Tara, Sabrina
Tech Needs	Caroline
Union-APSTA	Maureen, Sean
Behavior Plans/External Counseling	Erin, Adam, Amber
School-Tool	Sabrina
MTSS	Adam
Class Dojo	Jen

"It was powerful," Marie shares. "People started realizing that they could lean on each other, and I had a tool to point them toward rather than trying to solve every problem in the moment. And they saw the impact in me observing and coaching them more frequently. It was a win-win for everyone."[3]

Pick your Hound

When you think of a person who could be described as a hound, you imagine someone who pesters and cajoles someone to do something. That is precisely what you need as a principal—someone to hold you accountable to your time.

Rick Romain (from the Introduction) knew that he struggled with time management on his own. So, he turned it over to his secretary Donna Fleischman. "I told her the vision for my schedule," Rick shares, "including how much I wanted to observe and what meetings were essential. Then she became the master of it. She moved things around, set up ad hoc meetings. And I gave her the authority to hold me to it. It was one of the best decisions of my career."

Your "hound" has to be someone who you will listen to when they tell you that you aren't following your schedule, someone with the courage to act even if that means pulling you out of your office and sending you out to observe. They don't need a title (they are often like Rick's secretary!). All they need to know are your priorities and your agreed-upon schedule; where and how to redirect interruptions; and (most importantly), your commitment. You have to give them permission to hold you accountable, or it won't work. "Without Donna [Rick's secretary] playing this role," confirms Rick, "we don't get the results. Period."

So, what sort of schedule should they hold you to? Read on.

BUILD YOUR WEEKLY SCHEDULE

Every leader we have highlighted in this book shares something in common: they are relentless about how they schedule their time. Without a schedule that makes time for the most important actions you can take to fuel your school's growth, you're not building skyscrapers—you're fighting fires.

Core Idea

Without a high-leverage schedule, you're not building skyscrapers—you're fighting fires.

Marie's weekly schedule is sacred. "This is my go-to: I do not waver from it," she comments. So, how can we replicate her schedule? By learning from how she builds it step by step.

What does that look like? Let's try it—build your schedule right now. If you've never done this before, leave your old schedule to the side. Open up your Leverage Leadership App (LL App). Then decide to either work right in the App, or print out the weekly schedule template to do it by hand. (I still love filling it in by hand myself—with colored Post-its! So, feel free to choose.)

Pre-Work: Reflect and Distribute

The two pre-work variables that will influence your schedule are your own personal productivity (as we saw in *Atomic Habits* earlier) and how many teachers/instructional leaders you will manage directly. Take a moment and answer the following questions.

Stop & Jot

When are you most productive during the school day?

- For independent work (i.e., you can actually get something done)
- For observing classes (i.e., you don't get distracted/derailed by office work or other things)
- For meeting with teachers/teams
  - Do you like meetings back-to-back and then large chunks without meetings? Or
  - Do you prefer to take a break between meetings and spread them out more?

_____

_____

_____

_____

What is your Teacher-to-Instructional Leader ratio?

- How many teachers are in your school? _____ Teachers
- How many in your school are or could be instructional leaders? _____ FTE Leaders
  - Formal instructional leaders: asst principals, coaches, dept chairs, etc.
  - Others that could be leveraged this way: SPED Coordinators, lead teachers, etc.
- Ratio of Teachers to Leader _____ :1
  - (divide teachers by the number of total leaders—full-time equivalent):

If you are like most schools, you will have a leader-teacher ratio of 12:1 or less. That is the golden ratio: you can make the principles in this book work as is.

A Word on. . .When You Don't Have 12:1
What Do I Do Then?

Some of you might be in that small minority of schools that have larger than a 12:1 teacher-to-leader ratio. What then?

First, make sure no one else who can assist you in instructional leadership. This could include some of your strongest teachers whom you can give 1-2 teachers in exchange for a stipend or reduced responsibilities (see Chapter 7—Managing School Leadership Teams for a sample teacher schedule with instructional leadership responsibilities).

If you do that and you still have a larger ratio, then convert your whole schedule to bi-weekly. Rather than observe and meet with each teacher each week, you can double the ratio to 25:1, and observe/meet with 12 teachers one week and the remaining 13 teachers the next week. This still allows for a dramatic increase in teacher development and regular contact with each teacher.

Your next step is to distribute the teachers across your leadership team: which teachers will you manage directly and which will you delegate to others? In most cases, you should distribute teachers according to each instructional leader's strengths: their content expertise, and someone who is strong at working with novice teachers or teachers with management problems, etc. If you are leading a very large school and you have a large number of instructional leaders to lead yourself, you might decide to distribute all your teachers among them and focus on managing only the leaders.

Once you have made this choice, every other decision flows naturally. We're off! Let's take a deeper look at the way Marie builds her weekly schedule.

Step 1: Block Out Student Culture Times

As one of the super-levers, management of student culture is the most important thing to put on your schedule first. As mentioned in Chapter 5, there are a few critical moments when you have the biggest impact on student culture and when crises/challenges are most likely to happen. For every school, this is slightly different, but almost everyone would identify breakfast/arrival, lunch, and dismissal as key moments. Because these events occur at set times, they are the least flexible of the scheduling constraints and so should go first. Let's look at Marie's schedule as a guide:

Note that here Marie has left Thursday lunch free. This means that she will designate another leader to cover those moments. Remember that for a school that needs a student culture turnaround, your calendar will need to be filled with a lot more "green" to manage the challenge of making significant improvements to a struggling culture.

Step 2: Lock In Team Meetings

The next step to planning your schedule is to lock in group meetings, such as PD, staff meetings, and leadership team meetings. Be careful about too many meetings. Planning to attend all grade-level meetings every week—on top of your feedback meetings—won't work. Here's what Marie's schedule looks like:

Note the impact of distributed leadership that we mentioned back in Chapter 3 (Observation and Feedback): Marie is not leading all the grade-level planning meetings because her instructional coach Kelly is leading the other ones. "Her ability to lead the other data meetings and planning meetings is transformative: it gives me more time in classrooms and more focused work." Marie will periodically observe Kelly, but because she is not leading them every week, she keeps them off the schedule. What is on the schedule is what she must lead consistently.

Step 3: Lock In Teacher-Leader Meetings

Now it is time to add your standing individual meeting with teachers to give observational feedback, review lesson plans, and do data analysis. Marie holds these meetings

Marie Culihan's Schedule: Just Culture

DAILY SCHEDULE:		"If a school leader's main role is to drive student learning, then not observing and meeting with teachers means a leader did not do her job today. Despite the best intentions, she was only fighting fires."			
	MONDAY	TUESDAY	WEDNESDAY	THURSDAY	FRIDAY
6:30 7 AM					
:30					
8 AM	Arrival	Arrival	Arrival	Arrival	Arrival
:30					
9 AM					
:30					
10AM					
:30					
11 AM					
:30	LUNCH & Recess Check				
12 PM		LUNCH	LUNCH		
:30					LUNCH
1 PM					
:30					
2 PM					
:30	Dismissal	Dismissal	Dismissal	Dismissal	Dismissal
3 PM					
:30					
4 PM					
:30					
5 PM					

Marie Culihan's Schedule: Culture and Group Meetings

DAILY SCHEDULE:		"If a school leader's main role is to drive student learning, then not observing and meeting with teachers means a leader did not do her job today. Despite the best intentions, she was only fighting fires."			
	MONDAY	**TUESDAY**	**WEDNESDAY**	**THURSDAY**	**FRIDAY**
6:30 7 AM					
:30					
8 AM	Arrival	Arrival	Arrival	Arrival	Arrival
:30					BST Meeting
9 AM			4th Grade CPT	DISTRICT MEETING	
:30	4th Grade CPT				
10AM					
:30	1st Grade CPT				
11 AM		1st Grade CPT			
:30	LUNCH & Recess Check				
12 PM		LUNCH	LUNCH		
:30					LUNCH
1 PM					Leadership Team Meeting
:30					
2 PM					
:30	Dismissal	Dismissal	Dismissal	Dismissal	Dismissal
3 PM	Student Support Team		Faculty PD	Practice Clinic	
:30					
4 PM					
5 PM					

Marie Culihan's Schedule: Culture and All Meetings

DAILY SCHEDULE:		*"If a school leader's main role is to drive student learning, then not observing and meeting with teachers means a leader did not do her job today. Despite the best intentions, she was only fighting fires."*			
	MONDAY	TUESDAY	WEDNESDAY	THURSDAY	FRIDAY
6:30 7 AM					
:30					
8 AM	Arrival	Arrival	Arrival	Arrival	Arrival
:30				5th Grade CPT	BST Mtg
9 AM			4th Grade CPT	DISTRICT PD	
:30	4th Grade CPT	Feedback Mtg			
10AM			Attendance Meeting		
:30	1st Grade CPT				
11 AM		1st Grade CPT			
:30	LUNCH & Recess Check				Feedback Mtg
12 PM		LUNCH	LUNCH		Feedback Mtg
:30				Feedback Mtg	LUNCH
1 PM	Feedback Mtg			Feedback Mtg	Leadership Team Meeting
:30					
2 PM					
:30	Dismissal	Dismissal	Dismissal	Dismissal	Dismissal
3 PM	Student Support Team		Faculty PD	Practice Clinic	
:30					
4 PM					
:30					
5 PM					

dear because they're opportunities to dedicate focused time to whatever your teachers need most. The observation feedback you deliver to them could be guiding them in lesson planning, reteaching what the data tell you must be retaught, following up about techniques taught in PD, or perfecting student culture. In short, you can leverage one-on-one time with a teacher to coach them on any lever you need to.

Take out your school schedule and look for the prep periods of each teacher or leader you will coach. Pick a standing 30-minute window when they are not teaching. Marie locks in six teachers.

Some leaders prefer scheduling their meetings with teachers back-to-back whenever possible because that gives them longer open chunks of time to spend on other tasks. However, you may also schedule breaks between each check-in if that suits your schedule better. Remember the power of scheduling these meetings: you lock the time into the teacher's weekly plan as well, and then there is no need to chase down the teacher to find time to give him feedback! You also hold yourself accountable for observing each teacher, because you need to have observed before the feedback meeting to be able to discuss highest-leverage action steps when you get there.

Step 4: Lock In Observations

Now it is time to lock in your observations. Remember our core principle: weekly 10–15-minute observations are far more valuable than twice-yearly, full-length observations. Assuming you plan your observations back-to-back, we wouldn't recommend planning more than 3-4 observations in each hour time period: this way you schedule time to get from one classroom to the next and complete your observation tracker on the spot.

Note that Marie prefers to stack her Monday full with observations and meetings: "It gets me into the rhythm of not staying in my office, and I find it sets the habit for me for the entire week." But then she leaves more flexibility on Tuesday for whatever happens and what she couldn't get to on Monday. Also see how Marie schedules strategically to see whole grade levels or teams at a time—that allows her to draw best practices from one teacher to the next and see differences more clearly. Remember to schedule these observations strategically before your weekly meeting with each teacher, so that you have relevant observation data going into the meeting.

Marie Culihan's Schedule: Culture, Meetings and Observations

DAILY SCHEDULE:		*"If a school leader's main role is to drive student learning, then not observing and meeting with teachers means a leader did not do her job today. Despite the best intentions, she was only fighting fires."*			
	MONDAY	TUESDAY	WEDNESDAY	THURSDAY	FRIDAY
6:30 7 AM					
:30					
8 AM	Arrival	Arrival	Arrival	Arrival	Arrival
:30	Whole School Walkthrough		2nd Gr Walkthroughs	5th Grade CPT	BST Meeting
9 AM			4th Grade CPT	DISTRICT MEETING	
:30	4th Grade CPT	Wissman Wkly Mtg			
10AM			Attendance Meeting		
:30	1st Grade CPT				
11 AM		1st Grade CPT	4th Gr Walkthroughs		
:30	LUNCH & Recess Check		3rd Gr Walkthroughs		Feedback Meetings
12 PM		LUNCH	LUNCH	1st Gr Walkthroughs	Feedback Meetings
:30	K Walkthroughs			Feedback Meetings	LUNCH
1 PM	Feedback Meetings			Feedback Meetings	Leadership Team Meeting
:30	SPED Visits				
2 PM					
:30	Dismissal	Dismissal	Dismissal	Dismissal	Dismissal
3 PM	Student Support Team		Faculty PD	Practice Clinic	
:30					
4 PM					
:30					
5 PM					

A Note on Scheduling Staff Culture

Staff culture work doesn't always appear as a separate block on a leader's schedule, but it must always be intentional, planned, and woven into daily routines.

If you are introducing and rolling out Staff Culture, you will be scheduling and executing the Action Steps for Principals from Chapter 6 tailored to your needs (see Marie's "everything" schedule in the next section). But if your staff culture systems are up and running, you may either schedule a dedicated block for weekly check-ins with staff, or you may fold this work into existing routines: walking the building, greeting people, noticing the energy in shared spaces, and being deliberately present. Nothing instructional needs to happen during this time; it's about reinforcing the relationships and behaviors that make a strong staff culture possible and noticing "drift" before it gets out of hand.

Leaders won't always list this work explicitly on their calendars. Marie, for example, embeds culture building, leading by example, and monitoring into everyday interactions. Whether it shows up as its own line item or inside other routines, the key is that it's deliberate and consistent, never left to chance.

Step 5: Add Work Time for Big Projects

Your final task is to pick a block of time when you'll work on larger, non-daily projects. In reality, for most principals, this time will occur outside of the school day. Here's a simple fact: you cannot get work done in your office during the school day (let's be honest).

You need to find a different place to work (like the janitor's closet—only half-joking!) and have the rest of the leadership team cover for you (the advantage of a Whom to Go to For What document we highlighted earlier).

When we polled the exceptional leaders in this book, they were very realistic about the fact that they normally only have about three to five hours of weekly time for big picture work—their jobs consume everything else! We'll make sure you keep your big project work focused on the right things in the next section of the chapter. For the time being, lock in the planning time, as this final iteration of a weekly schedule:

Note Marie's intentionality. She likes to plan most of her meetings on Friday, and she ends Friday by adjusting her schedule for the following week to meet the needs of her staff and students. Building a detailed schedule doesn't limit you. On the contrary: it frees you to be intentional about where you spend your time.

Marie Culihan's Schedule: Everything

DAILY SCHEDULE:		"If a school leader's main role is to drive student learning, then not observing and meeting with teachers means a leader did not do her job today. Despite the best intentions, she was only fighting fires."			
	MONDAY	TUESDAY	WEDNESDAY	THURSDAY	FRIDAY
6:30 7 AM					Plan 4th Grade CPT
:30	Email/Coverage	Email/Coverage	Email/Coverage	Email/Coverage	
8 AM	Arrival	Arrival	Arrival	Arrival	Arrival
:30	Whole School Walkthrough		2nd Gr Walkthroughs	5th Grade CPT	BST Meeting
9 AM			4th Grade CPT	DISTRICT MEETING	
:30	4th Grade CPT	Wissman Wkly Mtg			Prep: 1st grade CPT Faculty PD
10AM			Attendance Meeting		
:30	1st Grade CPT				
11 AM		1st Grade CPT	4th Gr Walkthroughs		
:30	LUNCH/Recess		3rd Gr Walkthroughs		Feedback Meetings
12 PM		LUNCH	LUNCH	1st Gr Walkthroughs	Feedback Meetings
:30	K Walkthroughs			Feedback Meetings	LUNCH
1 PM	Feedback Meetings			Feedback Meetings	Leadership Team Meeting
:30	SPED Visits		Student Follow-up Time		
2 PM					
:30	Dismissal	Dismissal	Dismissal	Dismissal	Dismissal
3 PM	Student Support Team		Faculty PD	Practice Clinic	Closeout: Weekly Update Next Week Schedule
:30					
4 PM					
:30	Email/ Follow-Up	Email/ Follow-Up	Email/ Follow-Up	Email/ Follow-Up	Email/ Follow-Up
5 PM					

Take a Moment and Reflect on What You've Accomplished

Take a moment to consider what this schedule accomplishes. First, you have large chunks of your schedule still open, allowing time to address unforeseen daily issues and challenges. Thus, if a student issue occurs during your observation window on Monday, you can reschedule your observations to Tuesday. This is what makes the schedule feasible. If you don't have at least 30% unscheduled, the weekly schedule likely won't work. You'll need to cut down on some of your group meetings (that's the one variable that will make it untenable if you've limited yourself to managing 12 teachers directly on a weekly basis).

Look at the results:

➢ **Every teacher in the building is observed every week:** For schools that observed once a year, this is a 20-fold increase!

➢ **Every teacher is participating in weekly feedback, planning, and/or data meetings:** You've moved from 1-2 pieces of feedback in a year to 40: more feedback in one year than most teachers get in 20.

➢ **Staff are regularly receiving high quality professional development:** If done right, faculty meetings are now PD and not announcements, and practice clinics close the gaps.

➢ **Culture is monitored constantly:** You or another leader is present to drive student culture at each key moment of the day.

Most importantly, you have taken the critical step that each top-tier leader in this book has taken: you have taken control over your time. The seven previous chapters outlined the investments that make a school extraordinary. With this schedule, we've given you the tools to do the same.

It shouldn't take long for you to create a schedule of your own. Draft one yourself or click on the LL App to go faster.

Stop & Do
Leverage Leadership App
Weekly Schedule

Open the LL App. Have your list of standing meetings and teachers/leaders you manage ready. If you have a school schedule, use that as well.

Build your schedule tailored to what you need.
Key Takeaways:

_____

_____

_____

_____

Exceptional school leaders thrive not by working more hours than other school leaders, but by making their hours count. So, what next?

THE FINAL STEP
Keep the End in Mind and Manage Your Tasks

You're in the home stretch. You've scheduled your weekly routines and protected your time. The last piece is keeping the end in mind—an overall plan for everything you are doing—and to manage your tasks to that end: daily and monthly. To keep track of these tasks, leaders need something to "map" their actions, and to build a plan beyond the daily and weekly level.

One-on-One
Leading with the End in Mind

It's 2:30 on Monday afternoon at Colfax Elementary School, and the leadership team meeting is just getting started. "Let's open up our yearly calendar," instructs Michelle. "What are our priorities for this week and next?"

As all of the team members open the calendar, they review everything that is there side by side: a planned student attendance celebration, the new data cycle that is beginning, the plan for the Wednesday faulty PD, the observational feedback focus, and links to all the teachers' long-term unit planners.

"Ok, based on where we are, what adjustments do we need to make?" Michelle asks.

And the leadership team dives in—adjusting the PD to the needs that arose, delegating tasks, and planning their next coaching meetings. As they do, Michelle updates the calendar for use at the next meeting.

Michelle Koyama is no stranger to school leadership. A Denver native, she has spent two decades as a teacher, principal, principal supervisor, and then principal again—the place she loves the most. When she arrived at Colfax in 2021, COVID-19 had weakened any systems that had existed, and parents noted that the school was "on fire." While she worked to establish the student culture as her super-lever, she soon came to realize the second biggest problem: the school had no compass. Everyone was working in isolation with no sense of the end game.

Fast forward four years later, and Colfax is a different place; it was named one of the highlight schools in Denver for its improvement.

What was one of the biggest differences? Creating a yearlong calendar with everything in one place.

Build Your Yearly Calendar and Monthly Map

At the start of the year, Michelle sat down with her leadership team to create a full-year calendar with every component: unit plans, data-driven instruction calendar, faculty PD, leadership PD, student activities, and key teacher action steps of focus. The first time, they covered the walls with printed months and used sticky notes; later, they converted to a digital version. Then they made the plan visible for everyone—including teachers—to see. "Transparency changed everything," comments Michelle. "We all knew what we were working on, and we had a sense of purpose." Did they stick to the whole plan? No: they adjusted every week. But rather than adjusting like whack-a-mole, they had direction, and most importantly, coherence.[4]

With the end fully mapped, you make better decisions, and students get better outcomes.

Many leaders like Michelle convert their master calendar into a tool called the monthly map. The monthly map breaks your yearly plan into monthly segments, separating and highlighting your key tasks by month. Maia Heyck-Merlin, author of *The Together Teacher* and *The Together Leader*, calls this the Priority Plan. She notes that setting up a three-month Priority Plan is essential to mapping out a long-term view of your most important work—and a "Later List" will help you track the detailed long-term tasks.[5] You don't want your data-driven analysis meetings to sneak up on you, or to forget to schedule the dates of your interim assessments. (An important note: Data-driven instruction is much more a set of monthly tasks than weekly tasks. Thus, it is the lever that most needs a monthly map.)

Here's an example from Amanda McDonald of what two months of a leader's monthly map might look like. Full-length samples of monthly maps are available on the LL App that accompanies this book.

Her are two recommendations Michelle would share with you to make your own:

Better to work on fewer leadership levers well than all of them poorly. Michelle focused solely on culture and data-driven instruction in Year 1. "There was no time for anything else." She only added levers once those two were solidly in place.

Distribute actions as evenly as possible. Strategically distribute key actions across different weeks or months so that you aren't doing too much at one time. For example, when it comes to choosing dates for interim assessments, don't schedule them at the same time as report cards are due. That will mean teachers will be overwhelmed by trying to finish reports *and* analyze their results. Planning drivers for times when they are truly doable up front will protect your calendar from breaking down later in the year.

In the LL App, you can begin to build your own yearly calendar leveraging all the resources of the schools in this book, including blank print-ready templates for doing it visually.

Principal Monthly Map: On My Radar

LAKE MIDDLE SCHOOL

ILT Calendar			
Month	**Week**	**Building Capacity**	**Staff Fun**
Sept	Sept 9 & 13	• Walkthrough with Quarter 1 checklist on priorities • WDM PD—See it. Name it. • Plan first WDM agenda • Set Observation Schedule • Plan faculty PD and practice clinics • Attendance Data Review	**September: Back-to-School Kickoff** • Icebreaker Activities: team-building games • Goal Setting Session: staff share their personal and professional goals for the school year. **Staff Happy Hour 9/15**
	Sept 16 & 20	• Walkthrough with Quarter 1 checklist on priorities—look for progress • WDM PD—Do it. • Plan next WDM agenda & plan to film • Gradebook Audits	
	Sept 23 & 27	• Peer feedback: WDM videos • Review Staff Satisfaction Survey Results	
	Sept 30 & Oct 4	• Walkthrough with Quarter 1 checklist on priorities—look for progress • Norm on Lesson Plan Feedback • Plan faculty PD and practice clinics • PD from Cat on MLL supports	
Oct	Oct 7 & 11	• Review assessment Data • Relationship Data Review • ELD walkthrough, data analysis and action planning • Review SLO's and approve or give feedback	**October: Appreciation Month** • Dedicate a day to celebrate teachers with small gifts, notes of

LL App

The Daily/Weekly Action Plan

A Daily Action Plan gives you a way to organize tasks and hold yourself accountable for getting them done. The action plan coupled with a weekly schedule gives you everything you need to ensure that time and task management never get in the way of your school's success.

When I first wrote *Leverage Leadership*, I shared with you the tool that had worked best for me personally and with my school leaders: your tasks for the day, week, and month and place for notes for meetings and the weekly memo.

To DO	New Topics to Capture
Today	This Week
•	•
This Month [May]	Next Month [June]
•	•
Leadership Team Agenda Topics	Faculty Memo Topics
•	•

Since then, I have observed hundreds of tools that have worked as leaders have adjusted them to meet their style. You saw Marie lists her tasks right on her weekly schedule that she prints each week. And in *El Director Libre*, you can voice memo every task right into your AI app, and it will print a task list and completion schedule in less than a minute. Use the LL App to build the tool that works for you. If you have done all the other steps in this chapter—built a schedule, protected your time with your team, and selected a hound—you are already 80% of the way there. Onward!

Stop & Do
Leverage Leadership App
Task Management Tool

Open the LL App. Experiment with different options for managing your tasks until you come up with the one that works for you.

LL App

Key Takeaways:

_____

_____

_____

_____

_____

CONCLUSION

The heart of this book is simple: great leadership begins and ends with how you use your time. With the addition of your AI special assistant, it has never been easier to organize and take control of your time. Ultimately, then, the question is not whether it is feasible for leaders to pursue these systems but whether they can afford not to.

Four Keys to Finding The Time

➤ **Protect Your Time:** Build your support team to "block and tackle" for ycu (including AI)

➤ **Build Your Weekly Schedule:** Lock in instructional and cultural leadership and lock out most everything else

➤ **Build Your Yearly Calendar:** Lock in key milestones for instructional ard cultural leadership before anything else

➤ **Manage Your Tasks:** Utilize a monthly map and daily/weekly action plan to stay on top of the most important actions to be taken each week

Weekly Schedule Creation for School Leaders

Summary How-to Guide

Pre-work:

- Determine the number of instructional leaders you will need to manage directly (assistant principals, coaches, et al.)

- Determine the standing meetings you want to occur at least once/month (leadership team meeting, faculty PD)

- Determine the total number of teachers in your school and which people will lead which teachers directly. Determine the number of teachers you will manage directly (ranging from zero for a large-school leader to potentially all teachers for a small-school leader) *Note: Between leaders and teachers, you should have* **no more than 10–15 people** *you will lead personally*

- Get out your school's weekly schedule that shows when teachers are teaching and when they have prep periods

Weekly Schedule:

- Create a simple grid for the week in half-hour or hourly segments 7 AM–6 PM (modify the grid to match your school class schedule)
- Create the grid so that each hourly block is the size of the post-its you will use

Green Post-its—Student Culture:

- Place Green Post-its wherever you are likely to be focused on student culture and parental issues (likely breakfast/start of day, lunchtime, and at dismissal)

Yellow Post-its—Meetings:

- Make a decision: Do you work best with back-to-back-to-back meetings, or do you need breaks between meetings to stay focused? Use this criteria to complete the following tasks
- Each yellow Post-it represents a one-hour meeting
- Label Post-its for each of your team/large group meetings: leadership team, faculty PD, etc. Place them on the schedule. If they only happen every other week, note that on the Post-its
- Write the names of the 1–3 teachers you will lead on yellow post-its and place them on the schedule where they have a prep period
  - two teachers per post-it for 30-minute planning/feedback meetings
  - three teachers per post-it for 20-minute feedback check-ins
- Place on the schedule your check-ins with any other individuals
- Depending on your preferences, place these meetings as close together as possible or spread out

Orange Post-its—Observations:

- Calculate 3–4 observations for every hour (15-minute observations)
- Place one orange post-it for every 3–4 teachers you will be observing
  - If you have 16 teachers to observe, you need 4–5 post-its

Blue Post-its—Uninterrupted Work Time:

- Select three blocks of 2-3 hours of *uninterrupted* time and place blue Post-its on those areas
  - Unless you can get out of the building and have someone cover for you, these times have to be in the very early morning, very late afternoon, evenings, or weekends
- Designate one of those planning times for *no email: just large tasks from your monthly map*

Pulling the Lever

Action Planning Worksheet for FINDING THE TIME

Self-Assessment

- What percentage of your teachers currently gets feedback more than twice a month? _____ %
- What percentage of your time is currently devoted to instructional or cultural leadership? _____ %
- What are the biggest improvements you could make to your weekly schedule to increase the time you spend on instructional and cultural leadership?

_____

_____

_____

Planning for Action

- What tools from this book will you use to manage your time? Check all that you will use (you can find all in the LL App):

  ___ **How to Create a Weekly Schedule One-Pager**

  ___ **Sample Leader Weekly Schedule—ES, MS, and HS**

  ___ **How to Create a Monthly Map One-Pager**

  ___ **Monthly Map Template**

  ___ **Sample Monthly Maps**

  ___ **Daily Action Plan Template**

- What are your next steps for finding the time for instructional and cultural leadership?

Action:	Date:

Conclusion

The Stars Are Rising

Throughout this book, our focus has been on the use of time and on the strategies to drive learning. In each chapter, we've offered a system to drive school growth and the ways to put it into place. Taken together, we've offered a comprehensive blueprint for building an exceptional school.

Yet at the end of the day, this book's ultimate purpose is not time management; it's not even great school leadership. This book is about students like Isaiah.[1]

Katie Harshman remembers Isaiah, a third grader, who struggled deeply with reading. He'd freeze during decoding, avoid independent work, and quietly tell teachers he "just wasn't a reader." What changed his trajectory wasn't luck; it was skillful teaching. His teacher recognized exactly where his breakdowns were, planned intentionally for him every day, and celebrated every incremental improvement. Slowly, he began choosing books instead of avoiding them. Years later, Isaiah returned as a confident high schooler. He told his teachers he'd been accepted to college and wanted to work "with kids who struggle like I once did."

This book is also about students like Anthony. Corliss taught Anthony in first grade, when he was an average student—quietly diligent but not someone most would have predicted would one day stand out. As he entered middle school, Anthony began to struggle with reading comprehension, and it became clear he needed more targeted support. Corliss, then his principal, decided to tutor him. She worked with him through texts, questions, and strategies to help him truly understand what he was reading. "Watching his growth over time has been one of my greatest joys," she says fondly. Anthony went on to high school, where he is a thriving honor student and an active member of Junior ROTC, earning numerous accolades for his leadership and excellence.

Perhaps most of all, this book is about students like Aaliyah. As the eldest of three, Aaliyah's home life would have overwhelmed many. With her father incarcerated throughout her childhood and her mother a single parent with limited opportunity and fewer resources, responsibilities fell heavily on Aaliyah's shoulders. Guiding Aaliyah through this maze of competing high stakes needs required patience and empathy. "I worked with her to understand the importance of taking her time, reviewing her work, and prioritizing herself in her educational journey," notes Tiffany. Aaliyah responded. Her dedication culminated in a milestone achievement when she graduated from Xavier University in 2024. Now, she returns to Whittier as an educator herself—a full circle moment.

The stories of Isaiah, Aaliyah, and Anthony remind us that all students can move from struggle to confidence, from hesitation to mastery, from limited possibility to expanded opportunity. But they grow only if they have schools that see their greatness even when they don't see it themselves.

It's the essential motivating force that brings Leverage Leadership to life. We see it in the inspirational stories and experiences shared by LeVar, Rick, Candace, Taro, Kim, Jasmine, Amanda, Stephanie, Katie, Tiffany, Corliss, Marie, and so many more. They transformed learning from persistent failure to exceptional. They acted urgently to give every child the education they deserve. Treating time as a precious, limited resource, they made careful decisions about what to do and when to do it. And they aren't resting on their laurels. They know the work isn't done until every child rises—every Isaiah, Aaliyah, and Anthony.

That is the promise of *Leverage Leadership 3.0* and of the work ahead: schools around the world where every student experiences the joy of being supported and pushed to be their best. With the right systems and habits, leaders can take a dream and make it reality. The stars are rising.

Quick Reference Sheet

Highlights of the key concepts in *Leverage Leadership 3.0*

The Seven Levers

Instructional Levers:

1. **Data-Driven Instruction**—Continuously prioritize the learning and start from a high-quality end goal and adjust your teaching to meet students' needs

2. **Instructional Planning**—Plan backward to guarantee strong lessons

3. **Observation and Feedback**—Coach teachers to improve the learning

4. **Professional Development**—Strengthen teams with hands-on training that sticks

Cultural Levers:

5. **Student Culture**—Set the expectations, routines, and values that create an environment where learning can thrive

6. **Staff Culture**—Build shared values and behaviors that unite and guide adults to a common purpose

7. **Managing School Leadership Teams**—Increase instructional leadership capacity to achieve consistent coaching for every teacher every week

---

1. **Data-Driven Instruction:**
   - ➢ **Assessment:** set the road map for rigor
   - ➢ **Analysis:** identify the gaps in student understanding

- ➤ **Action:** re-teach key content to get students on track
- ➤ **Systems:** create systems and procedures to ensure constant data-driven improvement

2. **Planning:**
   - ➤ **Unit Plans:** craft data-driven unit plans that are aligned to the level of rigor you wish your students to reach
   - ➤ **Lesson Plans:** build effective day-to-day lesson plans that will drive student learning
   - ➤ **Coach Planning:** guide your teachers to master the skills that will ensure quality lessons
   - ➤ **Monitor Planning:** observe lessons in action to evaluate the impact

3. **Observation and Feedback:**
   - ➤ **Observe Frequently and Consistently:** lock in frequent and regular observations
   - ➤ **Identify the Key Action Step:** identify highest leverage, measurable, bite-sized, and sequenced action steps
   - ➤ **Give Effective Feedback:** Show models, name action steps, and guide the teacher through effective practice
   - ➤ **Monitor and Follow Up:** develop systems to monitor teacher development and follow up accordingly

4. **Professional Development:**
   - ➤ **What to Teach:** create objectives that are highest leverage, measurable, and bite-sized
   - ➤ **How to Teach:** See It. Name It. Do It. Reflect.
   - ➤ **Make it Stick:** Monitor implementation and coach for results

5. **Student Culture:**
   - ➤ **Set Your Vision:** identify what you want students and adults doing in school
   - ➤ **Roll It Out to Your Staff:** give multiple opportunities to practice and rehearse before stepping into the classroom
   - ➤ **Roll It Out to Your Students:** give multiple opportunities to practice to lock in habits across the school
   - ➤ **Monitor and Maintain:** lead publicly, manage individually, evaluate progress, and implement whole-school resets

6. **Staff Culture:**
   - ➤ **Set the Vision:** name the behaviors you wish to see and set clear roles and schedules

> **Roll It Out:** make visible via story the behaviors and values of the team and create a culture of practice

> **Make it durable:** lead by example, maximize strengths, and build accountability

7. **Managing School Leadership Teams**

> **Choose Your Team:** look for reliability and reflectiveness to reach the 12:1 ratio

> **Train Your Team:** set their schedule, lead PD, and use the one-pagers to guide them

> **Monitor the School:** walk the school and coach in real time

> **Lead Effective Meetings:** strengthen instructional leadership capacity through effective models and practice

8. **Finding the Time**

> **Build Your Weekly Schedule:** start with student culture, then add groups, one-on-one meetings, observations, staff culture, and work time

> **Protect Your Time:** Defeat distractions with a supportive team and clear division of labor

> **Keep the End in Mind and Manage Your Tasks:** build a yearly calendar and monthly map for the non-weekly tasks of instructional leadership, and utilize daily tools to manage your tasks

A Companion Text

A Principal Manager's Guide to Leverage Leadership

As inspiring as the single success of any single leader at any single school may be, *Leverage Leadership 3.0* isn't a book about individual leaders beating the odds. On the contrary, it's about the way leaders can change the odds altogether, at scale, when enough of them engage the right strategies. Principals accomplish this every day, but just like teachers, they accomplish much more and do so much more quickly when an instructional leader is there to make sure no instructor is an island. It's with this in mind that back in 2018 we wrote a supplementary guide to *Leverage Leadership 2.0*: one aimed at principal managers.

A Principal Manager's Guide to Leverage Leadership shows how to coach and develop principals around all the levers of leadership, with a particular deep dive on the two super-levers of school leadership: data-driven instruction and student culture. This guide is meant for anyone in a position to impact multiple school leaders:

- Principal managers/supervisors
- Superintendents and central office leaders
- Principal training organizations
- School boards
- State departments of education
- School turnaround programs

If your role is in any way to make principals better, this book applies to you. You can find it in any bookstore (with the unique grey cover). Pass it on to a leader who could use it!

Notes

INTRODUCTION

1. Recent studies affirm the long-established finding that sustained exposure to highly effective teachers produces cumulative, "gap-closing" learning gains across multiple years. See John Hattie, *Visible Learning: The Sequel* (London: Routledge, 2023), which updates the original meta-analyses and reiterates that teacher practices represent the strongest school-controlled influences on student learning. For cumulative, multi-year effects of strong teaching, see William L. Sanders and June C. Rivers, *Cumulative and Residual Effects of Teachers on Future Student Academic Achievement* (Knoxville: University of Tennessee Value-Added Research and Assessment Center, 1996), a foundational analysis demonstrating achievement differences of roughly fifty percentile points after three consecutive years with highly effective versus less effective teachers.

2. Education policy reviews also show broad state-level shifts toward evidence-based early literacy, including bans on three-cueing, updated training, early screening, and aligned materials. See National Council on Teacher Quality, *State of the States 2024: Five Policy Actions to Strengthen Elementary Reading Instruction* (Washington, DC: NCTQ, 2024). For the expansion of high-quality instructional materials (HQIMs), see Council of Chief State School Officers (CCSSO), "High-Quality Instructional Materials and Professional Development (IMPD) Network," launched 2017, which documents multi-state strategies to expand access; and Julia H. Kaufman, Sy Doan, Rudy B. Perez, et al., *Teachers' Use of Instructional Materials from 2019–2024* (Santa Monica, CA: RAND Corporation, 2025), a six-year national panel study showing steadily rising adoption across ELA, math, and science. For additional context on market pressure and district-level adoption dynamics, see

EdReports and The Decision Lab, *Beyond Selection: How Districts Adopt and Implement High-Quality Instructional Materials* (2025).

3. For more on the impact of effective time management on student achievement, see Sebastian W. Lee, Katja Pollock, and Georg Tulowitzki, eds., *How School Principals Use Their Time* (2020), a comprehensive and current international examination of time-use patterns and their implications for school improvement. See also Jason A. Grissom, Susanna Loeb, and Benjamin Master, "Effective Instructional Time Use for School Leaders," *Educational Researcher* 42, no. 8 (2013): 433–444, a longitudinal principal time-use study that identifies specific instructional investments associated with student achievement gains.

4. David Tyack and Larry Cuban, *Tinkering Toward Utopia: A Century of Public School Reform* (Cambridge, MA: Harvard University Press, 1995); and Michael Fullan, *The New Meaning of Educational Change*, 6th ed. (New York: Teachers College Press, 2024), which synthesizes six decades of research showing that lasting school improvement is both slow and capacity-dependent. See, for example, Robert J. *Marzano, Tony Frontier, and David Livingston, Effective Supervision: Supporting the Art and Science of Teaching* (Alexandria, VA: ASCD, 2011), 107.

AI PRIMER—LEVERAGE LEADERSHIP APP AS YOUR PERSONAL ASSISTANT

1. Bambrick-Santoyo, Paul, Ezequiel Molina, Carolina Lopez, and Octavio Lizama. *El Director LIBRE: El método de IA que libera horas de papeleo para liderar el aprendizaje*. Washington, DC: World Bank, 2025.

CHAPTER 1

1. Check out the Leverage Leadership Institute for all the states and countries served: www.leverageleaders.org. Check out all other publications written by Paul Bambrick-Santoyo for additional success stories.

2. To read more about the value of setting a clear standard for rigor—and checking in on learning "early and often"—see Grant Wiggins, "How Good Is Good Enough?," *Educational Leadership* 71, no. 4 (2013): 10–16; and Doug Lemov, "Rigor Checklist," *Teach Like a Champion* (2021).

3. For additional resources showing how assessments that reflect clear standards benefit students, see Olusola Adesope, Dominic Trevisan, and Narayankripa

Sundararajan, "Rethinking the Use of Tests: A Meta-Analysis of Practice Testing," *Review of Educational Research* 87, no. 3 (2017): 659–701; Richard Curwin, "Can Assessments Motivate?," *Educational Leadership* 72, no. 1 (2014): 38–40; and Kathleen Porter-Magee and Jennifer Borgioli, "The Four Biggest Myths of the Anti-Testing Backlash," *The Education Gadfly*, February 14, 2013. For a contemporary blueprint on aligning classroom, interim, and summative assessments within a coherent and instructionally useful system, see Center for Assessment (Scott Marion et al.), "A Tricky Balance: The Challenges and Opportunities of Balanced Assessment Systems" (2019/2021).

4. For a sampling of the many definitions of rigor that have been offered, see Nel Noddings, "The New Anti-Intellectualism in America," *Education Week* 26 (2007): 29, 32; Elliot Washor and Charles Mojkowski, "What Do You Mean by Rigor?," *Educational Leadership* 64 (2007); Daniel Baron, "Using Text-Based Protocols: The Five Rs," *Principal Leadership* 7 (2007); and W. Norton Grubb and Jeannie Oakes, *'Restoring Value' to the High School Diploma: The Rhetoric and Practice of Higher Standards* (Boulder, CO: Arizona State University, 2007). See also Richard DuFour, Robert E. Eaker, and Rebecca Burnette, *On Common Ground: The Power of Professional Learning Communities* (Bloomington, IN: National Educational Service, 2005). For additional contemporary perspectives, see Barbara Blackburn, "Rigor and Competency-Based Instruction: Are We Asking the Right Questions?," *EdCircuit*, January 3, 2017; and Learning Sciences International, "The Essentials for Achieving Rigor," materials aligned to Marzano's *The Art and Science of Teaching* (2017). For a large-scale empirical analysis of rigor in assessment design, see *Frontiers in Education* (2021), "The Position of Distractors in Multiple-Choice Test Items: The Case of a National Exam," a multi-year study illustrating how plausible versus non-functioning distractors shape item difficulty and discrimination. https://www.learningsciences.com/teach/core-instruction/, https://www.learningsciences.com/wp/wp-content/uploads/2017/06/Essentials-Executive-Summary-06-03-14.pdf, https://www.learningsciences.com/wp/wp-content/uploads/2017/06/School-Leader-Rigor-Paper-2014.pdf,

5. The original definition of rigor referenced here comes from "The Beginner's Guide to Understanding Rigor," by Barbara Blackburn, excerpted from *Rigor Made Easy* (Eye on Education, 2012). For more current treatments of the concept, see Barbara Blackburn, *Rigor Is NOT a Four-Letter Word*, new edition (Routledge, 2025); and Barbara Blackburn, *Rigor in Your Classroom: A Toolkit for Teachers*, 2nd ed. (New York: Taylor & Francis, 2022). Additional contemporary frameworks include

Quality Matters, "Academic Rigor: A Comprehensive Definition" (2019) and "Defining and Implementing Academic Rigor: A 5-Year Update" (2024), which synthesize research and practice guidance for designing rigorous learning experiences.

6. See Del Stover, "Up to the Challenge: Are You Doing All You Can to Provide Academic Rigor for Your Students?," *American School Board Journal* 202, no. 5 (2015): 42–43.

7. Many districts, in the rush to become data-driven, are over-assessing their students. Assessments are essential, but once every six to eight weeks in each subject is generally more than sufficient. The National Academy of Education's *Reimagining Balanced Assessment Systems* (2024) and the Center for Assessment's companion guidance recommend eliminating redundant tests and centering classroom formative assessment within a coherent instructional system. Districts can use WestEd's *Assessment Inventory Resource* (2020) to audit and reduce overlapping or low-value assessments; large-district data from the Council of the Great City Schools in *Student Testing in America's Great City Schools: An Inventory and Preliminary Analysis* (2015) document historical over-testing and misalignment. Most districts can monitor progress with two to three benchmark windows per year, paired with ongoing formative assessment. For approaches to reducing over-assessment, see Paul Bambrick-Santoyo, *Driven by Data 2.0*, 128. For additional system-level context, see RAND Corporation, *The Role of Benchmark Assessments in Coherent Instructional Systems (AIRS)* (2023), which shows that while benchmark assessments are nearly universal, their value depends on alignment with curriculum and professional learning rather than frequency.

8. See New Jersey state assessment results for North Star Academy Washington Park High School in Newark, NJ, as cited in previous editions of *Leverage Leadership*.

9. Research is clear that when students encounter material only once and don't return to it before a later assessment, they remember far less. In a middle-school science study, McDaniel et al. found that even brief retrieval after initial learning produced significantly better retention than a single study session. Walsh et al. show the same pattern experimentally: spacing practice across multiple sessions leads to stronger long-term learning than doing all practice at once. Mark A. McDaniel et al., "Retrieval Practice and Retention of Course Content in a Middle School Science Setting," accessed October 2025, https://pure.psu.edu/en/publications/retrieval-practice-and-retention-of-course-content-in-a-middle-sc; Matthew M. Walsh et al., "Enhancing Learning and Retention through the Distribution of Practice

Repetitions across Multiple Sessions," *Memory & Cognition* 51 (2023): 455–472, https://doi.org/10.3758/s13421-022-01361-8.

10. For background on Carolina Marín's athletic achievements, see "Carolina MARÍN – Athlete Profile," Olympics.com, accessed October 17, 2025, which summarizes her Rio 2016 Olympic gold medal and three world titles (2014, 2015, 2018).

11. For reporting on her use of data analytics, see "Will Big Data Help Carolina Marín to Badminton Gold at Tokyo 2020 in 2021?," *Olympics.com*, May 2021. For perspectives from her longtime coach, see Dev Sukumar, "Fernando Rivas: 'I'm Not a Slave of Data'," *BWF World Tour*, October 9, 2022; and "France in Good Position to Be Top Five in World," *BWF Olympics*, November 17, 2022. For commentary on the role of AI and emotional-state analysis in training, see "Fernando Rivas: 'Los algoritmos ayudan a entender las emociones'," *EFE / IUSPORT*, June 22, 2025. For reporting on Rivas's move toward an AI-driven performance project, see Jesús Garrido, "Fernando Rivas. . . deja Francia para iniciar un proyecto de IA de mejora del deportista," *El Confidencial*, June 16, 2025.

12. Paul Bambrick-Santoyo, and Stephen Chiger. *Love & Literacy: A Practical Guide to Finding the Magic in Literature (Grades 5–12)*. San Francisco: Jossey-Bass / John Wiley & Sons, 2021. (Google Books)

13. ACT, Inc. *Reading Between the Lines: What the ACT Reveals About College Readiness in Reading*. Iowa City, IA: ACT, January 19, 2006. https://www.act.org/content/dam/act/unsecured/documents/reading_report.pdf

14. Doug Lemov. *Teach Like a Champion 2.0: 62 Techniques That Put Students on the Path to College*. San Francisco: Jossey-Bass, 2015. (Colorado Mountain College)

15. Paul Bambrick-Santoyo. *Get Better Faster 2.0: A 90-Day Plan for Coaching New Teachers*. John Wiley & Sons / Jossey-Bass, 2025. (Google Books)

16. Muhammad Ali Center. (2025). *In his own words*. "The fight is won or lost far away from witnesses. . ." https://alicenter.org/meet-ali/in-his-own-words/ (Muhammad Ali Center)

17. For the foundational treatment of the "Good to Great" framework, see James Collins, *Good to Great: Why Some Companies Make the Leap. . . and Others Don't* (New York: Harper Business, 2001).

CHAPTER 2

1. For recent evidence on implementation barriers and national performance trends, see EdReports and The Decision Lab, *Beyond Selection* (2025), which identifies

persistent challenges in high-quality instructional materials uptake. Over the same period, national achievement data have shown limited improvement: NAEP 2024 Reading scores remain below 2019 levels, NAEP 2024 Mathematics shows only partial recovery from historic 2022 declines, PISA 2022 reports U.S. math declines and flat reading since 2018, and NWEA 2023–24 results indicate slow, incomplete recovery with persistent achievement gaps (RAND Corporation).

2. The research base for both rigor and critical thinking is extensive. For background knowledge as a prerequisite for comprehension, see E. D. Hirsch Jr., *Cultural Literacy: What Every American Needs to Know* (1988) and "How Schools Fail Democracy," *The Chronicle of Higher Education* (2012). See also Hirsch's recent work, *How to Educate a Citizen: The Power of Shared Knowledge to Unify a Nation* (New York: Harper, 2020). For peer-reviewed syntheses, see Gina N. Cervetti and Tanya S. Wright, "The Role of Knowledge in Understanding and Learning from Text," in *Handbook of Reading Research, Vol. V* (Taylor & Francis, 2020); and Hyo Jin Hwang, Sonia Q. Cabell, and Rachel Joyner, "Effects of Integrated Literacy and Content-Area Instruction on Vocabulary and Comprehension in the Elementary Years: A Meta-Analysis," *Scientific Studies of Reading* 26, no. 3 (2022): 223–249. For experimental evidence, see Tanya S. Wright, Gina N. Cervetti, Christopher Wise, and Nicole A. McClung, "The Impact of Knowledge-Building through Conceptually-Coherent Read-Alouds on Vocabulary and Comprehension," *Reading Psychology* 43, no. 1 (2022): 70–84. For assessment alignment, see College Board, "The Digital SAT Suite and Classroom Practice: ELA/Literacy" (2023), which notes that informational text complexity often reflects the knowledge demands placed on readers.

3. For contemporary treatments of critical thinking, see Diane F. Halpern and Dana S. Dunn, *Thought and Knowledge: An Introduction to Critical Thinking*, 6th ed. (New York: Routledge, 2022); and Robert H. Ennis, "Critical Thinking: A Streamlined Conception," in *The Palgrave Handbook of Critical Thinking in Higher Education*, ed. M. Davies and R. Barnett (New York: Palgrave Macmillan, 2015), 31–47. For quantitative evidence on effective approaches, see Philip C. Abrami et al., "Strategies for Teaching Students to Think Critically: A Meta-Analysis," *Review of Educational Research* (2015). Contemporary human neuroscience shows that schemas and prior knowledge scaffold the integration of new information into long-term memory. SeeSarah Audrain and M. P. McAndrews, "Schemas Provide a Scaffold for Neocortical Integration of New Memories over Time," *Nature Communications* 13 (2022): 5795; Sonia Crespo-García et al., "Reactivation of Schema Representation in Lateral Occipital Cortex Supports Integration of Novel

Information into Existing Knowledge," *Cerebral Cortex* 33, no. 10 (2023): 5968–5982; andShruti Ramanan and Brock Bellana, "Naïve to Expert: Considering the Role of Previous Knowledge in Memory," *Brain and Neuroscience Advances* 4 (2020): 1–13.

4. For an in-depth study of deeper learning across American high schools, see Jal Mehta and Sarah Fine, *In Search of Deeper Learning: The Quest to Remake the American High School* (Cambridge, MA: Harvard University Press, 2019), based on more than 750 hours of observation and 300 interviews. For a practitioner-oriented reflection, see Sarah Fine, "What Is the Secret Sauce for Deeper Learning?," *Cult of Pedagogy* (2023), interview and transcript. See also Steve Leinwand, personal interview with the author, 2023.

5. Leinwand, Steve. Personal interview with the author. 2023.

6. CMAS Achievement Test results: comparison of Trevista's pre-pandemic ELA performance in 2019 to 2025 results.

CHAPTER 3

1. Charlotte Danielson has long emphasized teacher development over teacher evaluation. See Charlotte Danielson, "Connecting Common Core to Teacher Evaluation," *School Administrator* 71, no. 3 (2014): 30–33, in which she argues that, particularly in light of heightened standards under the Common Core, evaluation is constructive only within a collaborative cycle where teachers engage in self-assessment, reflection, and professional conversation. Jon Saphier, also a long-standing advocate of teacher development, draws a direct connection between leaders' ability to develop teachers and improved student outcomes. See Jon Saphier and Pia Durkin, "Supervising Principals: How Central Office Administrators Can Improve Teaching and Learning in the Classroom," September 21, 2011.

2. Robert J. *Marzano, Tony Frontier, and David Livingston, Effective Supervision: Supporting the Art and Science of Teaching* (Alexandria, VA: ASCD, 2011), 69.

3. Marzano et al., page 97.

4. See New Jersey Department of Education, "AchieveNJ: Teacher Evaluation Overview," http://www.state.nj.us/education/AchieveNJ/intro/1PagerTeachers.pdf; and "Getting Classroom Observations Right," *Education Next*, http://educationnext.org/getting-classroom-observations-right/.

5. Daniel Coyle, *The Talent Code* (New York: Bantam, 2009), 82–84.

6. As AI tools grow more sophisticated, the research is clear that they can't replace the connection and trust that come from real human coaching. A recent national study shows that nearly 70 percent of U.S. teenagers are already forming "intimate" relationships with AI companions, highlighting how easily technology can stand in for interaction, but not the depth or accountability that comes from an actual person. At the same time, coaching research warns that AI systems miss core elements of effective human coaching: emotional intelligence, relational judgment, and the ability to read context. See Tatiana Bachkirova and Rob Kemp, "'AI Coaching': Democratising Coaching Service or Offering an Ersatz?," *Coaching: An International Journal of Theory, Research and Practice* 18, no. 1 (2025): 27–45; and Jonathan Passmore, Bergsveinn Olafsson, and David Tee, "A Systematic Literature Review of Artificial Intelligence (AI) in Coaching: Insights for Future Research and Product Development," *Journal of Work-Applied Management* (2025). For teen trends, see Common Sense Media, *Talk, Trust and Trade-Offs: How and Why Teens Use AI Companions* (Chicago: Common Sense Media, 2025), 3.

7. The importance of focusing on a small number of concrete, high-leverage changes is echoed across fields of learning and training. For example, Washington University in St. Louis, Center for Teaching and Learning, "Commenting on Student Writing," advises providing fewer, more targeted comments and warns that students are often overwhelmed by copious written feedback, recommending prioritization of higher-order issues first. See also Teaching@Tufts, "Giving Feedback on Student Writing" (2024), which explicitly recommends limiting comments—sometimes to as few as one or two per page—and emphasizes the value of summary comments as sufficient guidance in many cases.

CHAPTER 4

1. For recent work on designing professional learning with lasting impact, see Thomas R. Guskey, "Professional Learning with Staying Power," *Educational Leadership* 78, no. 5 (2021): 54–59, which reiterates that effective professional development must be anchored in specific student learning outcomes and aligned teacher practices. For empirical evidence, see Rachel Garrett, Qian Zhang, Michelle Citkowicz, and Lauren Burr, *How Learning Forward's Standards for Professional Learning Are Associated with Teacher Instruction and Student Achievement: A Meta-Analysis* (American Institutes for Research, 2021), a systematic review demonstrating associations between standards-aligned PD and student gains. For updated syntheses on

early-career teacher development, see EdResearch for Action (Rebecca Kwok and Eleanor Macfarlane), "Strengthening Early-Career Teachers: Effective Components of Teacher Induction Programs" (2025), which highlights individualized coaching, targeted PD, structured collaboration, administrative support, and workload adjustments. Complementing this upstream pipeline perspective, see EdResearch for Action (John Papay, Fareeha Qazilbash, and Taylor Claiborne), "From Candidate to Classroom: Research-Based Practices for Recruiting and Hiring Highly-Effective Teachers" (2025). Recent meta-analytic work (2019–2024) also continues to show that well-designed induction and mentoring programs yield statistically significant positive effects on retention, teacher efficacy, and student outcomes.

2. Giada Di Stefano, Francesca Gino, Gary P. Pisano, and Bradley Staats, "Making Experience Count: The Role of Reflection in Individual Learning," Harvard Business School Working Paper No. 14-093 (March 2014; revised June 2016).

3. Ibid. "Once an individual has accumulated experience with a task, the benefit of accumulating additional experience is inferior to the benefit of deliberately articulating and codifying the previously accumulated experience."

CHAPTER 5

1. Paul Bambrick-Santoyo, *Leverage Leadership 2.0: A Practical Guide to Building Exceptional Schools*, 2nd ed. (San Francisco: Jossey-Bass, 2018), 252–53.

2. TNTP. *Action Guide for Educators: Belonging*. New York: TNTP, 2024. https://tntp .org/wp-content/uploads/2024/09/Action-Guide-for-Educators_Belonging.pdf.

3. *Integrity is acting. . . so that conviction and conduct are one.* Aristotle, *Nicomachean Ethics*, trans. Terence Irwin, 3rd ed. (Indianapolis: Hackett, 2019), VI.1 (1138b18– 24) and II.6 (1107a1–2).

4. Brown, Chris B. "Bill Walsh: A Method for Game Planning." Smart Football. 2007.

5. Libertas Academy reported results 2025.

6. Common Sense Media, *Talk, Trust and Trade-Offs: How and Why Teens Use AI Companions* (San Francisco: Common Sense Media, 2025), 4. (commonsense media.org)

CHAPTER 6

1. Jon Saphier has written extensively on the research base demonstrating the impact of strong adult professional culture on student learning. See Jon Saphier,

The Skillful Teacher, 8th ed. (Research for Better Teaching/Jossey-Bass, 2025), which expands the argument that adult norms and professional culture are central to developing high-expertise teaching at scale. For a concise treatment, see Jon Saphier, "Adult Professional Culture: The Sine Qua Non of School Improvement," RBT white paper (c. 2019). For related perspectives, see Michael Fullan, *The Principal 2.0: Three Keys to Maximizing Impact* (Jossey-Bass/Wiley, 2023); and Michael Fullan, "The Right Drivers for Whole System Success," *CSE Leading Education Series* (2021), which emphasize collaborative culture, well-being, equity, and system alignment as levers for raising instructional quality. Judith Warren Little's seminal work on collegial norms, help-seeking, and professional community continues to form the canonical evidence base for the relationship between adult collaboration and student outcomes. Recent reviews—including Carrie Farrell, "Approaches to Studying Teacher Collaboration for Instructional Improvement," *Teaching and Teacher Education* (2021)—highlight Little's 1990 research as foundational and trace its influence through contemporary studies of teacher collaboration. For historical continuity, see also "The Three Generations of Effective Schools Research," ERIC (date unspecified), which summarizes the evolution from Edmonds' early work to current syntheses.

2. For a comprehensive synthesis of two decades of research on school leadership, see Jason A. Grissom, Anna J. Egalite, and Constance A. Lindsay, *How Principals Affect Students and Schools: A Systematic Synthesis of Two Decades of Research* (New York: The Wallace Foundation, 2021). For empirical evidence on effective instructional time use, see Jason A. Grissom, Susanna Loeb, and Benjamin Master, "Effective Instructional Time Use for School Leaders: Longitudinal Evidence from Observations of Principals," *Educational Researcher* 42, no. 8 (2013): 433–444.

3. Jon Saphier, *The Skillful Teacher*, 8th ed. (Research for Better Teaching/Jossey-Bass, 2025).

4. Jon Saphier, Matt King, and John D'Auria, "3 Strands Form Strong School Leadership," *Journal of Staff Development* 27, no. 2 (Spring 2006): 51–57.

5. Brené Brown, "Clear Is Kind. Unclear Is Unkind," *brenebrown.com*, October 15, 2018, https://brenebrown.com/articles/2018/10/15/clear-is-kind-unclear-is-unkind/.

6. https://tntp.org/assets/documents/TNTP_Greenhouse_Schools_2012.pdf

7. Ibid.

8. Recent organizational research underscores the connection between clarity and performance. See *Human Resource Management* (2021), "Crystal Clear: How

Leaders and Coworkers Together Shape Role Clarity and Well-Being," which finds that role clarity—clear expectations supported by both leaders and peers—is associated with improved well-being and work outcomes. For causal evidence, see *Journal of Public Administration Research & Theory* (2016), "Goal Clarity, Task Significance, and Performance—Evidence From a Lab Experiment," which demonstrates that specific, explicit goals improve individual task performance.

9. The notion that high expectations strengthen adult professional culture also appears in Robert Kegan, Matthew Miller, Lisa Lahey, and Andy Fleming, "Making Business Personal," *Harvard Business Review* 92, no. 4 (April 2014): 44–52, which identifies accountability, transparency, and support as the ingredients of cultures where error is normalized and professionals can focus on growth rather than impression management.

10. Research on adult professional culture shows that teachers grow fastest in environments where they regularly rehearse instruction together and receive feedback in cycles. Kraft and Papay find that schools with strong professional environments—where practice is part of daily work—produce far greater gains in teacher effectiveness. A meta-analysis by Kraft, Blazar, and Hogan shows that coaching improves instruction largely because it creates structured opportunities for repeated practice. Farrell's review of teacher collaboration highlights the same pattern: high-performing teams engage in joint work that includes modeling, rehearsal, and feedback. See Matthew A. Kraft and John P. Papay, "Can Professional Environments in Schools Promote Teacher Development? Explaining Heterogeneity in Returns to Teaching Experience," *Educational Evaluation and Policy Analysis* 36, no. 4 (2014): 476–500; Matthew A. Kraft, David Blazar, and Dylan Hogan, "The Effect of Teacher Coaching on Instruction and Achievement: A Meta-Analysis of the Causal Evidence," *Review of Educational Research* 88, no. 4 (2018): 547–588; Carrie Farrell, "Approaches to Studying Teacher Collaboration for Instructional Improvement," *Teaching and Teacher Education* 104 (2021): 103–338; and Deans for Impact, *Practice with Purpose: The Emerging Science of Teacher Expertise* (Austin, TX: Deans for Impact, 2016).

11. Jon Saphier, *Disrupting the Teacher Opportunity Gap: Aligning 12 Processes for High-Expertise Teaching* (Thousand Oaks, CA: Corwin, 2023), chap. 3, p. 77.

12. Tennessee Department of Education, "2023–24 Reward Schools," published November 22, 2024. For additional context on school performance and leadership, see Leadership Preparatory Charter School, "The Team."

13. Jason A. Grissom, Anna J. Egalite, and Constance A. Lindsay, *How Principals Affect Students and Schools: A Systematic Synthesis of Two Decades of Research* (New York: The Wallace Foundation, 2021).

14. Recent research underscores the importance of emotionally intelligent leadership for educator well-being and organizational health. See Jonathan L. Floman, Alexandra Ponnock, Jigna Jain, and Marc A. Brackett, "Emotionally Intelligent School Leadership Predicts Educator Well-Being Before and During a Crisis," *Frontiers in Psychology* 14 (2024): 1159382, which finds that leaders' emotional regulation and support skills predict higher job satisfaction and lower emotional exhaustion among educators. For related evidence, see Zorana Ivcevic, John Moeller, Jonas Menges, and Marc A. Brackett, "Supervisor Emotionally Intelligent Behavior and Employee Creativity," *Journal of Creative Behavior* 55, no. 1 (2021): 1–17, a large-scale U.S. study showing that employees with emotionally intelligent supervisors report greater happiness at work and more perceived growth opportunities.

15. For broader treatments of emotional intelligence and educator resilience, see Marc Brackett, *Permission to Feel: Unlocking the Power of Emotions to Help Our Kids, Ourselves, and Our Society Thrive* (New York: Celadon Books, 2019); Brené Brown, *Dare to Lead: Brave Work. Tough Conversations. Whole Hearts.* (New York: Random House, 2018); and Elena Aguilar, *Onward: Cultivating Emotional Resilience in Educators* (San Francisco: Jossey-Bass, 2018).

16. For accessible introductions to the science of well-being, see Laurie Santos, "The Science of Well-Being," Yale University/Coursera, 2018–present, https://www.coursera.org/learn/the-science-of-well-being (accessed October 26, 2025). See also Laurie Santos, host, *The Happiness Lab*, podcast, Pushkin Industries, 2019–present, https://www.happinesslab.fm (accessed October 26, 2025). For a related synthesis of positive psychology research, see Shawn Achor, *The Happiness Advantage* (New York: Crown Business, 2010).

17. Marc Brackett, *Permission to Feel: Unlocking the Power of Emotions to Help Our Kids, Ourselves, and Our Society Thrive* (New York: Celadon Books, 2019).

18. For evidence that high-quality teacher collaboration predicts improved student achievement and teacher growth, see Matthew Ronfeldt, Susanna Loeb, James H. Wyckoff, et al., "Teacher Collaboration in Instructional Teams and Student Achievement," *American Educational Research Journal* 52, no. 3 (2015): 475–514, a large K-12 study following more than 9,000 teachers in 336 schools. For broader evidence on professional learning communities, see the 2024 meta-analysis

reporting a significant positive association between school-level PLC implementation and student achievement (ScienceDirect).

19. For evidence on how clarity and feedback quality drive improved performance, see *Psychological Reports* (2019), "Effects of Leader Motivating Language on Employee Task and Contextual Performance," which reports that direction-giving language—clear expectations paired with actionable feedback—predicts higher employee performance, with feedback quality mediating the effect.

20. Jon Saphier, *Disrupting the Teacher Opportunity Gap: Aligning 12 Processes for High-Expertise Teaching* (Thousand Oaks, CA: Corwin, 2023), 77.

CHAPTER 7

1. For current school performance data, see DC School Report Card 2024, https://schoolreportcard.dc.gov/lea/1/school/338/report#measure-100.

2. A 2017 article entitled "Gauging Goodness of Fit: Teachers' Responses to Their Instructional Teams in High-Poverty Schools" by Megin Charner-Laird, Monica Ng, Susan Moore Johnson, Matthew Kraft, John Papay, and Stefanie Reinhorn affirmed the value of leadership team meetings that focus on learning. Having principals act as thought partners, comfortable exchange of feedback between colleagues, and meeting agendas rooted in assessment data were some of the keys to doing this effectively. *American Journal of Education*, August 2017 (Vol. 123, #4, p. 553-584)

3. Paul Bambrick-Santoyo, *The Principal Manager's Guide to Leverage Leadership 2.0* (San Francisco: Jossey-Bass, 2016)

CHAPTER 8

1. Kim Marshall, "How I Confronted HSPS (Hyperactive Superficial Principal Syndrome) and Began to Deal with the Heart of the Matter," *Phi Delta Kappan* 77 (1996): 336–345.

2. For evidence on how small, consistent actions compound into meaningful change, see James Clear, *Atomic Habits* (New York: Penguin Random House, 2018), which provides an evidence-based framework for 1% improvements and habit stacking. See also B. J. Fogg, *Tiny Habits* (New York: HarperCollins, 2019), in which the Stanford behavior scientist argues that durable behavior change comes from starting with small actions anchored to existing routines (prompt × ability × motivation).

3. The National SAM® Innovation Project (NSIP) partners with over 900 schools in 22 states to increase the amount of time school leaders spend on instruction. Researchers have found that SAM principals, on average, increase their instructional time from roughly 30 percent to 65 percent of the day within one year. Formal research studies by PSA, Vanderbilt University, and others are available at the NSIP website, www.SamsConnect.com.

4. For research and case studies illustrating the importance of coherence, consistency, and belonging in driving student learning, see TNTP, *The Opportunity Makers: How a Diverse Group of Public Schools Helps Students Catch Up and How Far More Can*, https://tntp.org/publication/the-opportunity-makers. This report documents how schools with coherent instructional systems, consistent expectations, and strong cultures of belonging accelerate student progress.

5. Maia Heyck-Merlin, *The Together Leader: Get Organized for Your Success—and Sanity!* (San Francisco: Jossey-Bass, 2016).

CONCLUSION

1. We are using pseudonyms to protect the identity of these students, but the stories are real!

Index